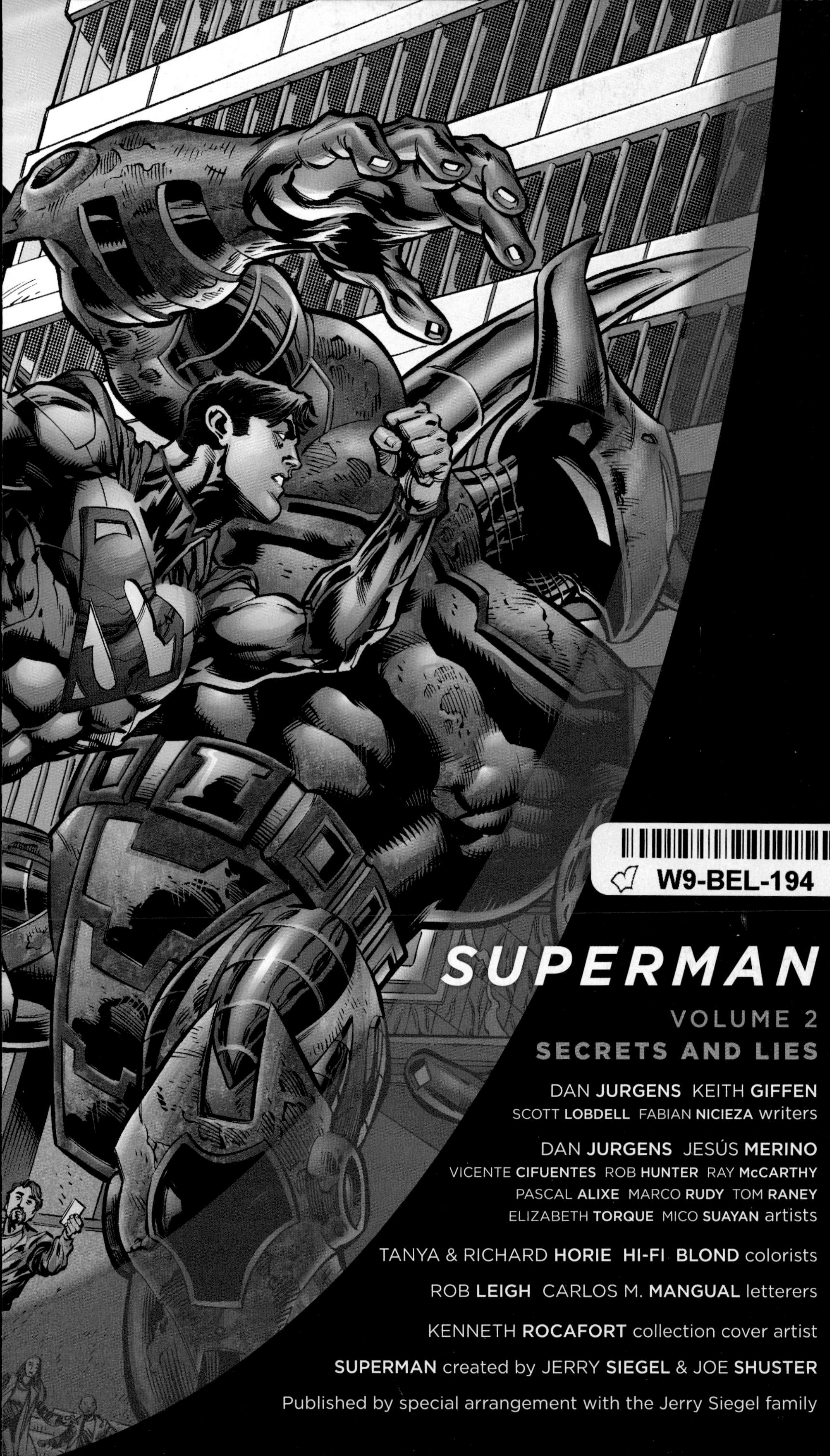

SUPERMAN

VOLUME 2
SECRETS AND LIES

DAN **JURGENS** KEITH **GIFFEN**
SCOTT **LOBDELL** FABIAN **NICIEZA** writers

DAN **JURGENS** JESÚS **MERINO**
VICENTE **CIFUENTES** ROB **HUNTER** RAY **McCARTHY**
PASCAL **ALIXE** MARCO **RUDY** TOM **RANEY**
ELIZABETH **TORQUE** MICO **SUAYAN** artists

TANYA & RICHARD **HORIE** **HI-FI** **BLOND** colorists

ROB **LEIGH** CARLOS M. **MANGUAL** letterers

KENNETH **ROCAFORT** collection cover artist

SUPERMAN created by JERRY **SIEGEL** & JOE **SHUSTER**

Published by special arrangement with the Jerry Siegel family

MATT IDELSON EDDIE BERGANZA Editors – Original Series WIL MOSS Associate Editor – Original Series
DARREN SHAN Assistant Editor – Original Series ROWENA YOW Editor
ROBBIN BROSTERMAN Design Director – Books ROBBIE BIEDERMAN Publication Design

BOB HARRAS Senior VP – Editor-in-Chief, DC Comics

DIANE NELSON President DAN DIDIO and JIM LEE Co-Publishers GEOFF JOHNS Chief Creative Officer
JOHN ROOD Executive VP – Sales, Marketing and Business Development AMY GENKINS Senior VP – Business and Legal Affairs
NAIRI GARDINER Senior VP – Finance JEFF BOISON VP – Publishing Planning
MARK CHIARELLO VP – Art Direction and Design JOHN CUNNINGHAM VP – Marketing
TERRI CUNNINGHAM VP – Editorial Administration ALISON GILL Senior VP – Manufacturing and Operations
HANK KANALZ Senior VP – Vertigo and Integrated Publishing JAY KOGAN VP – Business and Legal Affairs, Publishing
JACK MAHAN VP – Business Affairs, Talent NICK NAPOLITANO VP – Manufacturing Administration
SUE POHJA VP – Book Sales COURTNEY SIMMONS Senior VP – Publicity BOB WAYNE Senior VP – Sales

SUPERMAN VOLUME 2: SECRETS AND LIES

DC Comics, 1700 Broadway, New York, NY 10019
A Warner Bros. Entertainment Company.
Printed by RR Donnelley, Salem, VA, USA. 12/6/13. First Printing.

ISBN: 978-1-4012-4257-2

Library of Congress Cataloging-in-Publication Data

Jurgens, Dan, author.
Superman : secrets and lies / Dan Jurgens, Keith Giffen.
pages cm
"Originally published in single magazine form in Superman 7-12, Superman Annual 1."
ISBN 978-1-4012-4028-8
1. Graphic novels. I. Giffen, Keith, illustrator. II. Title. III. Title: Secrets and lies.
PN6728.S9J8786 2013
741.5'973—dc23
2013009122

PN6728.S9P47 2012

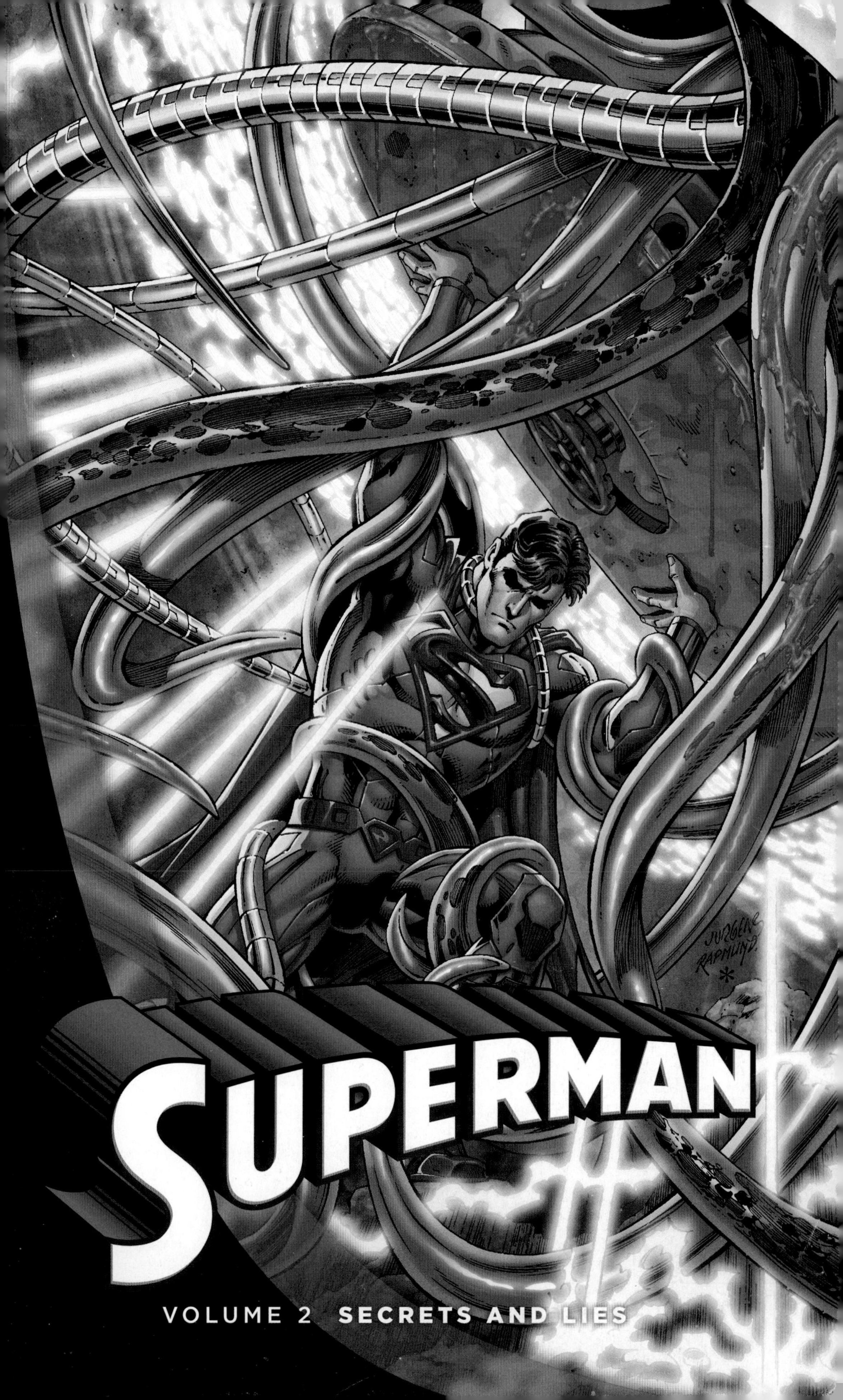

SUPERMAN

VOLUME 2 **SECRETS AND LIES**

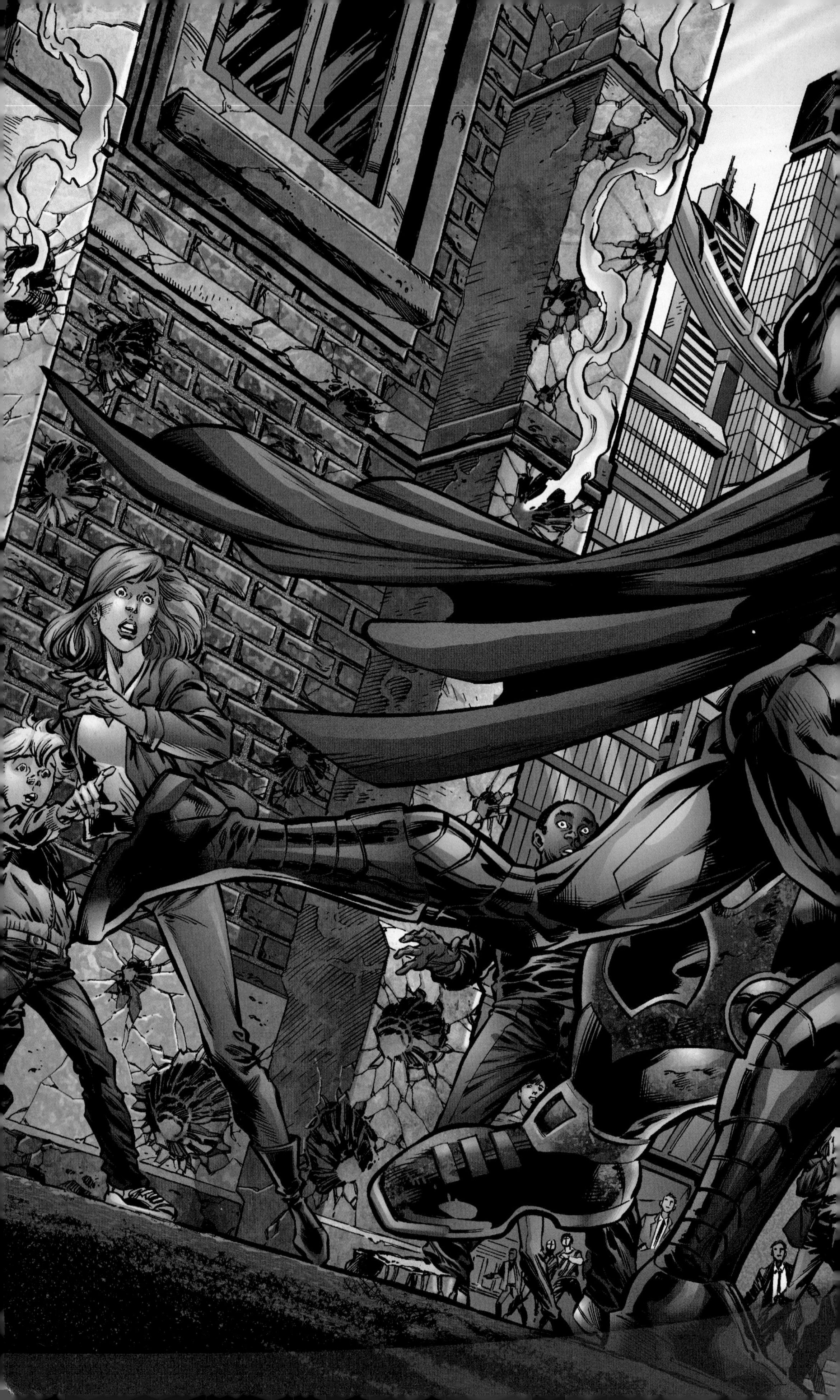

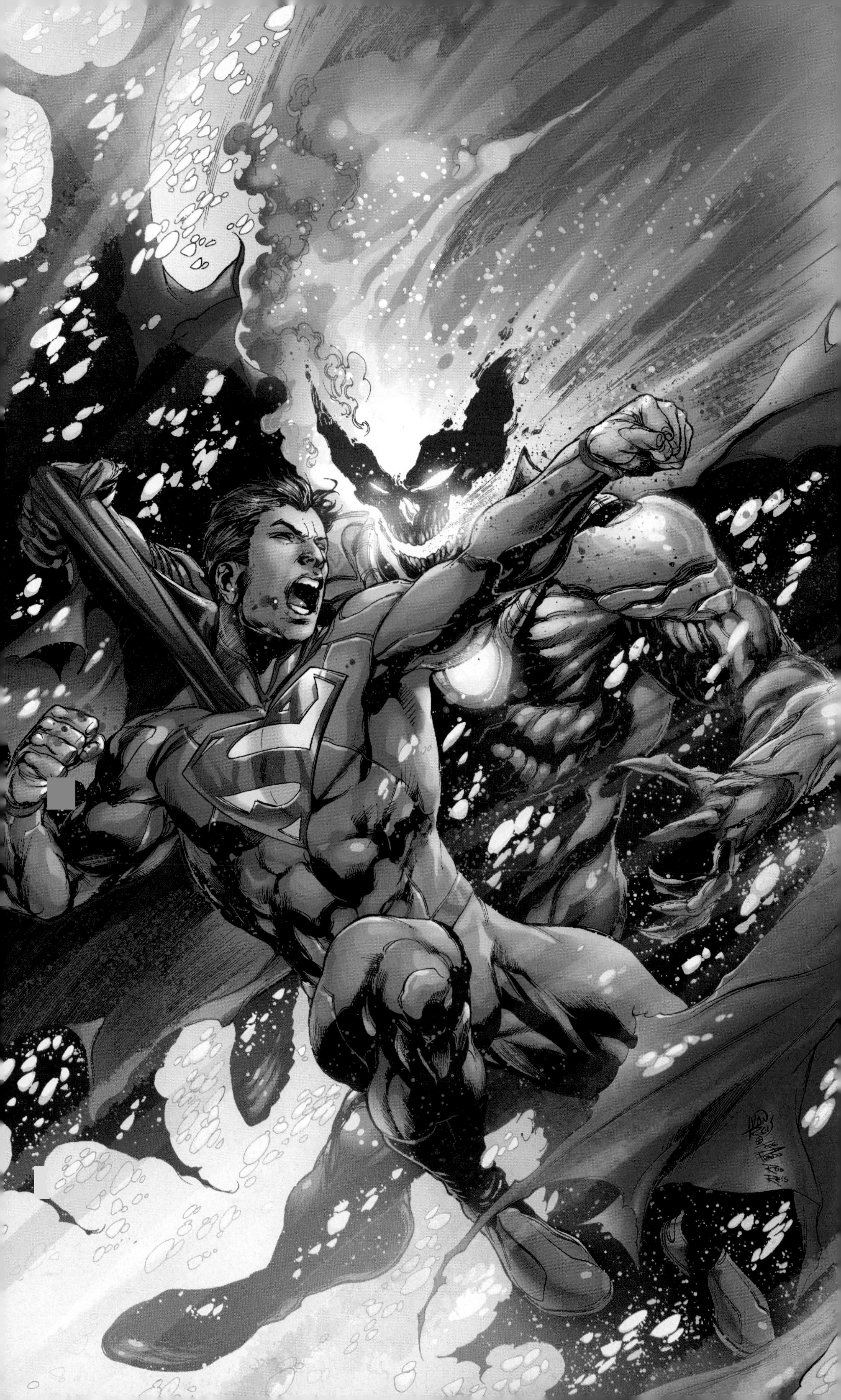

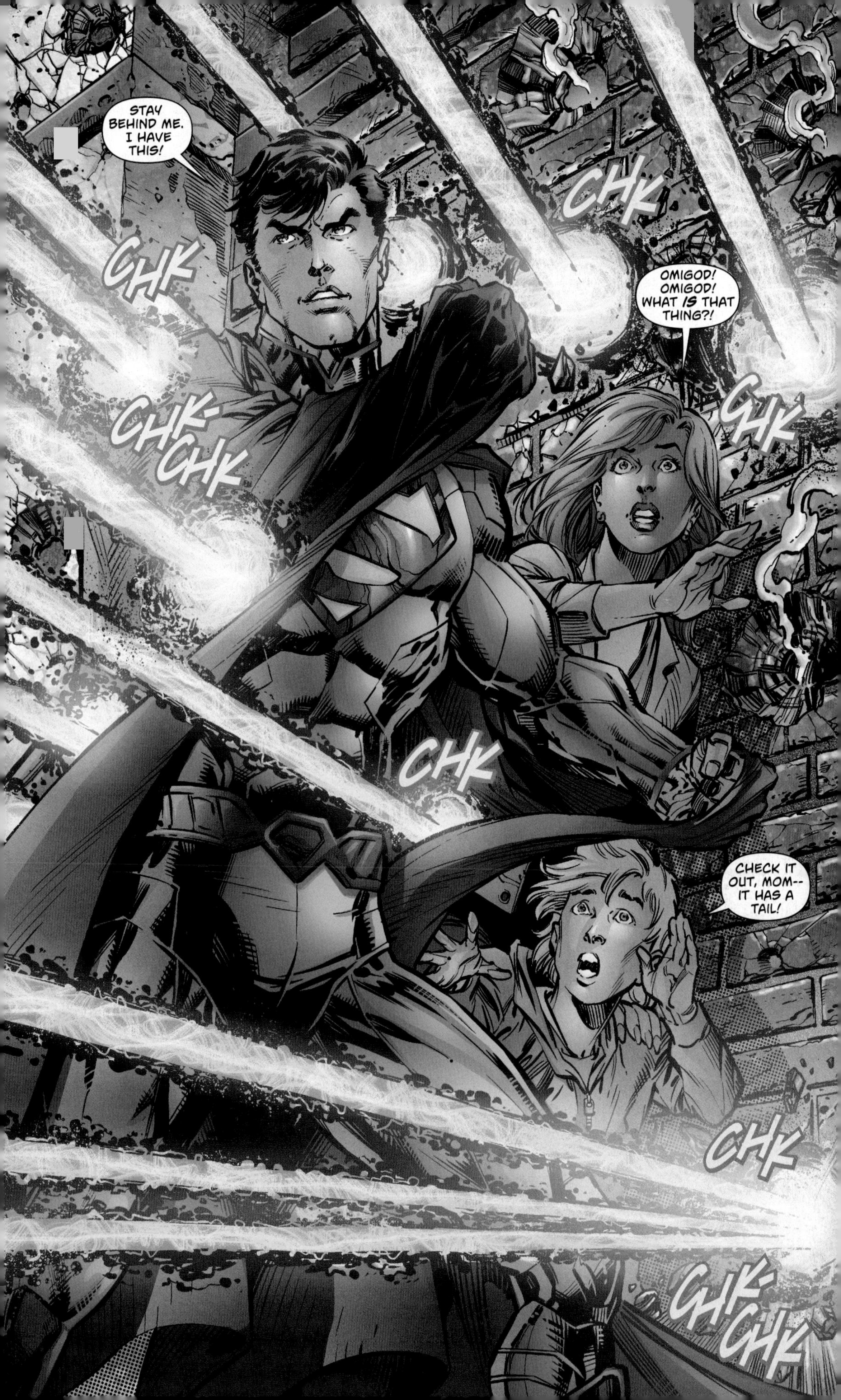
STAY BEHIND ME. I HAVE THIS!
CHK
CHK-CHK
OMIGOD! OMIGOD! WHAT IS THAT THING?!
CHK
CHK
CHK
CHECK IT OUT, MOM-- IT HAS A TAIL!
CHK
CHK-CHK

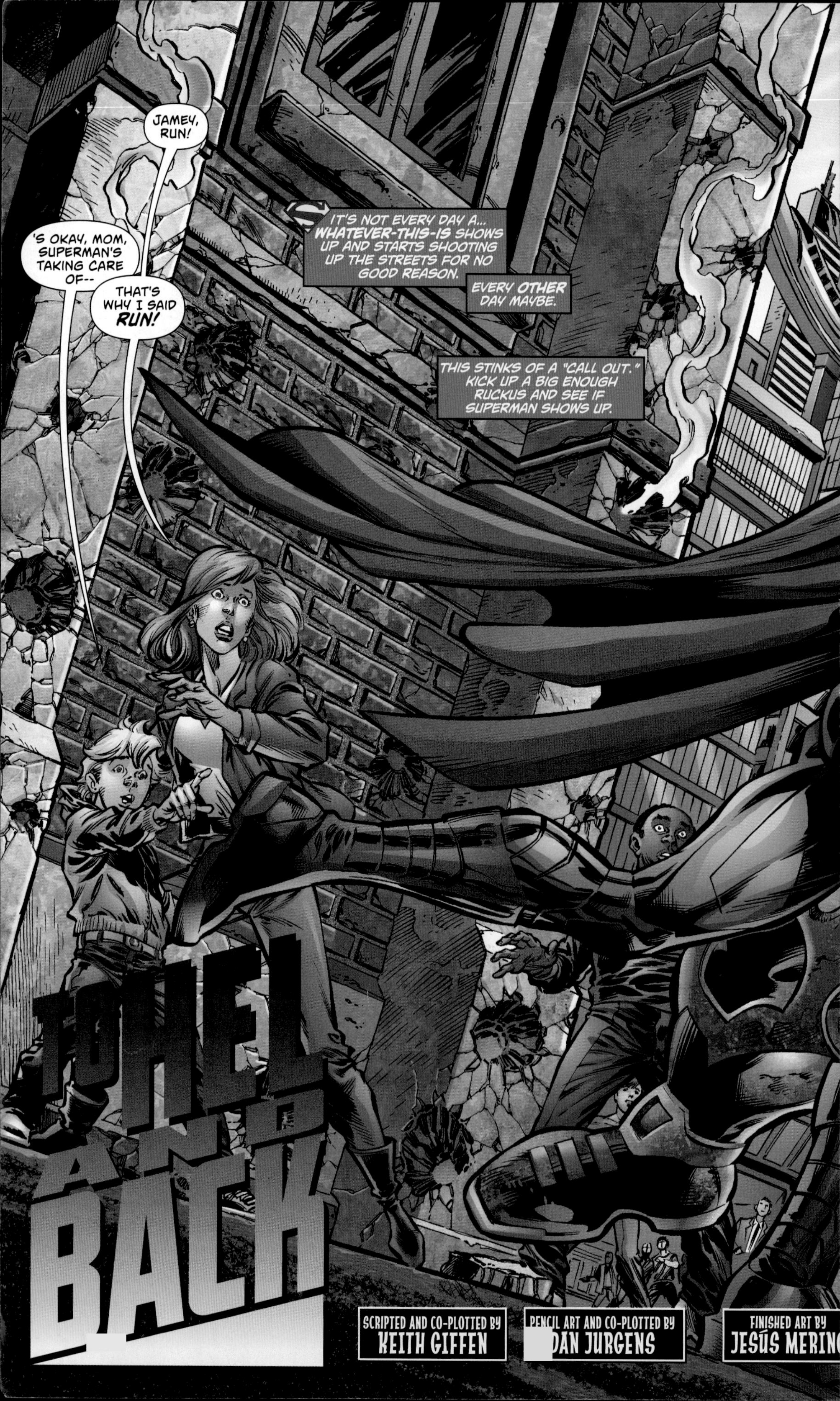
JAMEY, RUN!
IT'S NOT EVERY DAY A... WHATEVER-THIS-IS SHOWS UP AND STARTS SHOOTING UP THE STREETS FOR NO GOOD REASON.
EVERY OTHER DAY MAYBE.
'S OKAY, MOM, SUPERMAN'S TAKING CARE OF--
THAT'S WHY I SAID RUN!
THIS STINKS OF A "CALL OUT." KICK UP A BIG ENOUGH RUCKUS AND SEE IF SUPERMAN SHOWS UP.
TO HELL AND BACK
SCRIPTED AND CO-PLOTTED BY KEITH GIFFEN
PENCIL ART AND CO-PLOTTED BY DAN JURGENS
FINISHED ART BY JESÚS MERIN

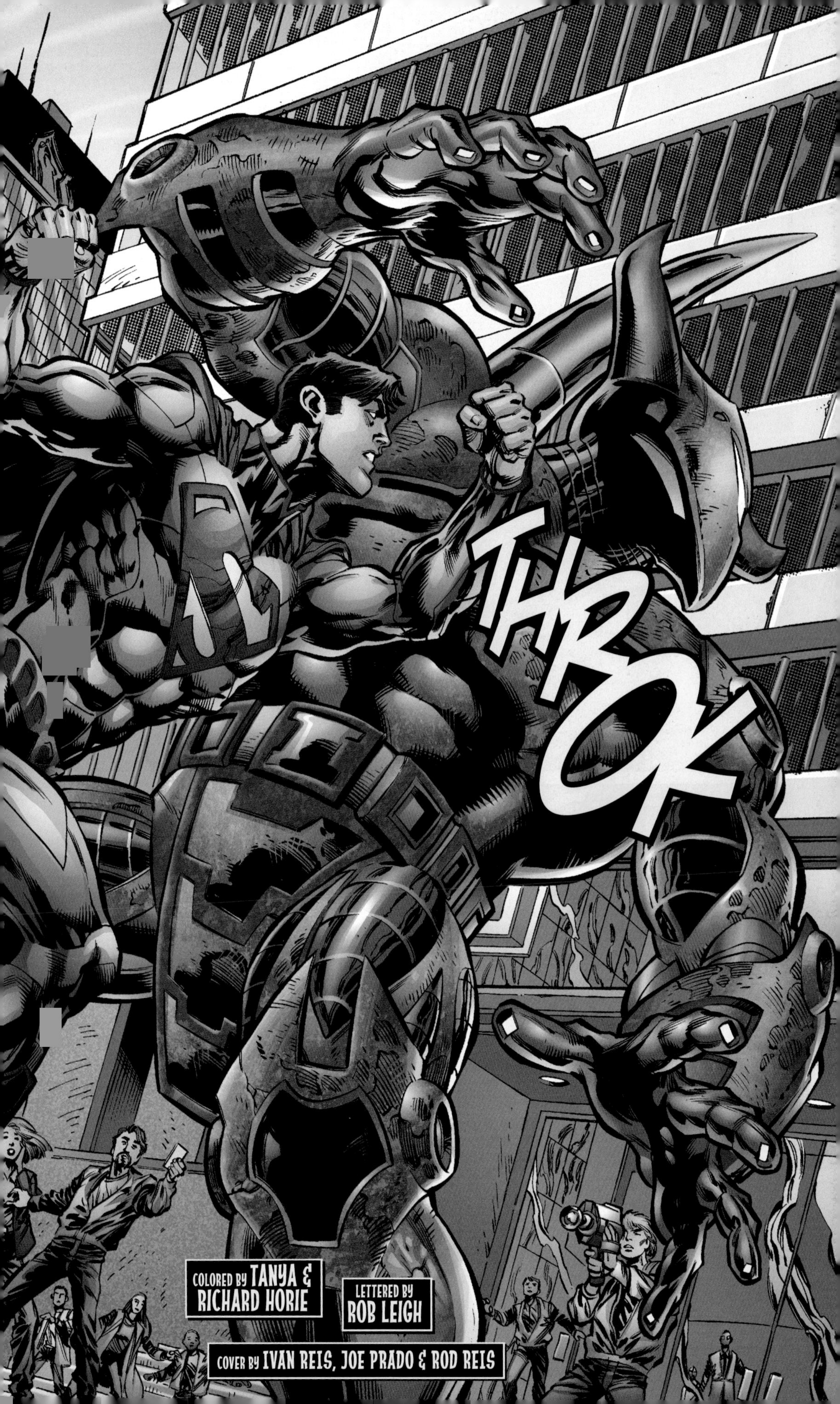
THROK
COLORED BY TANYA & RICHARD HORIE
LETTERED BY ROB LEIGH
COVER BY IVAN REIS, JOE PRADO & ROD REIS

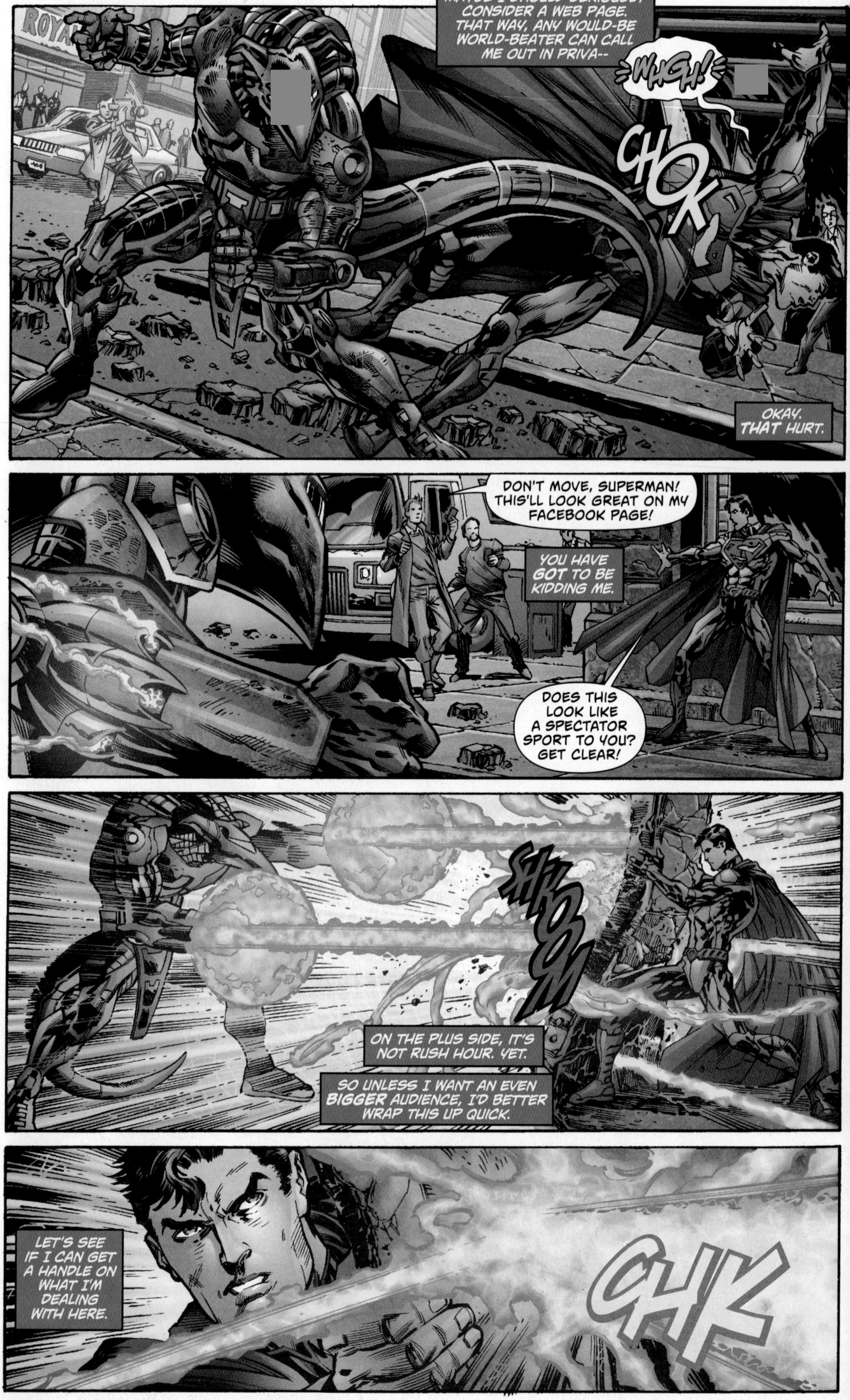

MAYBE I SHOULD SERIOUSLY CONSIDER A WEB PAGE. THAT WAY, ANY WOULD-BE WORLD-BEATER CAN CALL ME OUT IN PRIVA--
WHGH!
CHOK
OKAY. THAT HURT.
DON'T MOVE, SUPERMAN! THIS'LL LOOK GREAT ON MY FACEBOOK PAGE!
YOU HAVE GOT TO BE KIDDING ME.
DOES THIS LOOK LIKE A SPECTATOR SPORT TO YOU? GET CLEAR!
SHKOOM
ON THE PLUS SIDE, IT'S NOT RUSH HOUR. YET.
SO UNLESS I WANT AN EVEN BIGGER AUDIENCE, I'D BETTER WRAP THIS UP QUICK.
LET'S SEE IF I CAN GET A HANDLE ON WHAT I'M DEALING WITH HERE.
CHK

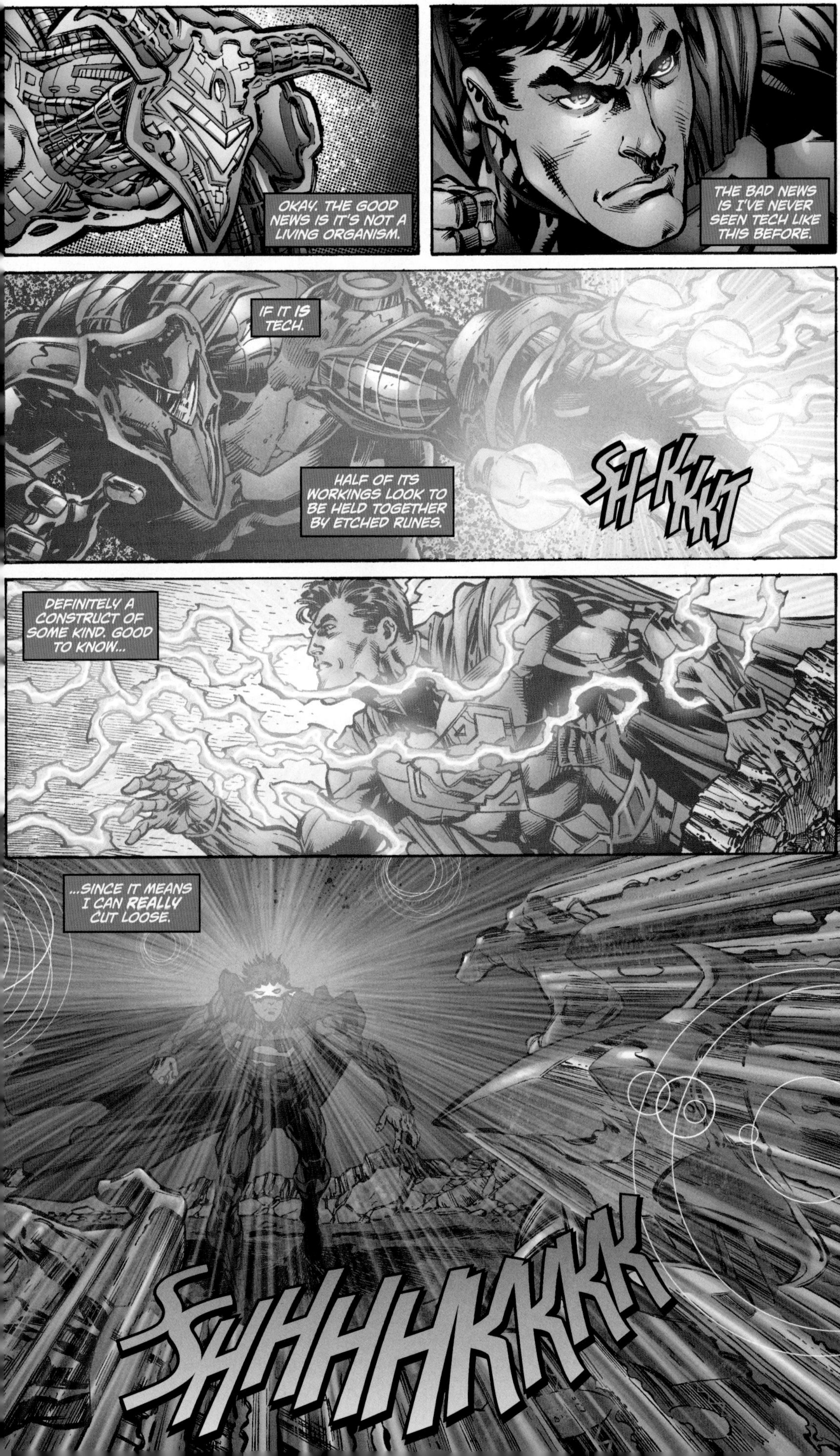
OKAY. THE GOOD NEWS IS IT'S NOT A LIVING ORGANISM.
THE BAD NEWS IS I'VE NEVER SEEN TECH LIKE THIS BEFORE.
IF IT IS TECH.
HALF OF ITS WORKINGS LOOK TO BE HELD TOGETHER BY ETCHED RUNES.
SH-KKKT
DEFINITELY A CONSTRUCT OF SOME KIND. GOOD TO KNOW...
...SINCE IT MEANS I CAN REALLY CUT LOOSE.
SHHHKKKK

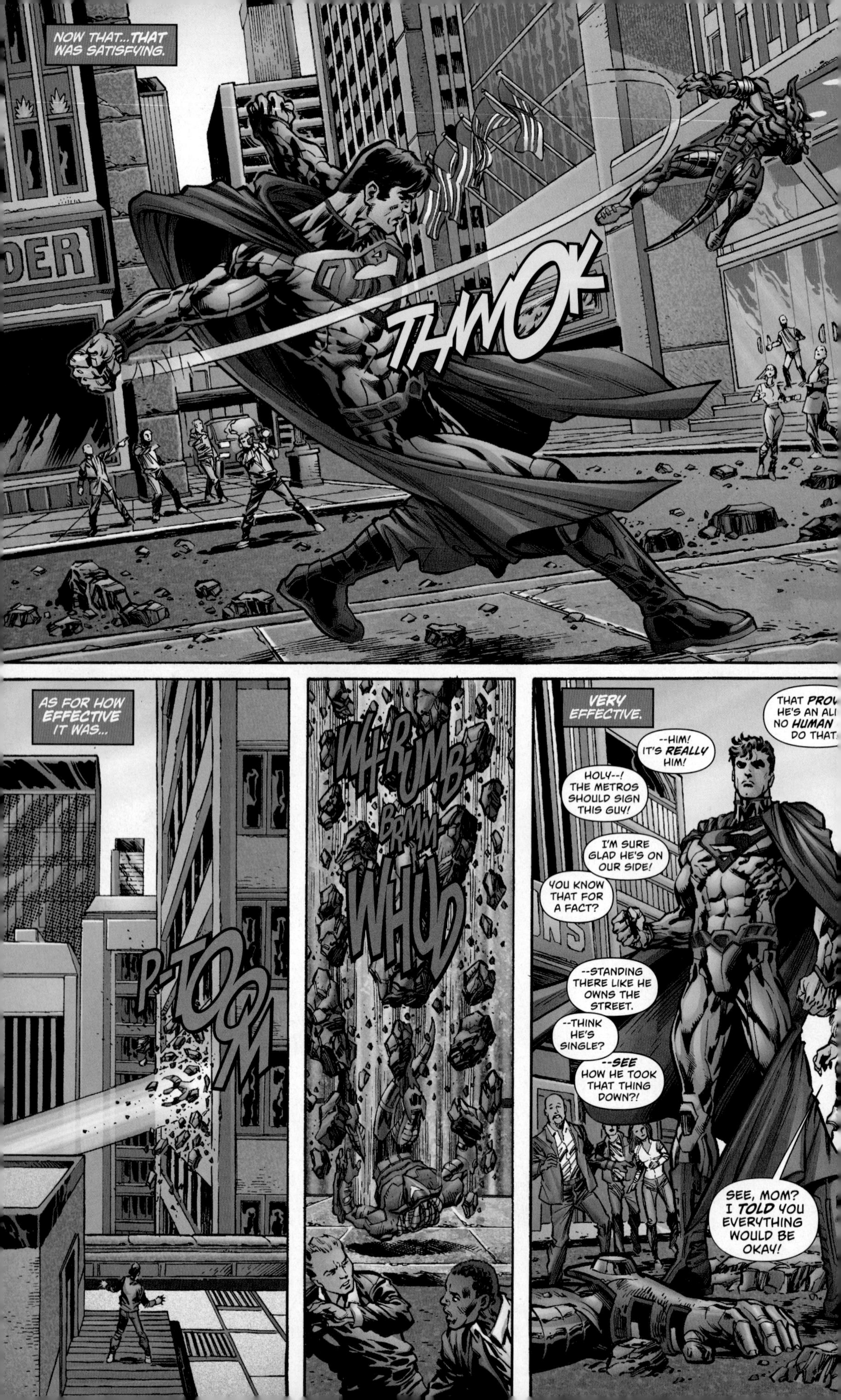

NOW THAT...**THAT** WAS SATISFYING.
THWOK
AS FOR HOW **EFFECTIVE** IT WAS...
P-TOOM
WH-RUMB-
BRMM-
WHUD
VERY EFFECTIVE.
THAT **PROV** HE'S AN ALI NO **HUMAN** DO THAT.
--HIM! IT'S **REALLY** HIM!
HOLY--! THE METROS SHOULD SIGN THIS GUY!
I'M SURE GLAD HE'S ON OUR SIDE!
YOU KNOW THAT FOR A FACT?
--STANDING THERE LIKE HE OWNS THE STREET.
--THINK HE'S SINGLE?
--SEE HOW HE TOOK THAT THING DOWN?!
SEE, MOM? I **TOLD** YOU EVERYTHING WOULD BE OKAY!

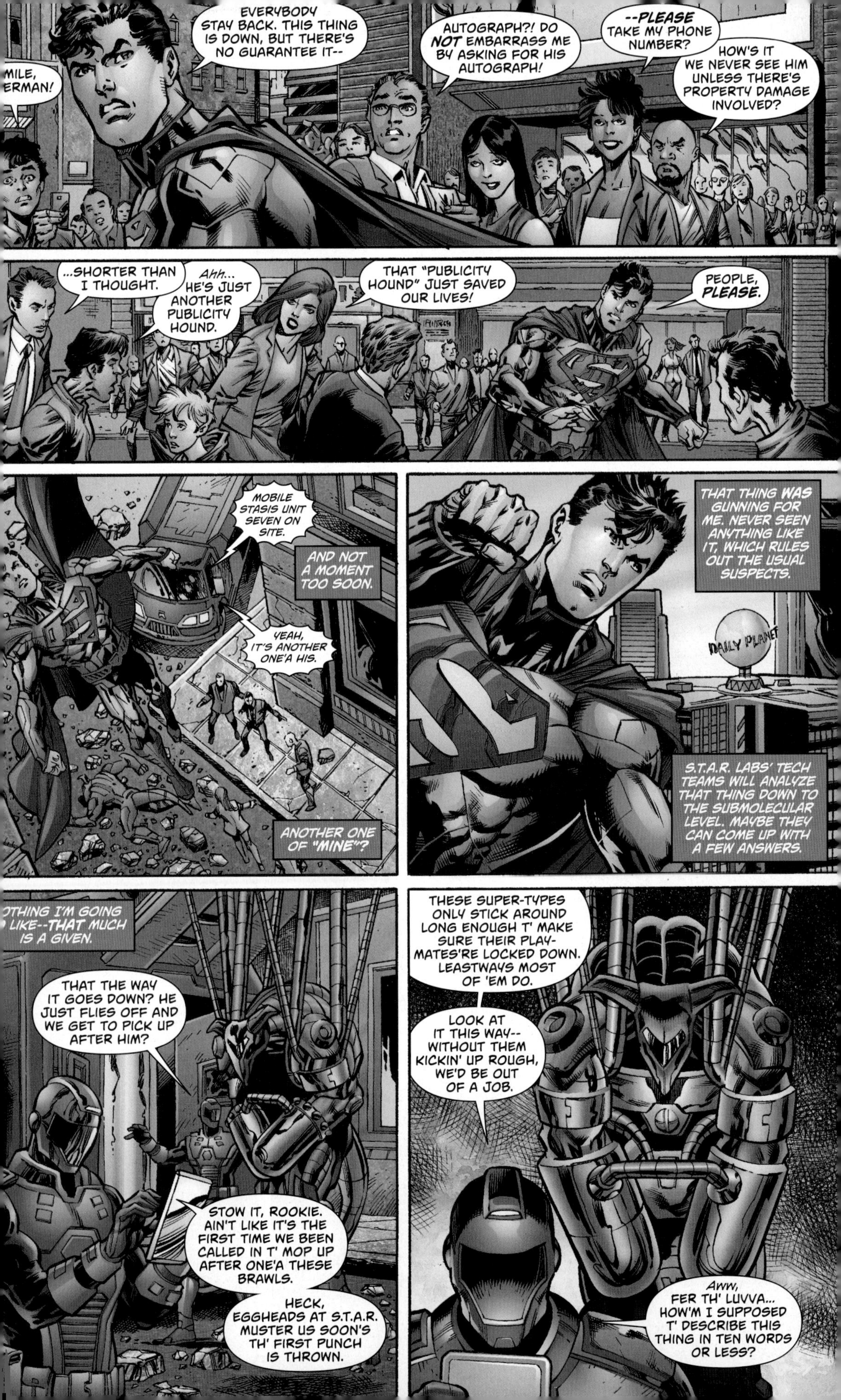
MILE,
ERMAN!
EVERYBODY STAY BACK. THIS THING IS DOWN, BUT THERE'S NO GUARANTEE IT--
AUTOGRAPH?! DO NOT EMBARRASS ME BY ASKING FOR HIS AUTOGRAPH!
--PLEASE TAKE MY PHONE NUMBER?
HOW'S IT WE NEVER SEE HIM UNLESS THERE'S PROPERTY DAMAGE INVOLVED?
...SHORTER THAN I THOUGHT.
Ahh... HE'S JUST ANOTHER PUBLICITY HOUND.
THAT "PUBLICITY HOUND" JUST SAVED OUR LIVES!
PEOPLE, PLEASE.
MOBILE STASIS UNIT SEVEN ON SITE.
AND NOT A MOMENT TOO SOON.
YEAH, IT'S ANOTHER ONE'A HIS.
ANOTHER ONE OF "MINE"?
THAT THING WAS GUNNING FOR ME. NEVER SEEN ANYTHING LIKE IT, WHICH RULES OUT THE USUAL SUSPECTS.
DAILY PLANET
S.T.A.R. LABS' TECH TEAMS WILL ANALYZE THAT THING DOWN TO THE SUBMOLECULAR LEVEL. MAYBE THEY CAN COME UP WITH A FEW ANSWERS.
OTHING I'M GOING
LIKE--THAT MUCH IS A GIVEN.
THAT THE WAY IT GOES DOWN? HE JUST FLIES OFF AND WE GET TO PICK UP AFTER HIM?
STOW IT, ROOKIE. AIN'T LIKE IT'S THE FIRST TIME WE BEEN CALLED IN T' MOP UP AFTER ONE'A THESE BRAWLS.
HECK, EGGHEADS AT S.T.A.R. MUSTER US SOON'S TH' FIRST PUNCH IS THROWN.
THESE SUPER-TYPES ONLY STICK AROUND LONG ENOUGH T' MAKE SURE THEIR PLAY-MATES'RE LOCKED DOWN. LEASTWAYS MOST OF 'EM DO.
LOOK AT IT THIS WAY-- WITHOUT THEM KICKIN' UP ROUGH, WE'D BE OUT OF A JOB.
Aww, FER TH' LUVVA... HOW'M I SUPPOSED T' DESCRIBE THIS THING IN TEN WORDS OR LESS?

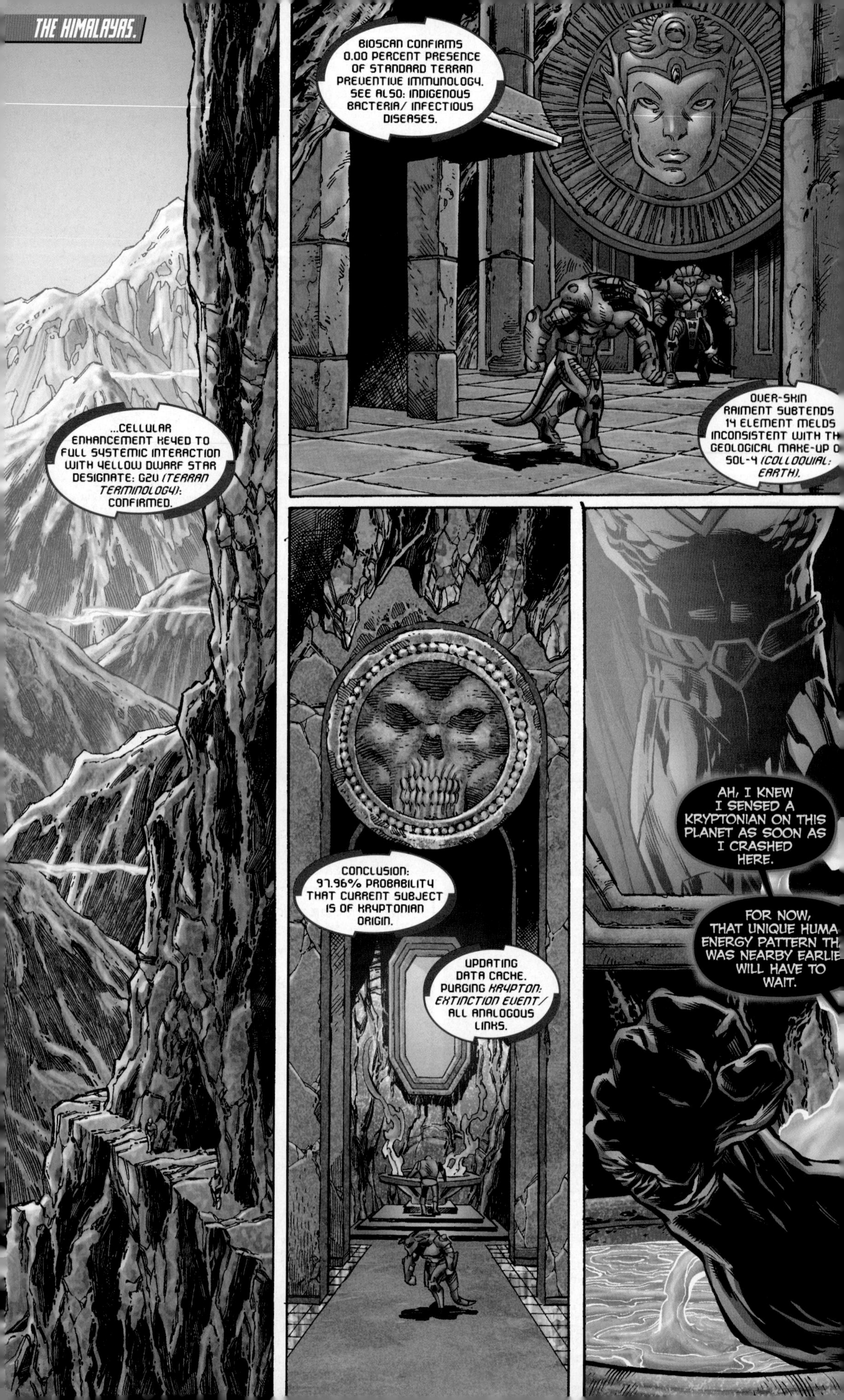
THE HIMALAYAS.
...CELLULAR ENHANCEMENT KEYED TO FULL SYSTEMIC INTERACTION WITH YELLOW DWARF STAR DESIGNATE: G2V (TERRAN TERMINOLOGY): CONFIRMED.
BIOSCAN CONFIRMS 0.00 PERCENT PRESENCE OF STANDARD TERRAN PREVENTIVE IMMUNOLOGY. SEE ALSO: INDIGENOUS BACTERIA/ INFECTIOUS DISEASES.
OVER-SKIN RAIMENT SUBTENDS 14 ELEMENT MELDS INCONSISTENT WITH TH GEOLOGICAL MAKE-UP O SOL-4 (COLLOQUIAL: EARTH).
CONCLUSION: 97.96% PROBABILITY THAT CURRENT SUBJECT IS OF KRYPTONIAN ORIGIN.
UPDATING DATA CACHE. PURGING KRYPTON: EXTINCTION EVENT/ ALL ANALOGOUS LINKS.
AH, I KNEW I SENSED A KRYPTONIAN ON THIS PLANET AS SOON AS I CRASHED HERE.
FOR NOW, THAT UNIQUE HUMA ENERGY PATTERN TH WAS NEARBY EARLIE WILL HAVE TO WAIT.

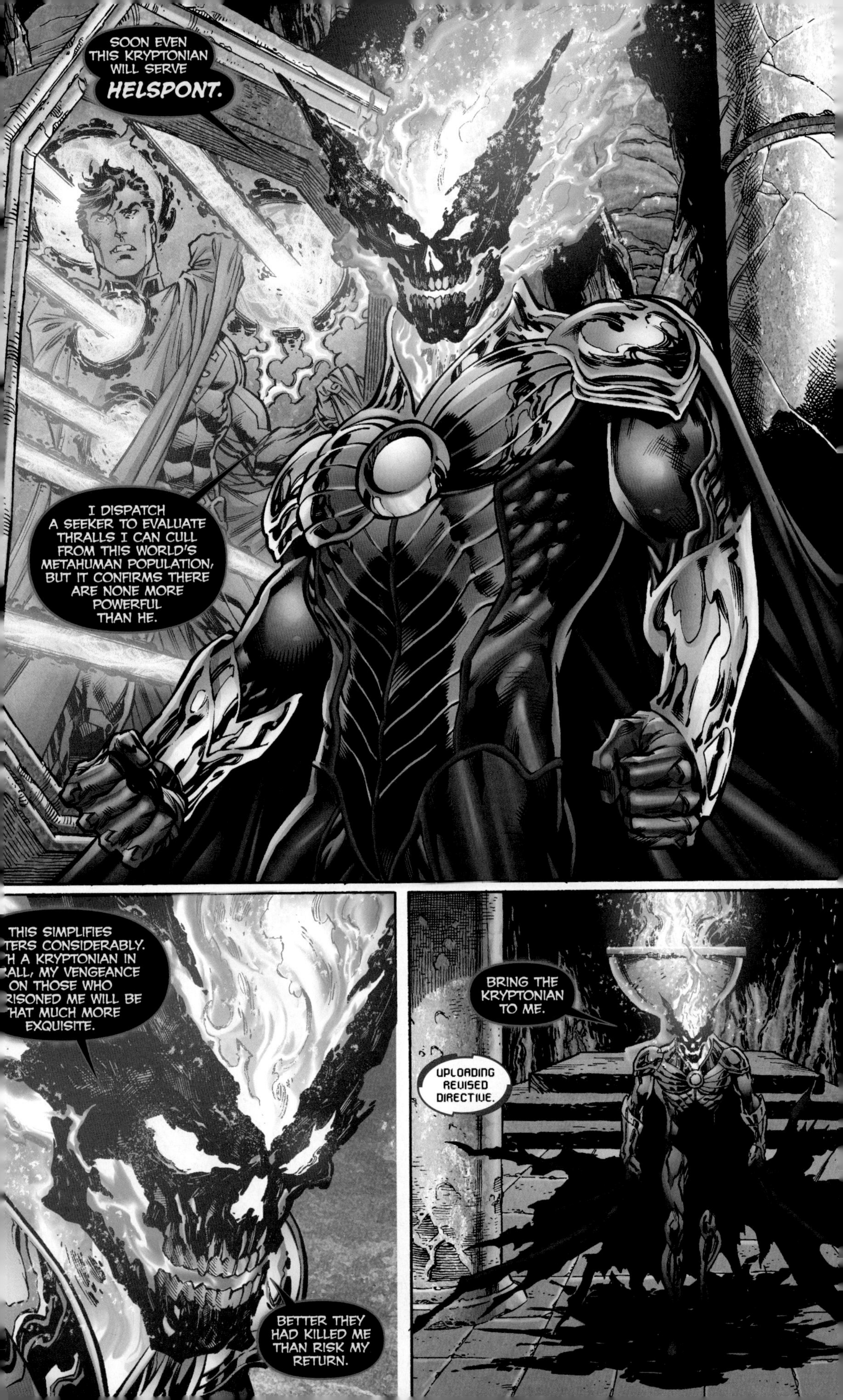
SOON EVEN THIS KRYPTONIAN WILL SERVE HELSPONT.
I DISPATCH A SEEKER TO EVALUATE THRALLS I CAN CULL FROM THIS WORLD'S METAHUMAN POPULATION, BUT IT CONFIRMS THERE ARE NONE MORE POWERFUL THAN HE.
THIS SIMPLIFIES TERS CONSIDERABLY. H A KRYPTONIAN IN ALL, MY VENGEANCE ON THOSE WHO RISONED ME WILL BE HAT MUCH MORE EXQUISITE.
BETTER THEY HAD KILLED ME THAN RISK MY RETURN.
BRING THE KRYPTONIAN TO ME.
UPLOADING REVISED DIRECTIVE.

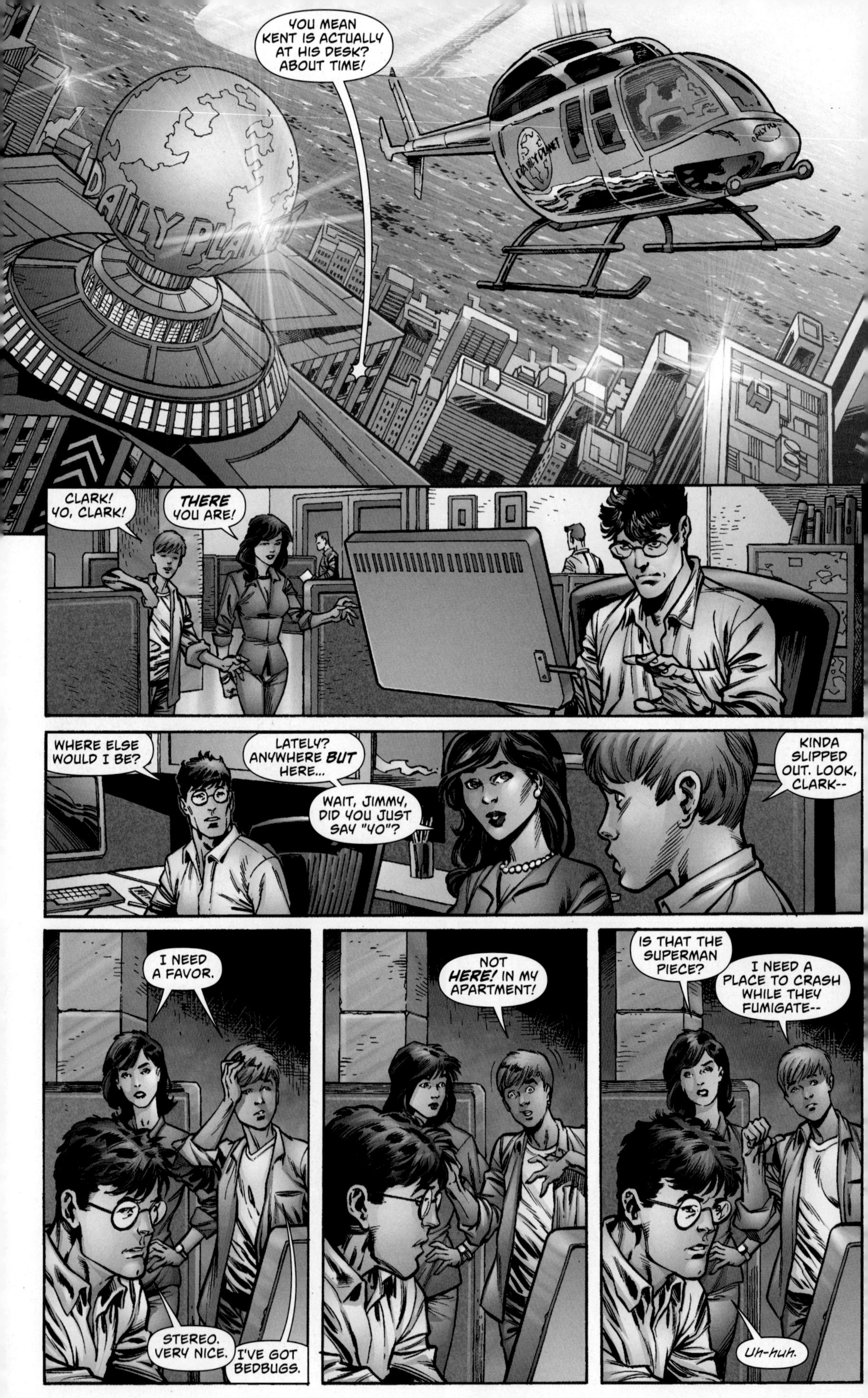
YOU MEAN KENT IS ACTUALLY AT HIS DESK? ABOUT TIME!
CLARK! YO, CLARK!
THERE YOU ARE!
WHERE ELSE WOULD I BE?
LATELY? ANYWHERE BUT HERE...
WAIT, JIMMY, DID YOU JUST SAY "YO"?
KINDA SLIPPED OUT. LOOK, CLARK--
I NEED A FAVOR.
STEREO. VERY NICE.
I'VE GOT BEDBUGS.
NOT HERE! IN MY APARTMENT!
IS THAT THE SUPERMAN PIECE?
I NEED A PLACE TO CRASH WHILE THEY FUMIGATE--
Uh-huh.

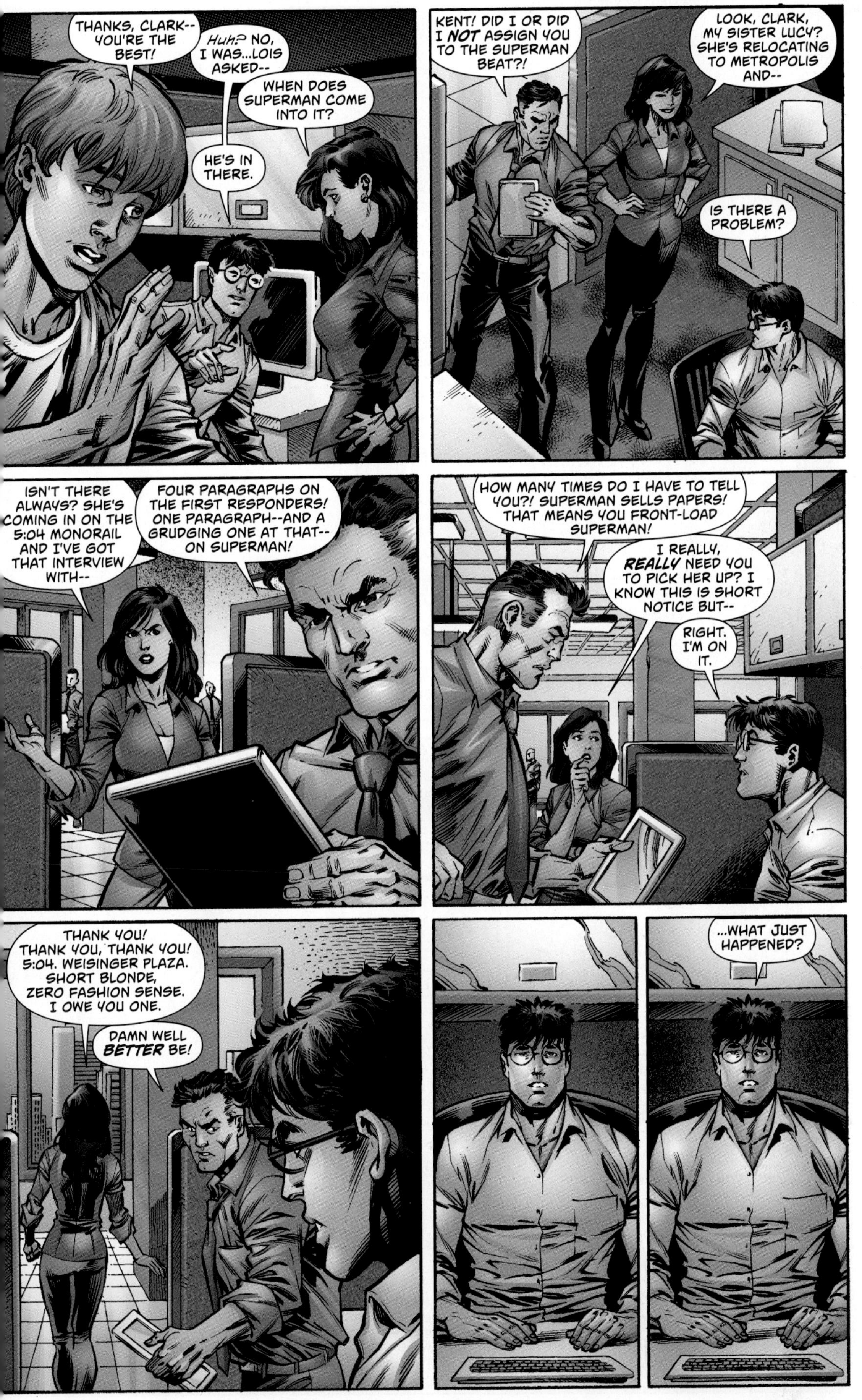

THANKS, CLARK-- YOU'RE THE BEST!
Huh? NO, I WAS...LOIS ASKED--
WHEN DOES SUPERMAN COME INTO IT?
HE'S IN THERE.
KENT! DID I OR DID I ***NOT*** ASSIGN YOU TO THE SUPERMAN BEAT?!
LOOK, CLARK, MY SISTER LUCY? SHE'S RELOCATING TO METROPOLIS AND--
IS THERE A PROBLEM?
ISN'T THERE ALWAYS? SHE'S COMING IN ON THE 5:04 MONORAIL AND I'VE GOT THAT INTERVIEW WITH--
FOUR PARAGRAPHS ON THE FIRST RESPONDERS! ONE PARAGRAPH--AND A GRUDGING ONE AT THAT--ON SUPERMAN!
HOW MANY TIMES DO I HAVE TO TELL YOU?! SUPERMAN SELLS PAPERS! THAT MEANS YOU FRONT-LOAD SUPERMAN!
I REALLY, ***REALLY*** NEED YOU TO PICK HER UP? I KNOW THIS IS SHORT NOTICE BUT--
RIGHT. I'M ON IT.
THANK YOU! THANK YOU, THANK YOU! 5:04. WEISINGER PLAZA. SHORT BLONDE, ZERO FASHION SENSE. I OWE YOU ONE.
DAMN WELL ***BETTER*** BE!
...WHAT JUST HAPPENED?

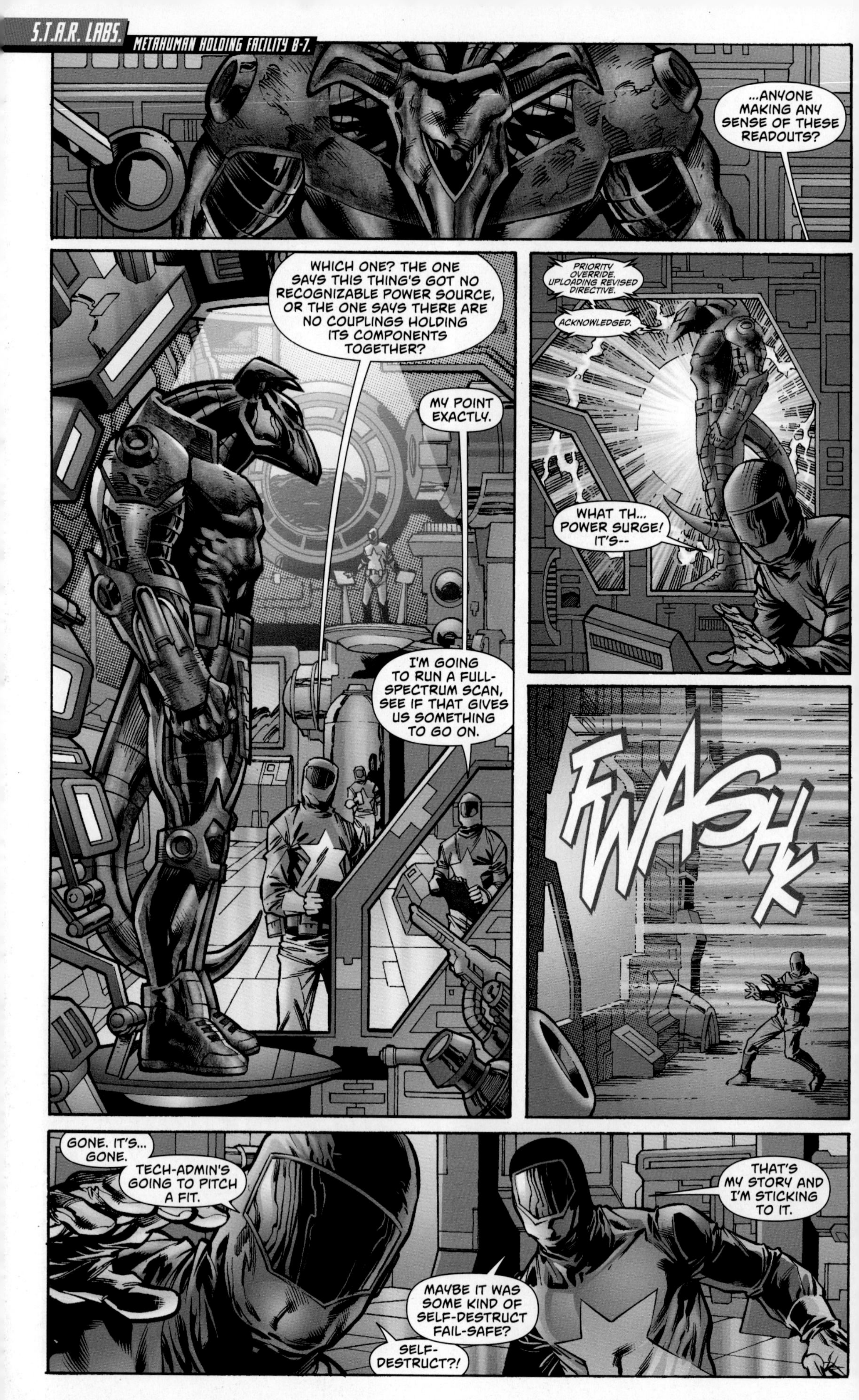
S.T.A.R. LABS.
METAHUMAN HOLDING FACILITY 8-7.
...ANYONE MAKING ANY SENSE OF THESE READOUTS?
WHICH ONE? THE ONE SAYS THIS THING'S GOT NO RECOGNIZABLE POWER SOURCE, OR THE ONE SAYS THERE ARE NO COUPLINGS HOLDING ITS COMPONENTS TOGETHER?
MY POINT EXACTLY.
I'M GOING TO RUN A FULL-SPECTRUM SCAN, SEE IF THAT GIVES US SOMETHING TO GO ON.
PRIORITY OVERRIDE. UPLOADING REVISED DIRECTIVE.
ACKNOWLEDGED.
WHAT TH... POWER SURGE! IT'S--
FWASHK
GONE. IT'S... GONE.
TECH-ADMIN'S GOING TO PITCH A FIT.
MAYBE IT WAS SOME KIND OF SELF-DESTRUCT FAIL-SAFE?
SELF-DESTRUCT?!
THAT'S MY STORY AND I'M STICKING TO IT.

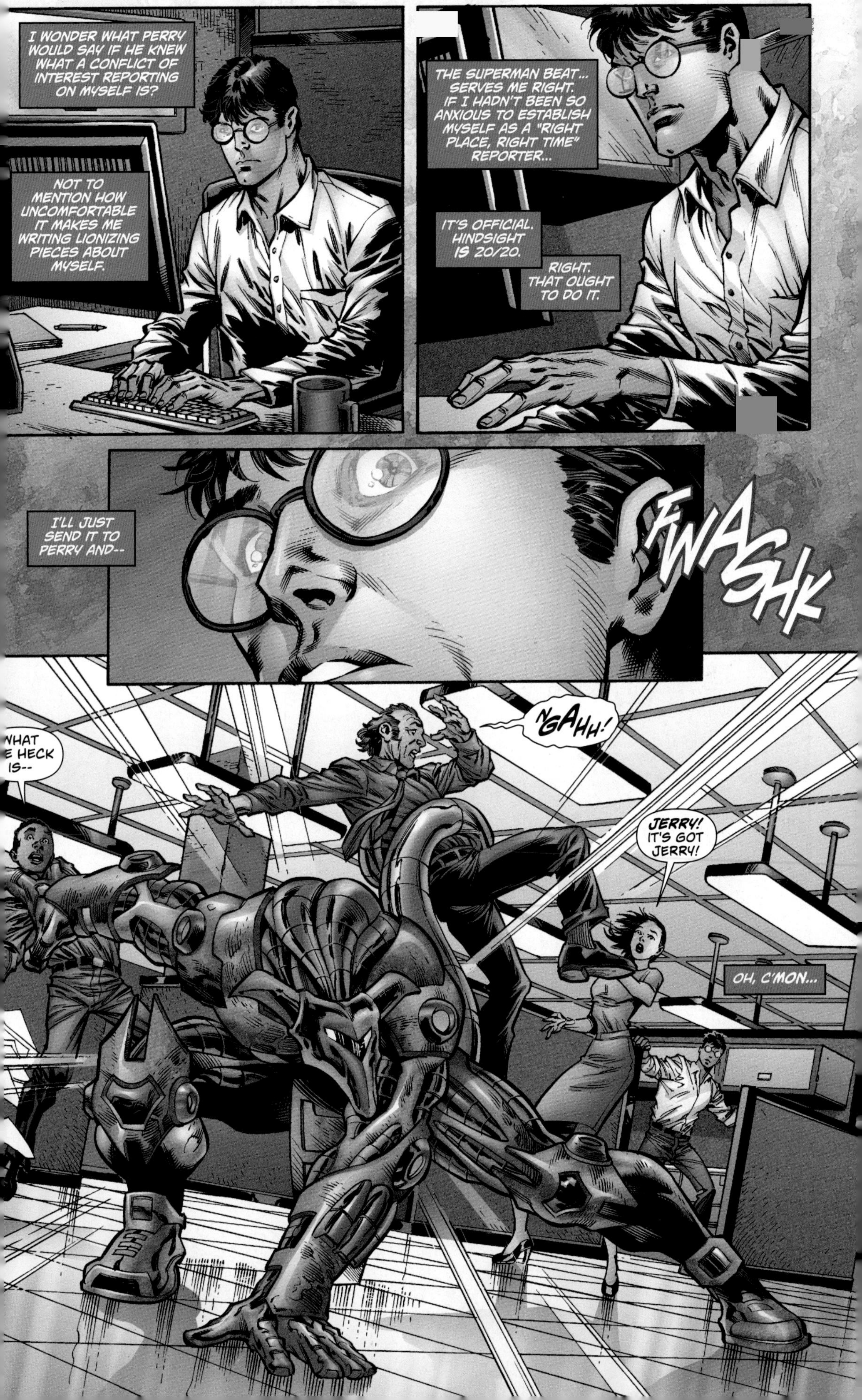

I WONDER WHAT PERRY WOULD SAY IF HE KNEW WHAT A CONFLICT OF INTEREST REPORTING ON MYSELF IS?
NOT TO MENTION HOW UNCOMFORTABLE IT MAKES ME WRITING LIONIZING PIECES ABOUT MYSELF.
THE SUPERMAN BEAT... SERVES ME RIGHT. IF I HADN'T BEEN SO ANXIOUS TO ESTABLISH MYSELF AS A "RIGHT PLACE, RIGHT TIME" REPORTER...
IT'S OFFICIAL. HINDSIGHT IS 20/20.
RIGHT. THAT OUGHT TO DO IT.
I'LL JUST SEND IT TO PERRY AND--
FWASHK
NGAHH!
JERRY! IT'S GOT JERRY!
OH, C'MON...

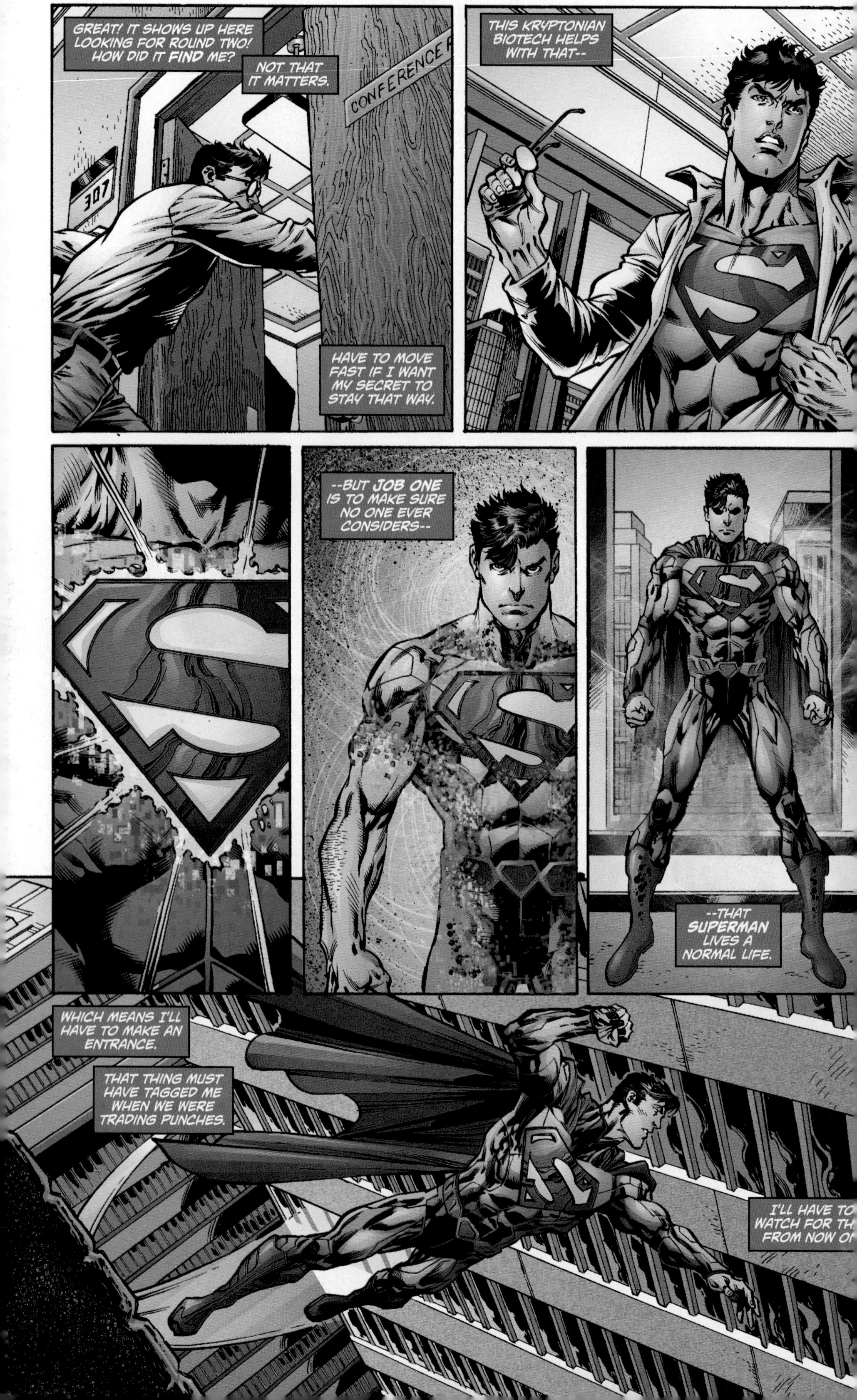

GREAT! IT SHOWS UP HERE LOOKING FOR ROUND TWO! HOW DID IT FIND ME?
NOT THAT IT MATTERS.
CONFERENCE
307
HAVE TO MOVE FAST IF I WANT MY SECRET TO STAY THAT WAY.
THIS KRYPTONIAN BIOTECH HELPS WITH THAT--
--BUT JOB ONE IS TO MAKE SURE NO ONE EVER CONSIDERS--
--THAT SUPERMAN LIVES A NORMAL LIFE.
WHICH MEANS I'LL HAVE TO MAKE AN ENTRANCE.
THAT THING MUST HAVE TAGGED ME WHEN WE WERE TRADING PUNCHES.

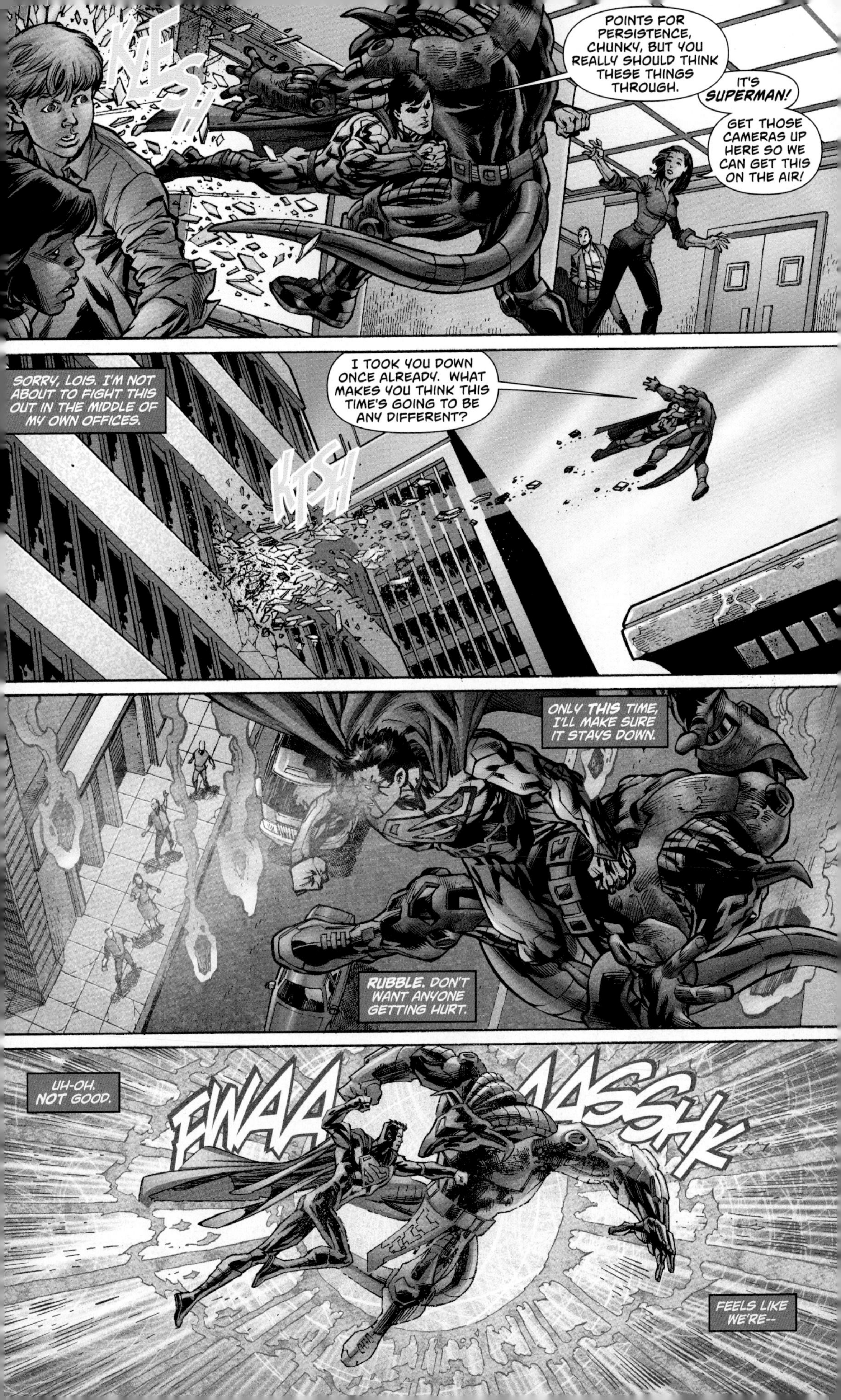

KLESH
POINTS FOR PERSISTENCE, CHUNKY, BUT YOU REALLY SHOULD THINK THESE THINGS THROUGH.
IT'S SUPERMAN!
GET THOSE CAMERAS UP HERE SO WE CAN GET THIS ON THE AIR!
SORRY, LOIS. I'M NOT ABOUT TO FIGHT THIS OUT IN THE MIDDLE OF MY OWN OFFICES.
I TOOK YOU DOWN ONCE ALREADY. WHAT MAKES YOU THINK THIS TIME'S GOING TO BE ANY DIFFERENT?
KTSH
ONLY THIS TIME, I'LL MAKE SURE IT STAYS DOWN.
RUBBLE. DON'T WANT ANYONE GETTING HURT.
UH-OH. NOT GOOD.
FWAAAASSHK
FEELS LIKE WE'RE--

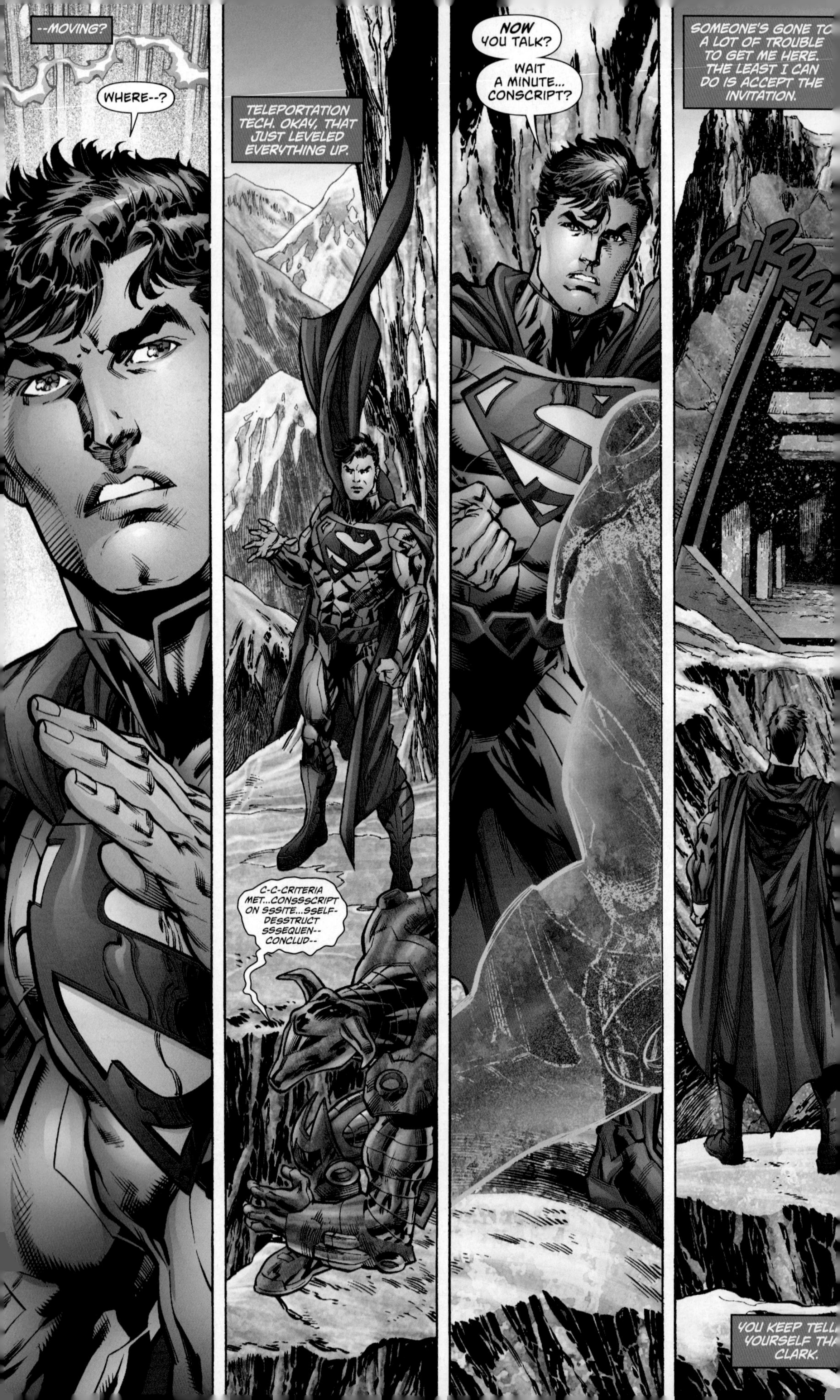

--MOVING?
WHERE--?
TELEPORTATION TECH. OKAY, THAT JUST LEVELED EVERYTHING UP.
C-C-CRITERIA MET...CONSSSCRIPT ON SSSITE...SSELF-DESSTRUCT SSSEQUEN-- CONCLUD--
NOW YOU TALK?
WAIT A MINUTE... CONSCRIPT?
SOMEONE'S GONE TO A LOT OF TROUBLE TO GET ME HERE. THE LEAST I CAN DO IS ACCEPT THE INVITATION.
YOU KEEP TELL YOURSELF TH CLARK.

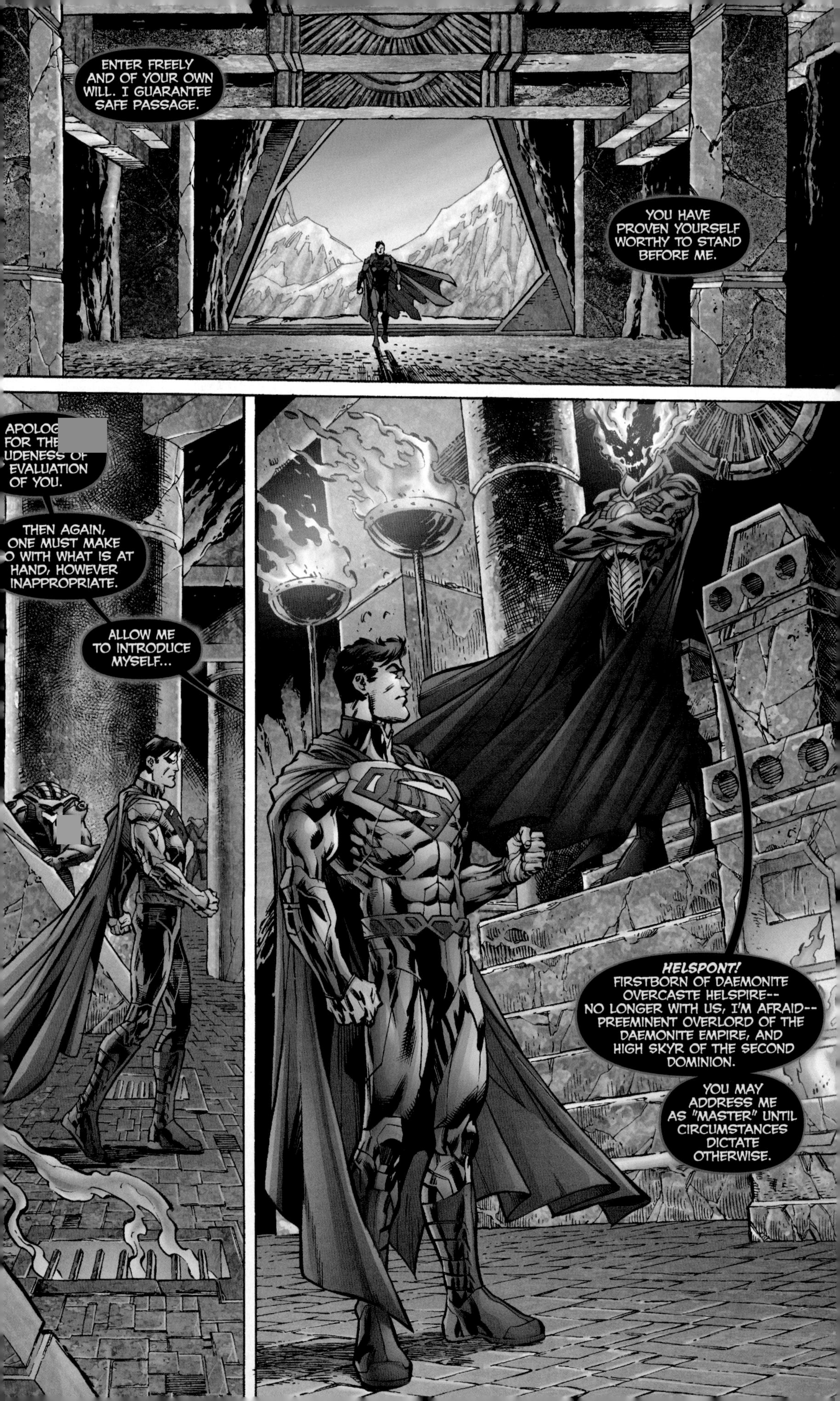
ENTER FREELY AND OF YOUR OWN WILL. I GUARANTEE SAFE PASSAGE.
YOU HAVE PROVEN YOURSELF WORTHY TO STAND BEFORE ME.
APOLOG FOR THE UDENESS OF EVALUATION OF YOU.
THEN AGAIN, ONE MUST MAKE O WITH WHAT IS AT HAND, HOWEVER INAPPROPRIATE.
ALLOW ME TO INTRODUCE MYSELF...
HELSPONT! FIRSTBORN OF DAEMONITE OVERCASTE HELSPIRE-- NO LONGER WITH US, I'M AFRAID-- PREEMINENT OVERLORD OF THE DAEMONITE EMPIRE, AND HIGH SKYR OF THE SECOND DOMINION.
YOU MAY ADDRESS ME AS "MASTER" UNTIL CIRCUMSTANCES DICTATE OTHERWISE.

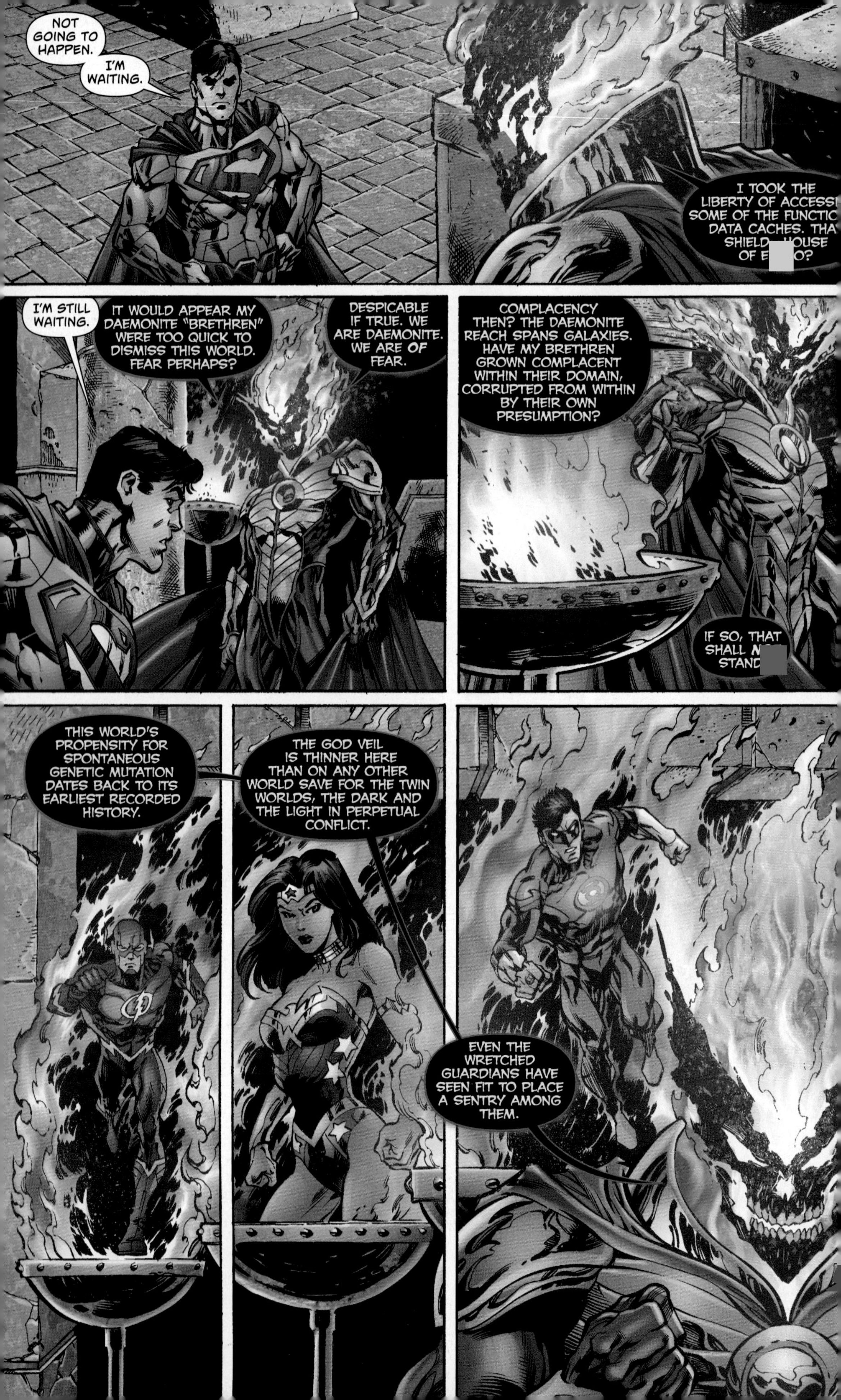

NOT GOING TO HAPPEN.
I'M WAITING.
I TOOK THE LIBERTY OF ACCESS SOME OF THE FUNCTIC DATA CACHES. THA SHIELD HOUSE OF E O?
I'M STILL WAITING.
IT WOULD APPEAR MY DAEMONITE "BRETHREN" WERE TOO QUICK TO DISMISS THIS WORLD. FEAR PERHAPS?
DESPICABLE IF TRUE. WE ARE DAEMONITE. WE ARE OF FEAR.
COMPLACENCY THEN? THE DAEMONITE REACH SPANS GALAXIES. HAVE MY BRETHREN GROWN COMPLACENT WITHIN THEIR DOMAIN, CORRUPTED FROM WITHIN BY THEIR OWN PRESUMPTION?
IF SO, THAT SHALL N STAND
THIS WORLD'S PROPENSITY FOR SPONTANEOUS GENETIC MUTATION DATES BACK TO ITS EARLIEST RECORDED HISTORY.
THE GOD VEIL IS THINNER HERE THAN ON ANY OTHER WORLD SAVE FOR THE TWIN WORLDS, THE DARK AND THE LIGHT IN PERPETUAL CONFLICT.
EVEN THE WRETCHED GUARDIANS HAVE SEEN FIT TO PLACE A SENTRY AMONG THEM.

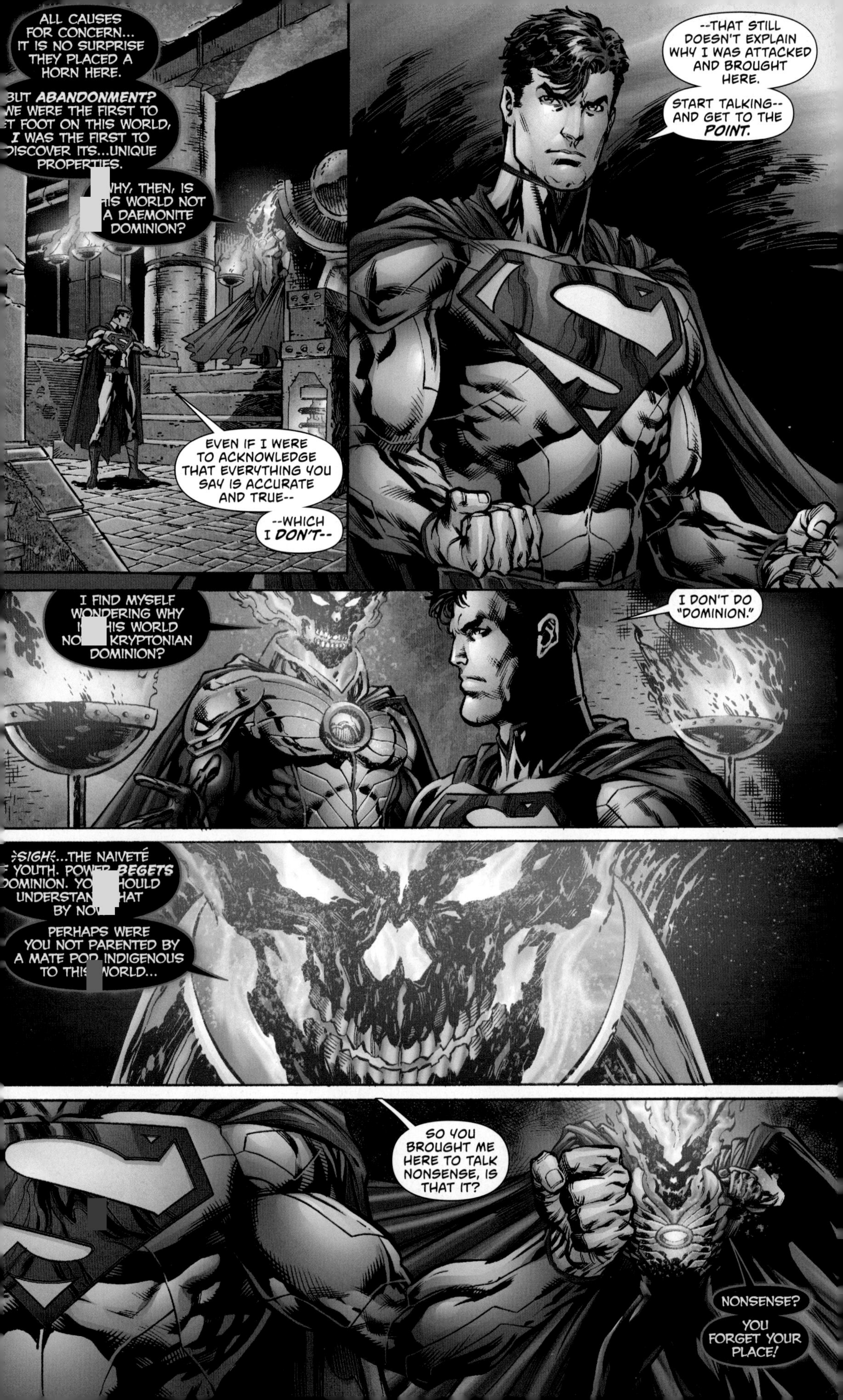
ALL CAUSES FOR CONCERN... IT IS NO SURPRISE THEY PLACED A HORN HERE.
BUT *ABANDONMENT?* WE WERE THE FIRST TO T FOOT ON THIS WORLD, *I* WAS THE FIRST TO ISCOVER ITS...UNIQUE PROPERTIES.
HY, THEN, IS HIS WORLD NOT A DAEMONITE DOMINION?
EVEN IF I WERE TO ACKNOWLEDGE THAT EVERYTHING YOU SAY IS ACCURATE AND TRUE--
--WHICH I *DON'T*--
--THAT STILL DOESN'T EXPLAIN WHY I WAS ATTACKED AND BROUGHT HERE.
START TALKING-- AND GET TO THE *POINT.*
I FIND MYSELF WONDERING WHY HIS WORLD NO KRYPTONIAN DOMINION?
I DON'T DO "DOMINION."
SIGH...THE NAIVETÉ YOUTH. POWE *BEGETS* OMINION. YO HOULD UNDERSTAN HAT BY NO
PERHAPS WERE YOU NOT PARENTED BY A MATE POD INDIGENOUS TO THIS WORLD...
SO YOU BROUGHT ME HERE TO TALK NONSENSE, IS THAT IT?
NONSENSE?
YOU FORGET YOUR PLACE!

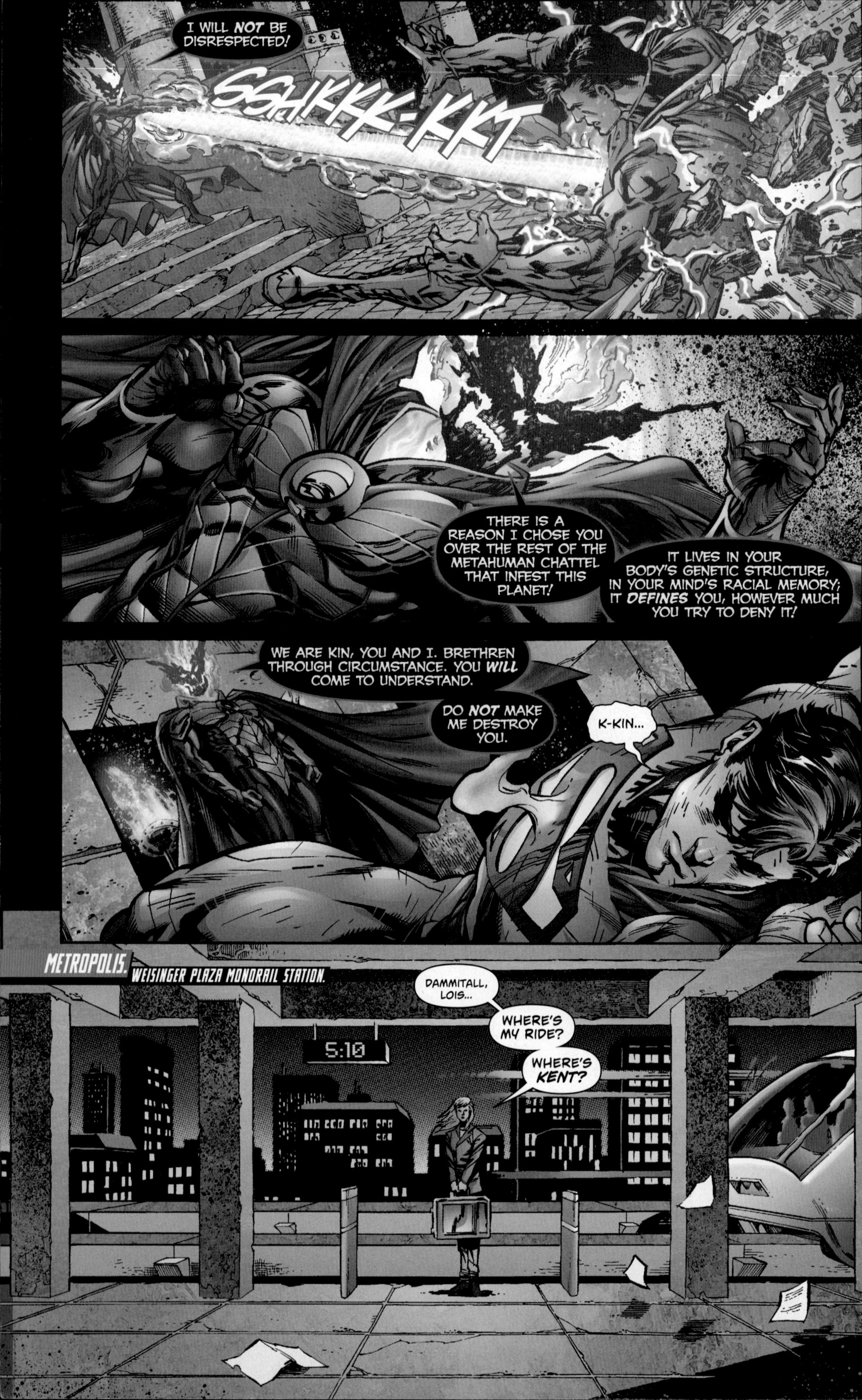
I WILL NOT BE DISRESPECTED!
SSHKKK-KKT
THERE IS A REASON I CHOSE YOU OVER THE REST OF THE METAHUMAN CHATTEL THAT INFEST THIS PLANET!
IT LIVES IN YOUR BODY'S GENETIC STRUCTURE, IN YOUR MIND'S RACIAL MEMORY; IT DEFINES YOU, HOWEVER MUCH YOU TRY TO DENY IT!
WE ARE KIN, YOU AND I. BRETHREN THROUGH CIRCUMSTANCE. YOU WILL COME TO UNDERSTAND.
DO NOT MAKE ME DESTROY YOU.
K-KIN...
METROPOLIS.
WEISINGER PLAZA MONORAIL STATION.
5:10
DAMMITALL, LOIS...
WHERE'S MY RIDE?
WHERE'S KENT?

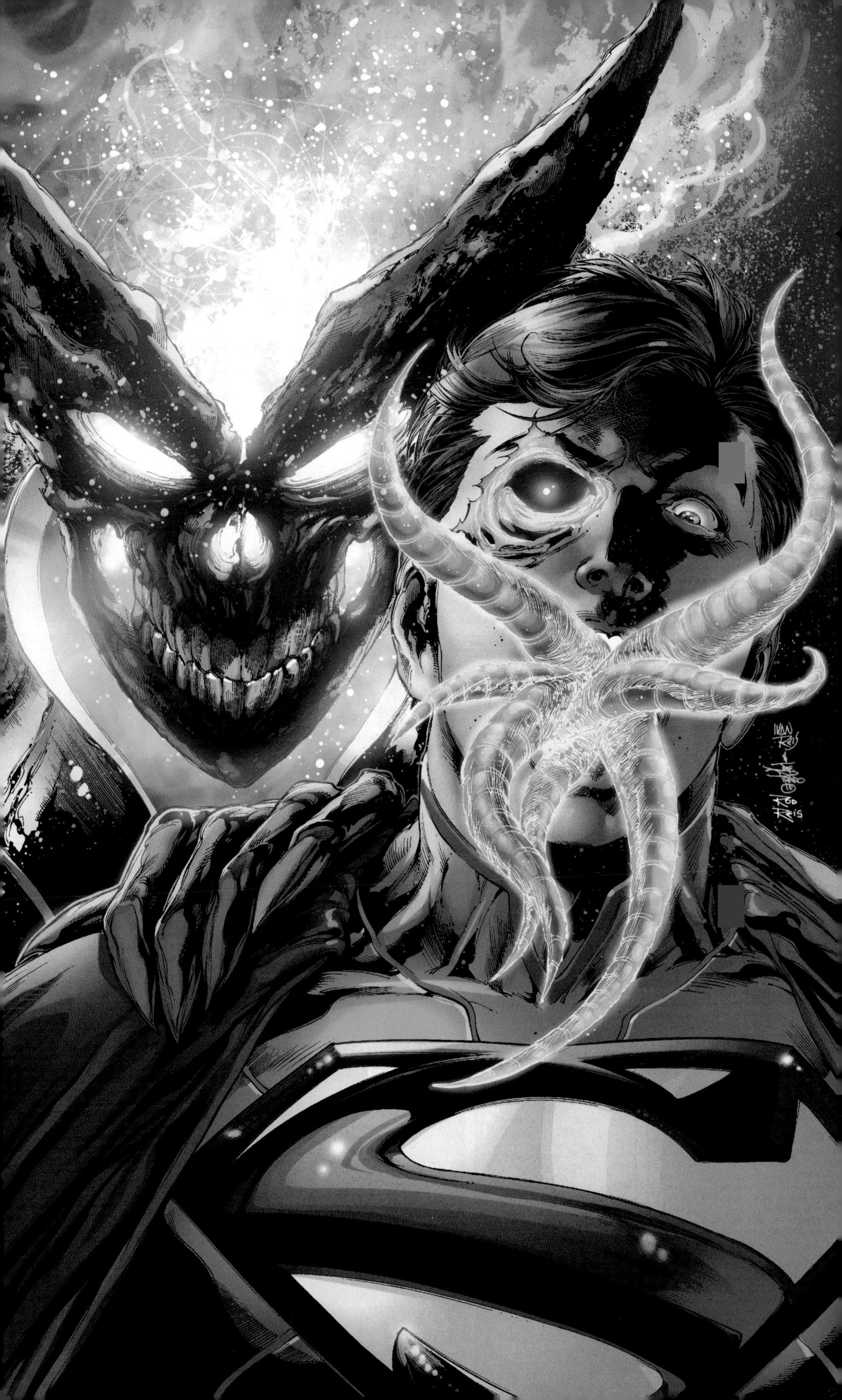
IVAN REIS
ROD REIS

WELL FORGIVE *ME* FOR FEELING BAD ABOUT LEAVING MY LITTLE SISTER STRANDED.

STRANDED? I WAS AT THE METROPOLIS MONORAIL STATION, NOT THE AMAZON RAIN FOREST.

HEY, I'M A BIG GIRL NOW; I CAN TAKE CARE OF MYSELF.

LOIS, WOULD YOU *PLEASE*, FOR THE LOVE OF GOD, STOP APOLOGIZING?

THIS IS *SO* UNLIKE CLARK.

HIS NAME IS "CLARK." DO THE MATH.

THERE'S THE LUCY LANE WE'VE COME TO KNOW AND LOVE.

YOU HAVEN'T EVEN MET THE MAN AND YOU'RE ALREADY--

YOU KNOW, I'D KILL FOR A CUP OF COFFEE.

FOR WHAT IT'S WORTH, I'M GLAD YOU'RE HERE. YOU'LL LOVE METROPOLIS. THE NIGHTLIFE ALONE--

AAGH! CAFFEINE WITHDRAWAL! DO I HAVE TO WAIT FOR CLARK TO BRING ME THE COFFEE TOO?

WONDERFUL. N EVEN ONE DAY AND SHE'S FOU SOMEONE TO P A BULL'S-EYE C

SMOOTH DODGE.

I THOUGHT SO.

I HOPE YOU'VE A GOOD REASC FOR NOT PICKI HER UP, CLAR

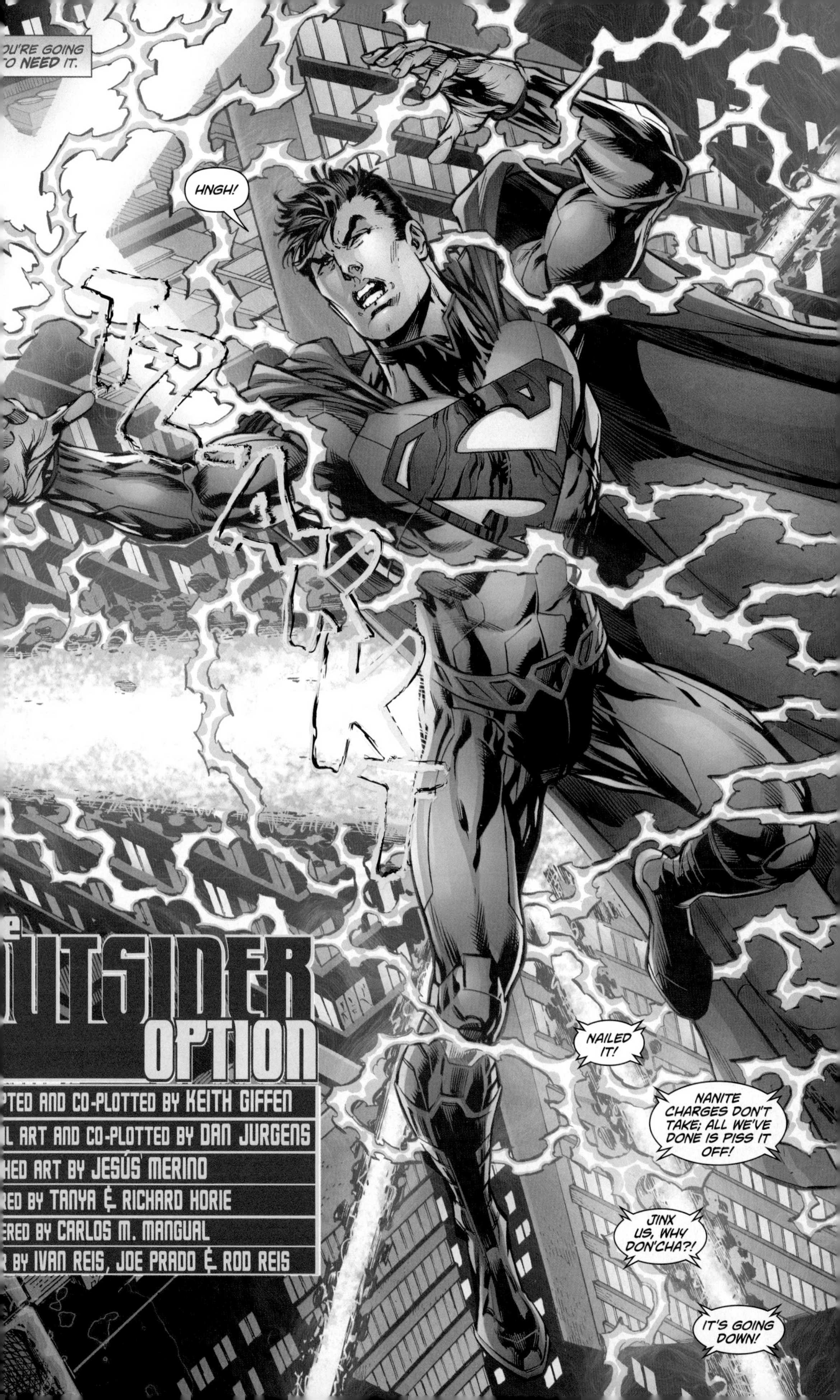

OU'RE GOING
O NEED IT.
HNGH!
TZAK
UTSIDER
OPTION
PTED AND CO-PLOTTED BY KEITH GIFFEN
L ART AND CO-PLOTTED BY DAN JURGENS
HED ART BY JESÚS MERINO
RED BY TANYA & RICHARD HORIE
ERED BY CARLOS M. MANGUAL
R BY IVAN REIS, JOE PRADO & ROD REIS
NAILED IT!
NANITE CHARGES DON'T TAKE; ALL WE'VE DONE IS PISS IT OFF!
JINX US, WHY DON'CHA?!
IT'S GOING DOWN!

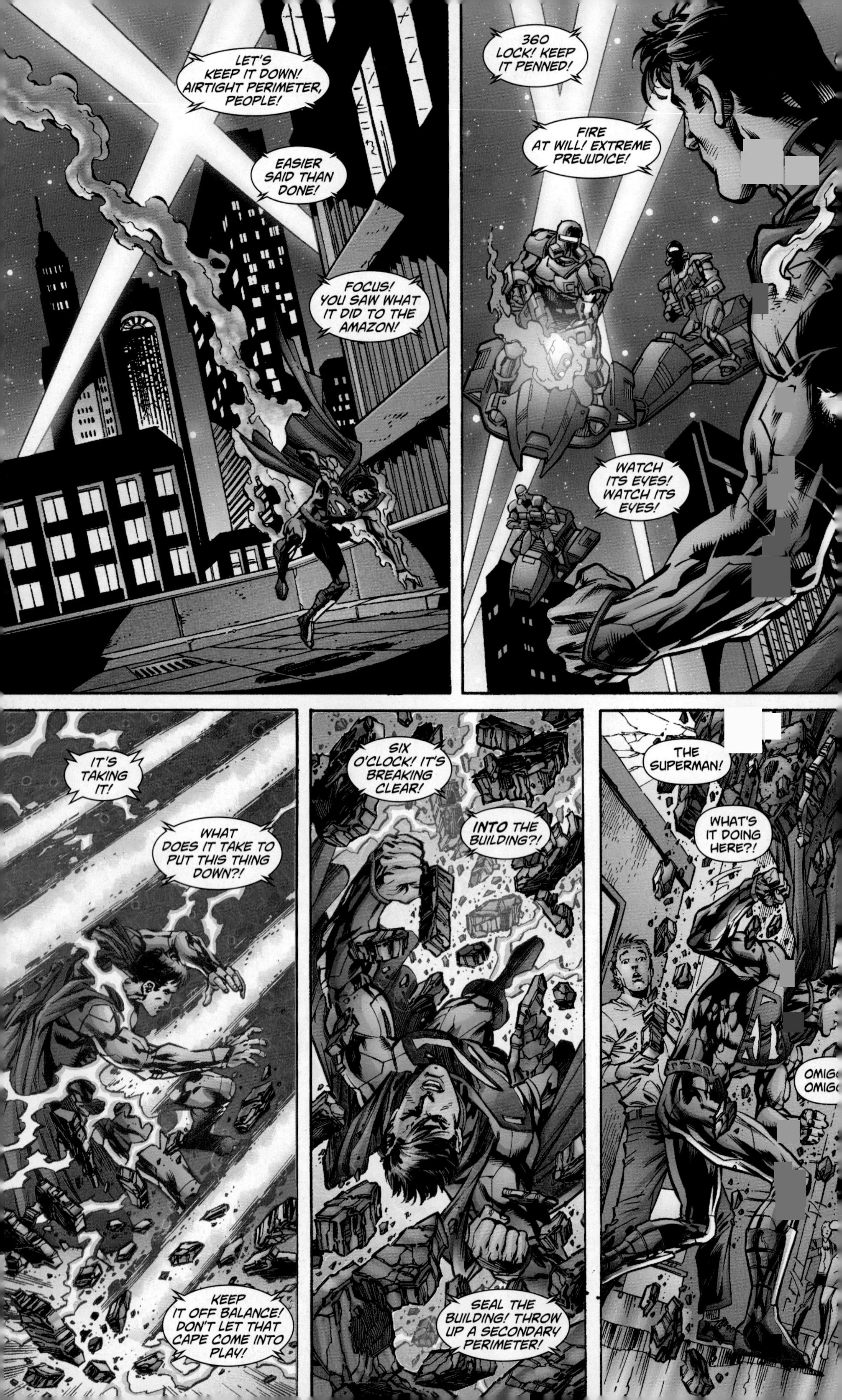
LET'S KEEP IT DOWN! AIRTIGHT PERIMETER, PEOPLE!
EASIER SAID THAN DONE!
FOCUS! YOU SAW WHAT IT DID TO THE AMAZON!
360 LOCK! KEEP IT PENNED!
FIRE AT WILL! EXTREME PREJUDICE!
WATCH ITS EYES! WATCH ITS EYES!
IT'S TAKING IT!
WHAT DOES IT TAKE TO PUT THIS THING DOWN?!
KEEP IT OFF BALANCE! DON'T LET THAT CAPE COME INTO PLAY!
SIX O'CLOCK! IT'S BREAKING CLEAR!
INTO THE BUILDING?!
SEAL THE BUILDING! THROW UP A SECONDARY PERIMETER!
THE SUPERMAN!
WHAT'S IT DOING HERE?!

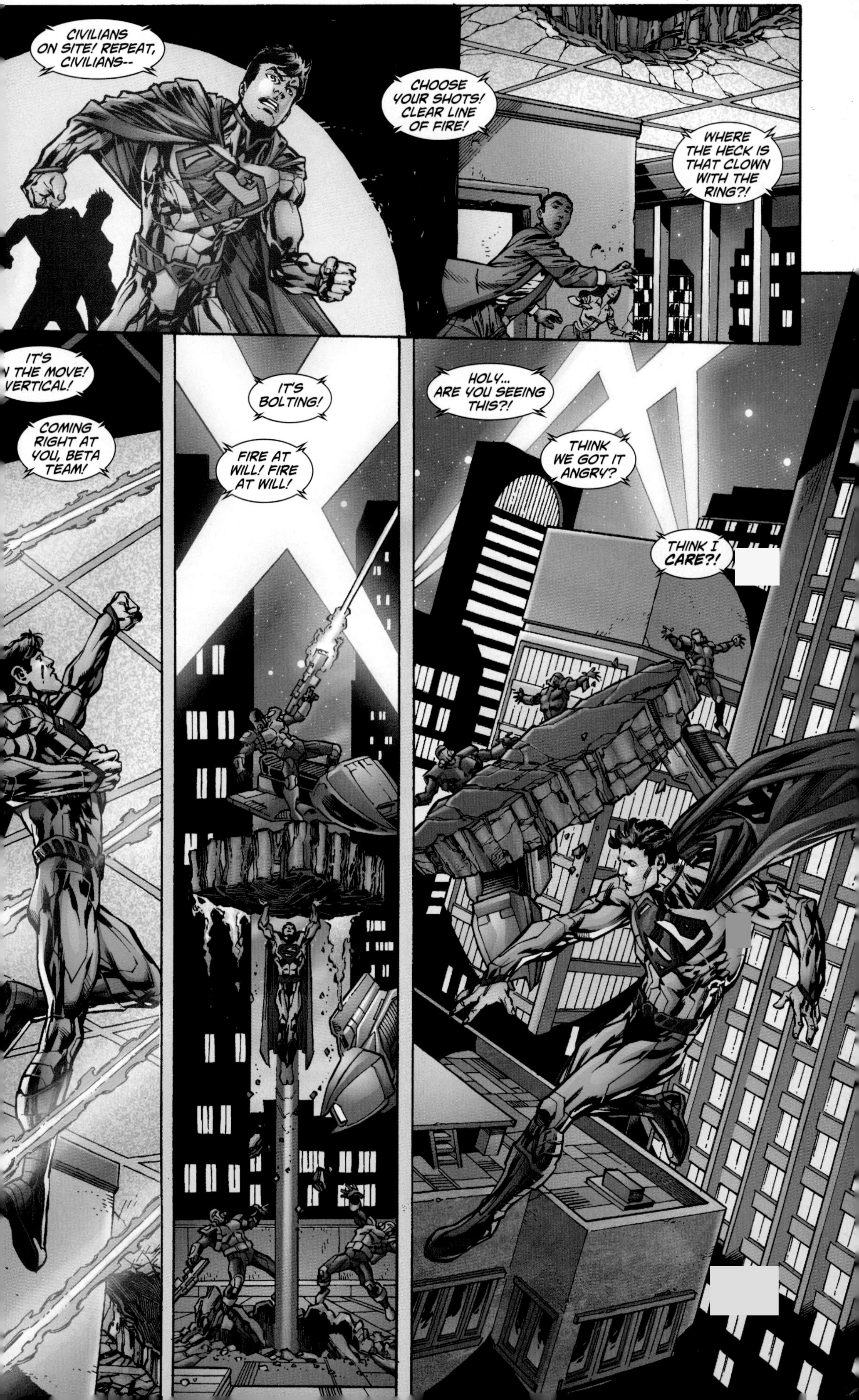

CIVILIANS ON SITE! REPEAT, CIVILIANS--
CHOOSE YOUR SHOTS! CLEAR LINE OF FIRE!
WHERE THE HECK IS THAT CLOWN WITH THE RING?!
IT'S N THE MOVE! VERTICAL!
COMING RIGHT AT YOU, BETA TEAM!
IT'S BOLTING!
FIRE AT WILL! FIRE AT WILL!
HOLY... ARE YOU SEEING THIS?!
THINK WE GOT IT ANGRY?
THINK I CARE?!

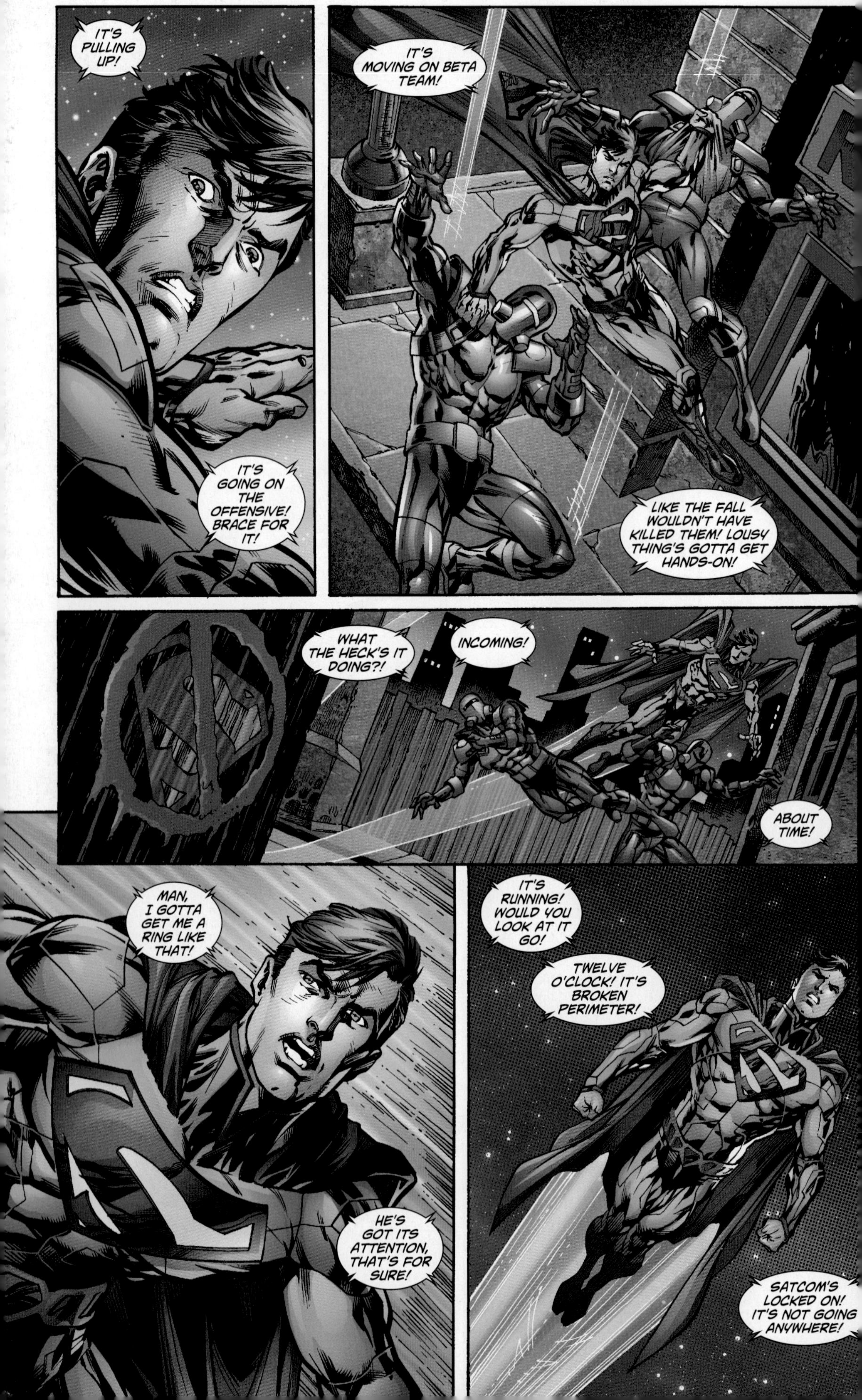
IT'S PULLING UP!
IT'S GOING ON THE OFFENSIVE! BRACE FOR IT!
IT'S MOVING ON BETA TEAM!
LIKE THE FALL WOULDN'T HAVE KILLED THEM! LOUSY THING'S GOTTA GET HANDS-ON!
WHAT THE HECK'S IT DOING?!
INCOMING!
ABOUT TIME!
MAN, I GOTTA GET ME A RING LIKE THAT!
HE'S GOT ITS ATTENTION, THAT'S FOR SURE!
IT'S RUNNING! WOULD YOU LOOK AT IT GO!
TWELVE O'CLOCK! IT'S BROKEN PERIMETER!
SATCOM'S LOCKED ON! IT'S NOT GOING ANYWHERE!

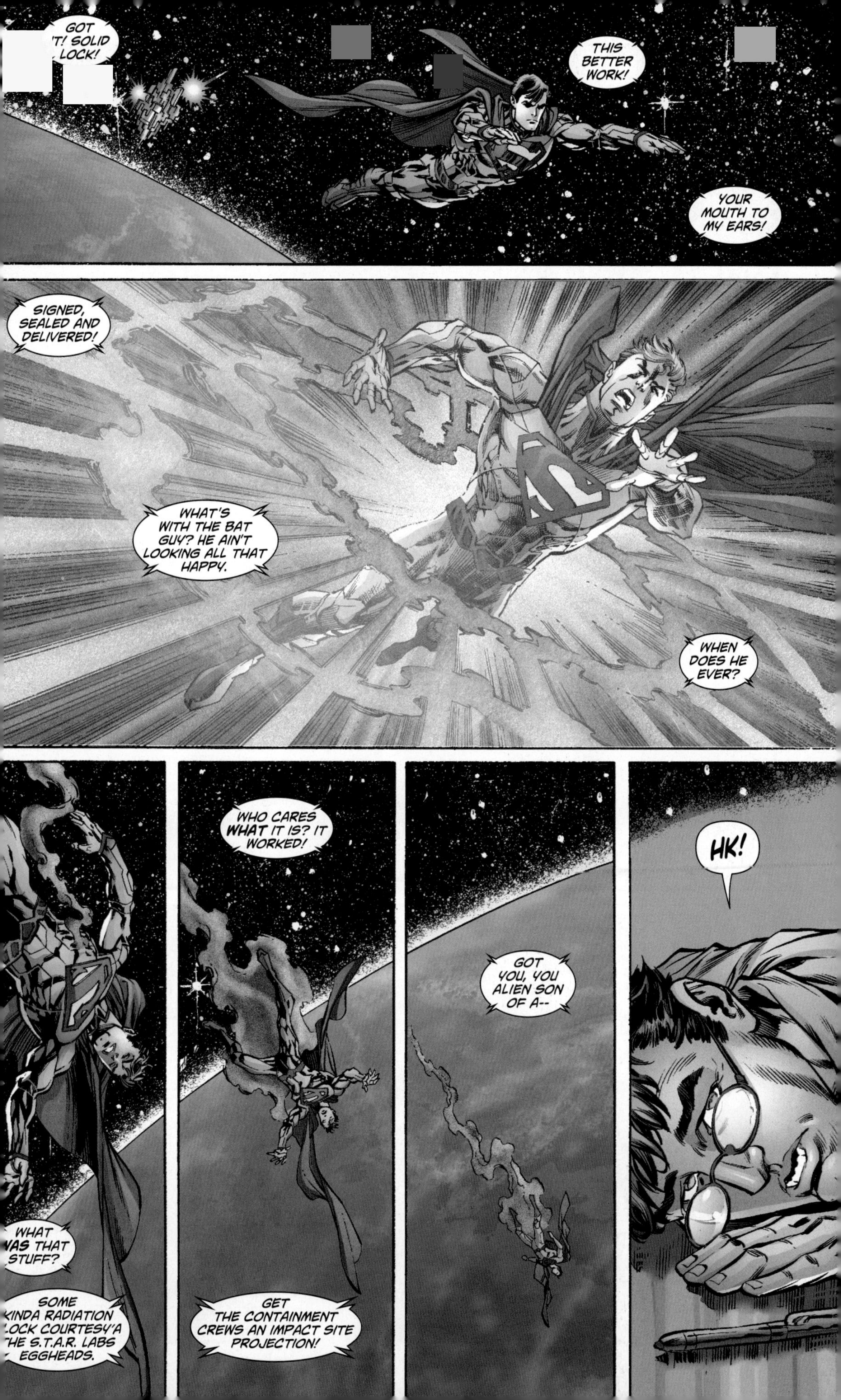
GOT T! SOLID LOCK!
THIS BETTER WORK!
YOUR MOUTH TO MY EARS!
SIGNED, SEALED AND DELIVERED!
WHAT'S WITH THE BAT GUY? HE AIN'T LOOKING ALL THAT HAPPY.
WHEN DOES HE EVER?
WHAT WAS THAT STUFF?
SOME KINDA RADIATION LOCK COURTESY'A THE S.T.A.R. LABS EGGHEADS.
WHO CARES WHAT IT IS? IT WORKED!
GET THE CONTAINMENT CREWS AN IMPACT SITE PROJECTION!
GOT YOU, YOU ALIEN SON OF A--
HK!

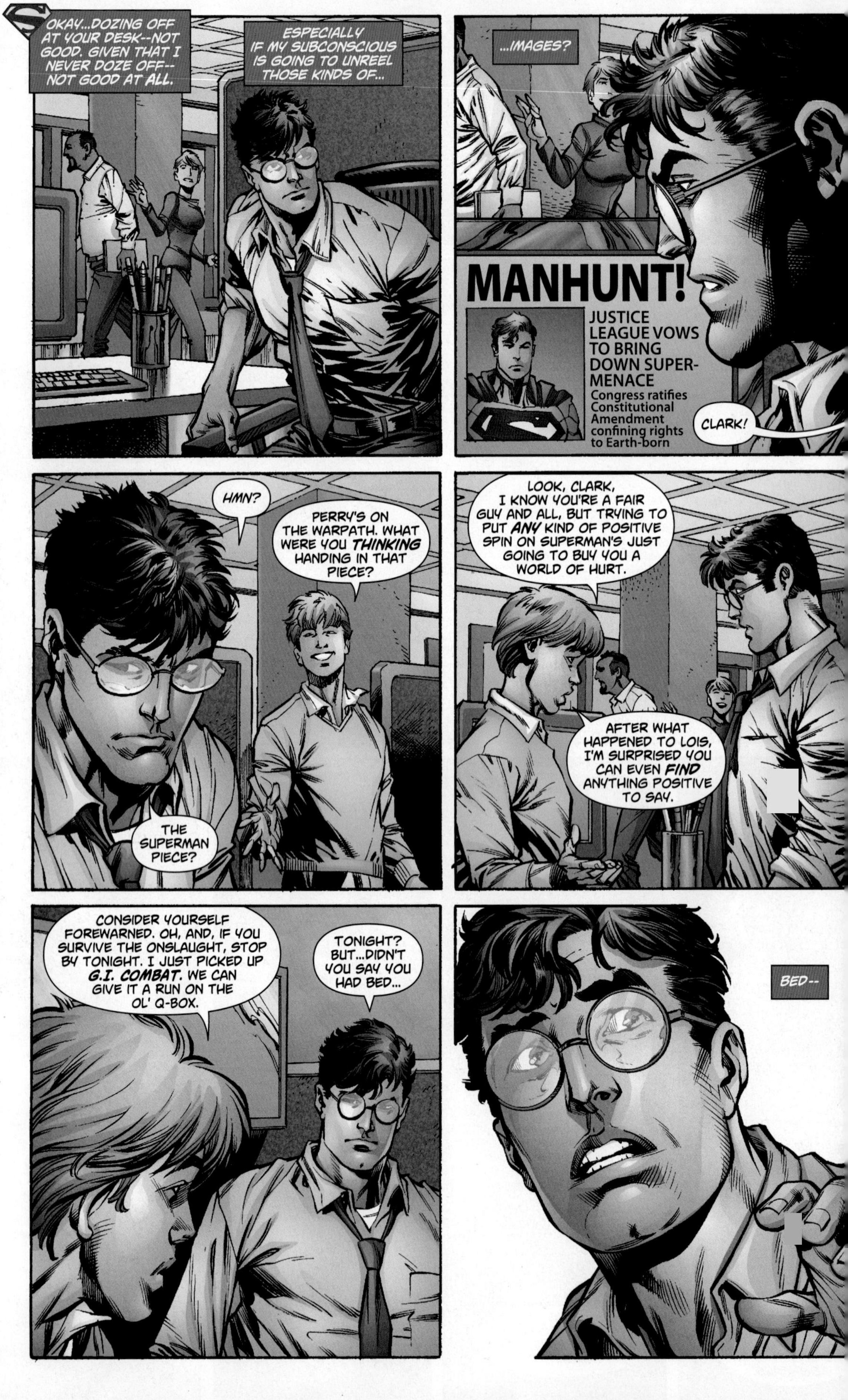
OKAY...DOZING OFF AT YOUR DESK--NOT GOOD. GIVEN THAT I NEVER DOZE OFF--NOT GOOD AT ALL.
ESPECIALLY IF MY SUBCONSCIOUS IS GOING TO UNREEL THOSE KINDS OF...
...IMAGES?
MANHUNT!
JUSTICE LEAGUE VOWS TO BRING DOWN SUPER-MENACE
Congress ratifies Constitutional Amendment confining rights to Earth-born
CLARK!
HMN?
PERRY'S ON THE WARPATH. WHAT WERE YOU THINKING HANDING IN THAT PIECE?
THE SUPERMAN PIECE?
LOOK, CLARK, I KNOW YOU'RE A FAIR GUY AND ALL, BUT TRYING TO PUT ANY KIND OF POSITIVE SPIN ON SUPERMAN'S JUST GOING TO BUY YOU A WORLD OF HURT.
AFTER WHAT HAPPENED TO LOIS, I'M SURPRISED YOU CAN EVEN FIND ANYTHING POSITIVE TO SAY.
CONSIDER YOURSELF FOREWARNED. OH, AND, IF YOU SURVIVE THE ONSLAUGHT, STOP BY TONIGHT. I JUST PICKED UP G.I. COMBAT. WE CAN GIVE IT A RUN ON THE OL' Q-BOX.
TONIGHT? BUT...DIDN'T YOU SAY YOU HAD BED...
BED--

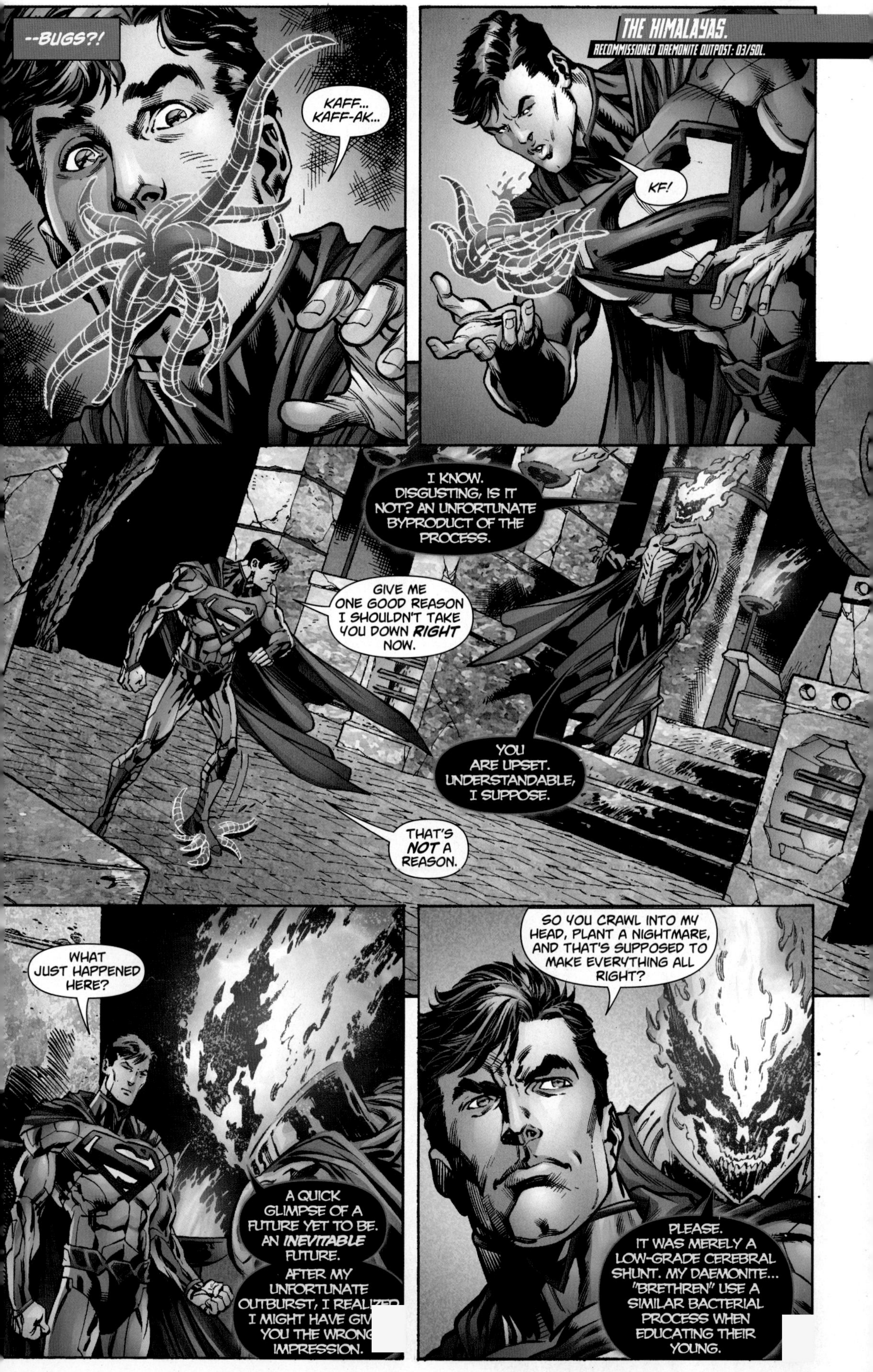
--BUGS?!
KAFF... KAFF-AK...
THE HIMALAYAS.
RECOMMISSIONED DAEMONITE OUTPOST: 03/SOL.
KF!
I KNOW. DISGUSTING, IS IT NOT? AN UNFORTUNATE BYPRODUCT OF THE PROCESS.
GIVE ME ONE GOOD REASON I SHOULDN'T TAKE YOU DOWN RIGHT NOW.
YOU ARE UPSET. UNDERSTANDABLE, I SUPPOSE.
THAT'S NOT A REASON.
WHAT JUST HAPPENED HERE?
A QUICK GLIMPSE OF A FUTURE YET TO BE. AN INEVITABLE FUTURE.
AFTER MY UNFORTUNATE OUTBURST, I REALIZ I MIGHT HAVE GIV YOU THE WRONG IMPRESSION.
SO YOU CRAWL INTO MY HEAD, PLANT A NIGHTMARE, AND THAT'S SUPPOSED TO MAKE EVERYTHING ALL RIGHT?
PLEASE. IT WAS MERELY A LOW-GRADE CEREBRAL SHUNT. MY DAEMONITE... "BRETHREN" USE A SIMILAR BACTERIAL PROCESS WHEN EDUCATING THEIR YOUNG.

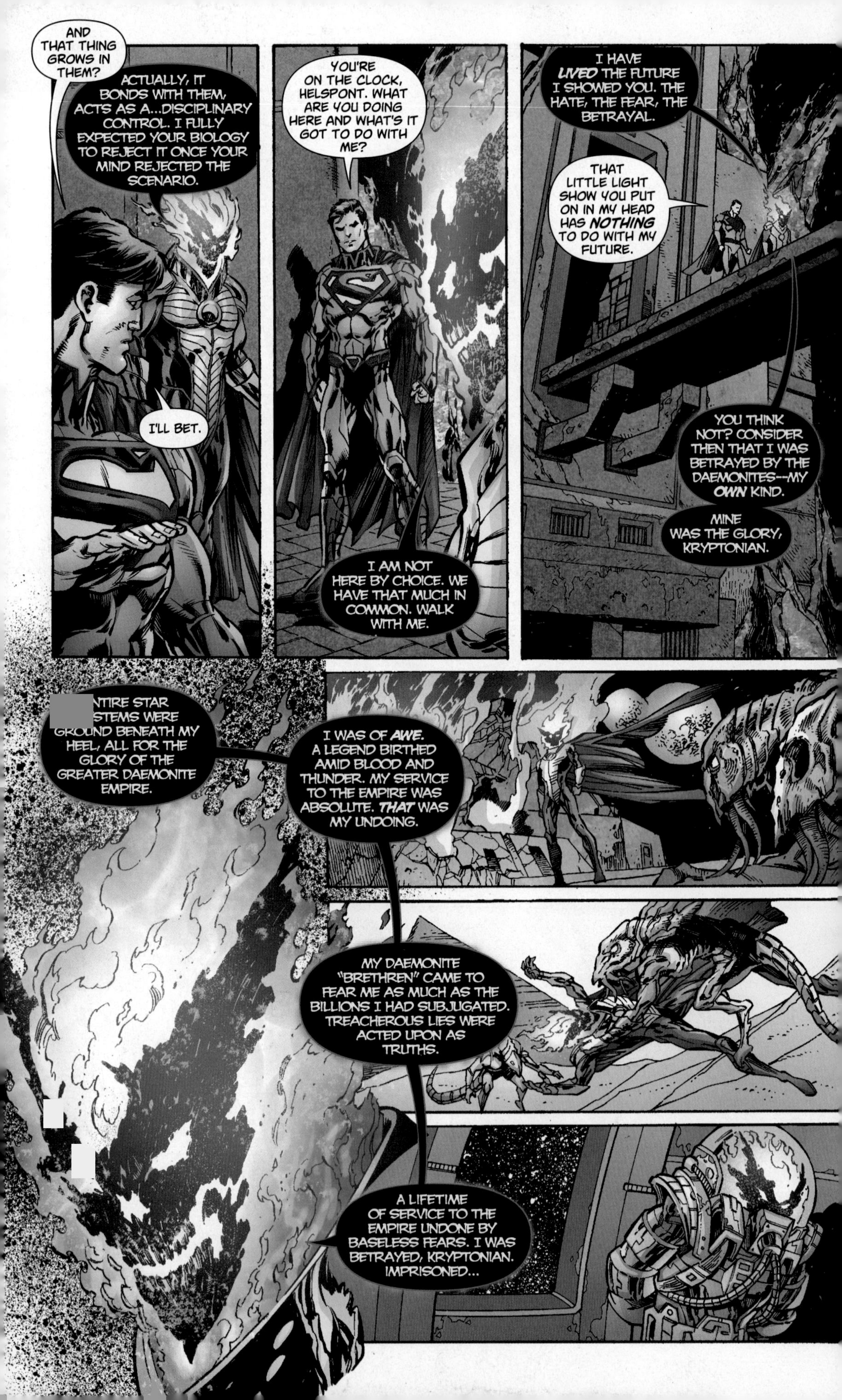
AND THAT THING GROWS IN THEM?
ACTUALLY, IT BONDS WITH THEM, ACTS AS A...DISCIPLINARY CONTROL. I FULLY EXPECTED YOUR BIOLOGY TO REJECT IT ONCE YOUR MIND REJECTED THE SCENARIO.
I'LL BET.
YOU'RE ON THE CLOCK, HELSPONT. WHAT ARE YOU DOING HERE AND WHAT'S IT GOT TO DO WITH ME?
I AM NOT HERE BY CHOICE. WE HAVE THAT MUCH IN COMMON. WALK WITH ME.
I HAVE LIVED THE FUTURE I SHOWED YOU. THE HATE, THE FEAR, THE BETRAYAL.
THAT LITTLE LIGHT SHOW YOU PUT ON IN MY HEAD HAS NOTHING TO DO WITH MY FUTURE.
YOU THINK NOT? CONSIDER THEN THAT I WAS BETRAYED BY THE DAEMONITES--MY OWN KIND.
MINE WAS THE GLORY, KRYPTONIAN.
NTIRE STAR STEMS WERE GROUND BENEATH MY HEEL, ALL FOR THE GLORY OF THE GREATER DAEMONITE EMPIRE.
I WAS OF AWE. A LEGEND BIRTHED AMID BLOOD AND THUNDER. MY SERVICE TO THE EMPIRE WAS ABSOLUTE. THAT WAS MY UNDOING.
MY DAEMONITE "BRETHREN" CAME TO FEAR ME AS MUCH AS THE BILLIONS I HAD SUBJUGATED. TREACHEROUS LIES WERE ACTED UPON AS TRUTHS.
A LIFETIME OF SERVICE TO THE EMPIRE UNDONE BY BASELESS FEARS. I WAS BETRAYED, KRYPTONIAN. IMPRISONED...

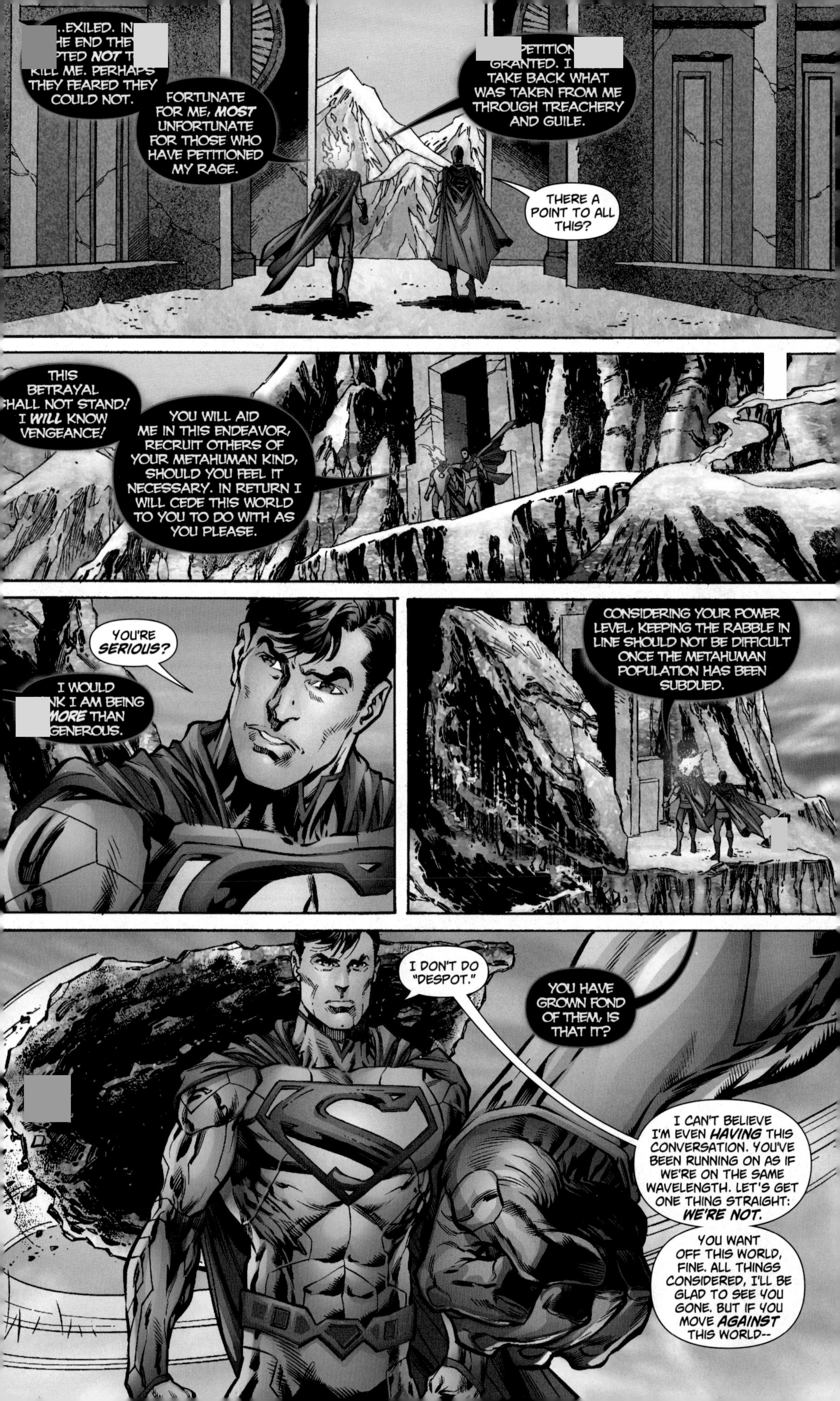

...EXILED. IN
HE END THE
PTED NOT T
KILL ME. PERHAPS THEY FEARED THEY COULD NOT.
FORTUNATE FOR ME, MOST UNFORTUNATE FOR THOSE WHO HAVE PETITIONED MY RAGE.
PETITION
GRANTED. I
TAKE BACK WHAT WAS TAKEN FROM ME THROUGH TREACHERY AND GUILE.
THERE A POINT TO ALL THIS?
THIS BETRAYAL HALL NOT STAND! I WILL KNOW VENGEANCE!
YOU WILL AID ME IN THIS ENDEAVOR, RECRUIT OTHERS OF YOUR METAHUMAN KIND, SHOULD YOU FEEL IT NECESSARY. IN RETURN I WILL CEDE THIS WORLD TO YOU TO DO WITH AS YOU PLEASE.
YOU'RE SERIOUS?
I WOULD NK I AM BEING MORE THAN GENEROUS.
CONSIDERING YOUR POWER LEVEL, KEEPING THE RABBLE IN LINE SHOULD NOT BE DIFFICULT ONCE THE METAHUMAN POPULATION HAS BEEN SUBDUED.
I DON'T DO "DESPOT."
YOU HAVE GROWN FOND OF THEM, IS THAT IT?
I CAN'T BELIEVE I'M EVEN HAVING THIS CONVERSATION. YOU'VE BEEN RUNNING ON AS IF WE'RE ON THE SAME WAVELENGTH. LET'S GET ONE THING STRAIGHT: WE'RE NOT.
YOU WANT OFF THIS WORLD, FINE. ALL THINGS CONSIDERED, I'LL BE GLAD TO SEE YOU GONE. BUT IF YOU MOVE AGAINST THIS WORLD--

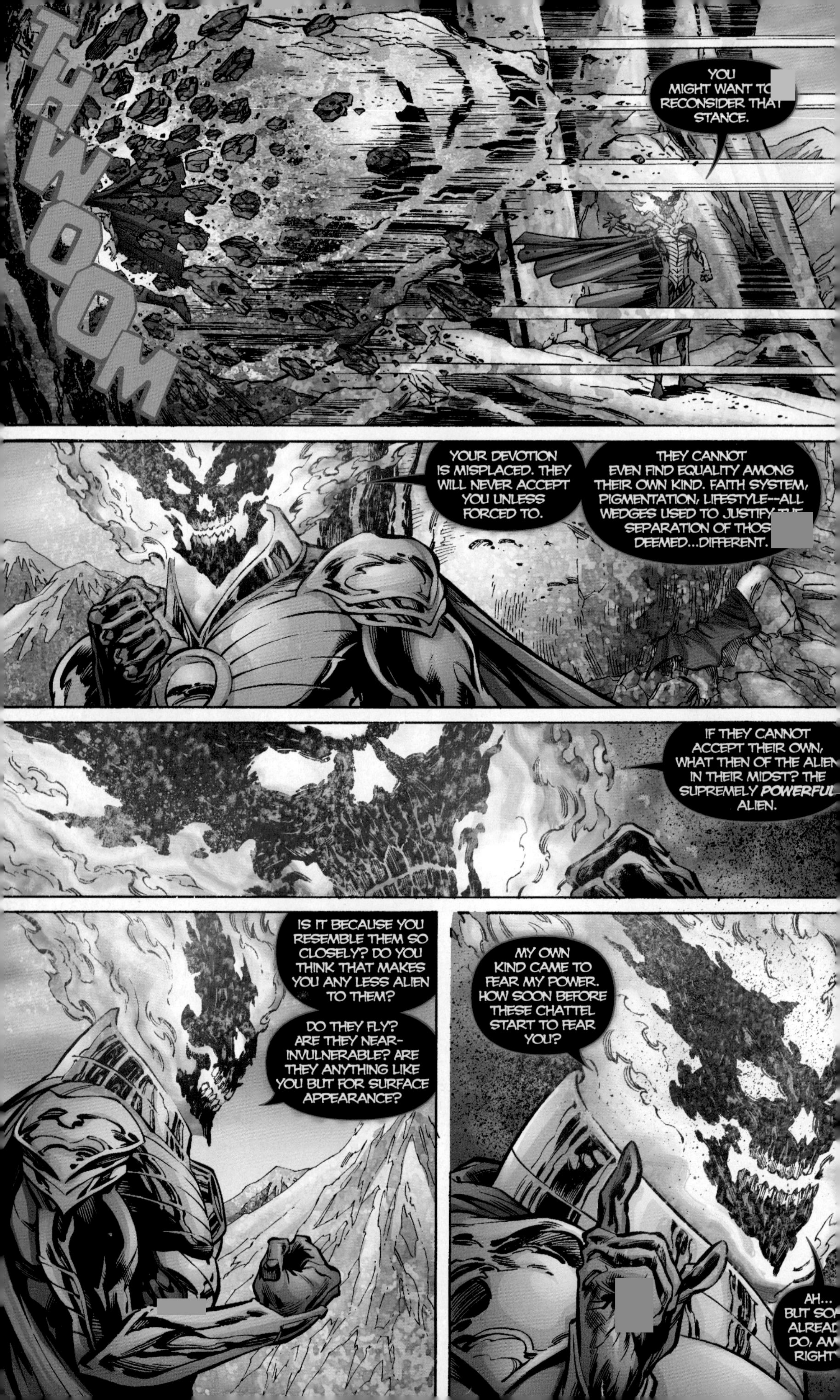
THWOOM
YOU MIGHT WANT T RECONSIDER THA STANCE.
YOUR DEVOTION IS MISPLACED. THEY WILL NEVER ACCEPT YOU UNLESS FORCED TO.
THEY CANNOT EVEN FIND EQUALITY AMONG THEIR OWN KIND. FAITH SYSTEM, PIGMENTATION, LIFESTYLE--ALL WEDGES USED TO JUSTIFY SEPARATION OF THOS DEEMED...DIFFERENT.
IF THEY CANNOT ACCEPT THEIR OWN, WHAT THEN OF THE ALIE IN THEIR MIDST? THE SUPREMELY *POWERFUL* ALIEN.
IS IT BECAUSE YOU RESEMBLE THEM SO CLOSELY? DO YOU THINK THAT MAKES YOU ANY LESS ALIEN TO THEM?
DO THEY FLY? ARE THEY NEAR-INVULNERABLE? ARE THEY ANYTHING LIKE YOU BUT FOR SURFACE APPEARANCE?
MY OWN KIND CAME TO FEAR MY POWER. HOW SOON BEFORE THESE CHATTEL START TO FEAR YOU?
AH... BUT SO ALREAD DO, AM RIGHT

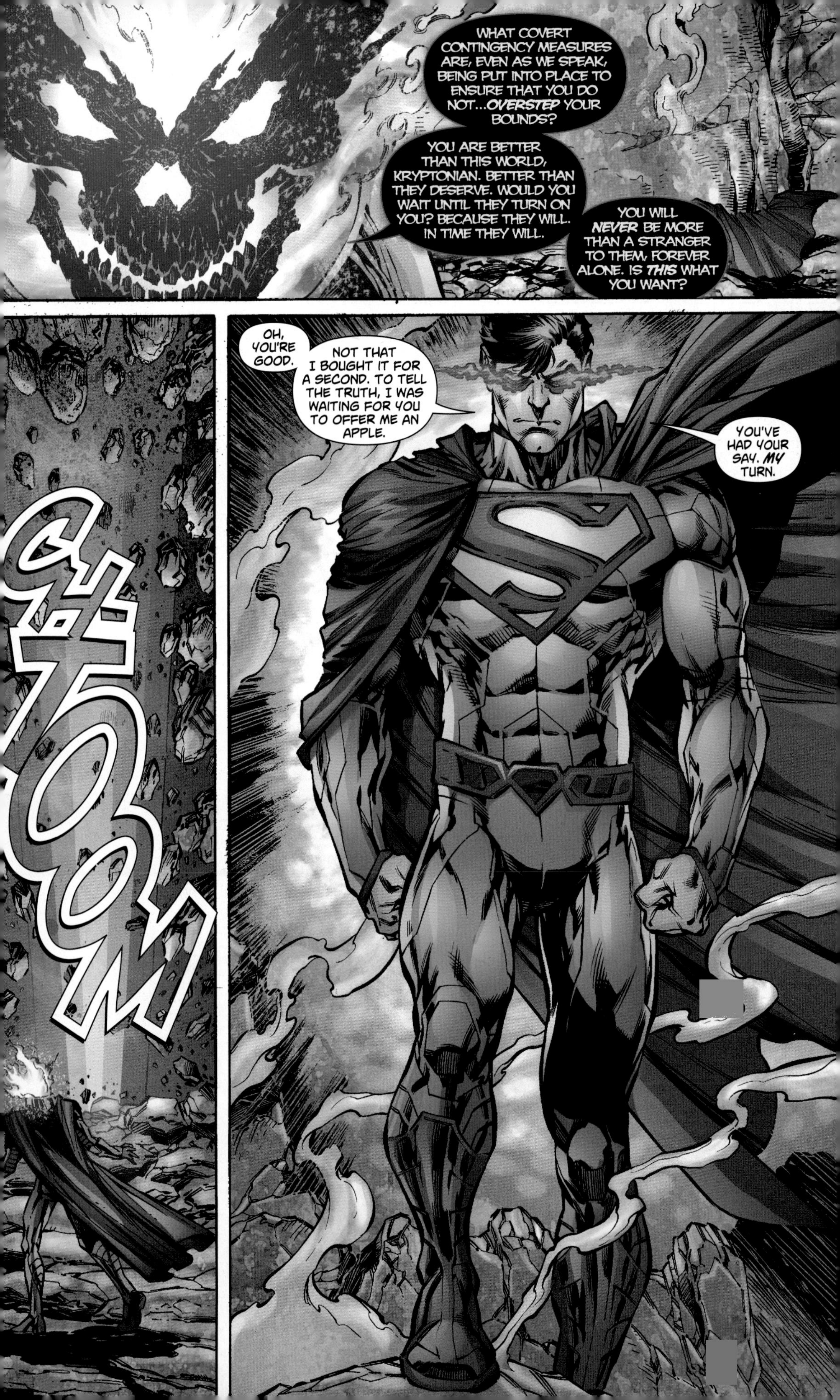
WHAT COVERT CONTINGENCY MEASURES ARE, EVEN AS WE SPEAK, BEING PUT INTO PLACE TO ENSURE THAT YOU DO NOT...OVERSTEP YOUR BOUNDS?
YOU ARE BETTER THAN THIS WORLD, KRYPTONIAN. BETTER THAN THEY DESERVE. WOULD YOU WAIT UNTIL THEY TURN ON YOU? BECAUSE THEY WILL. IN TIME THEY WILL.
YOU WILL NEVER BE MORE THAN A STRANGER TO THEM, FOREVER ALONE. IS THIS WHAT YOU WANT?
CHTOOM
OH, YOU'RE GOOD.
NOT THAT I BOUGHT IT FOR A SECOND. TO TELL THE TRUTH, I WAS WAITING FOR YOU TO OFFER ME AN APPLE.
YOU'VE HAD YOUR SAY. MY TURN.

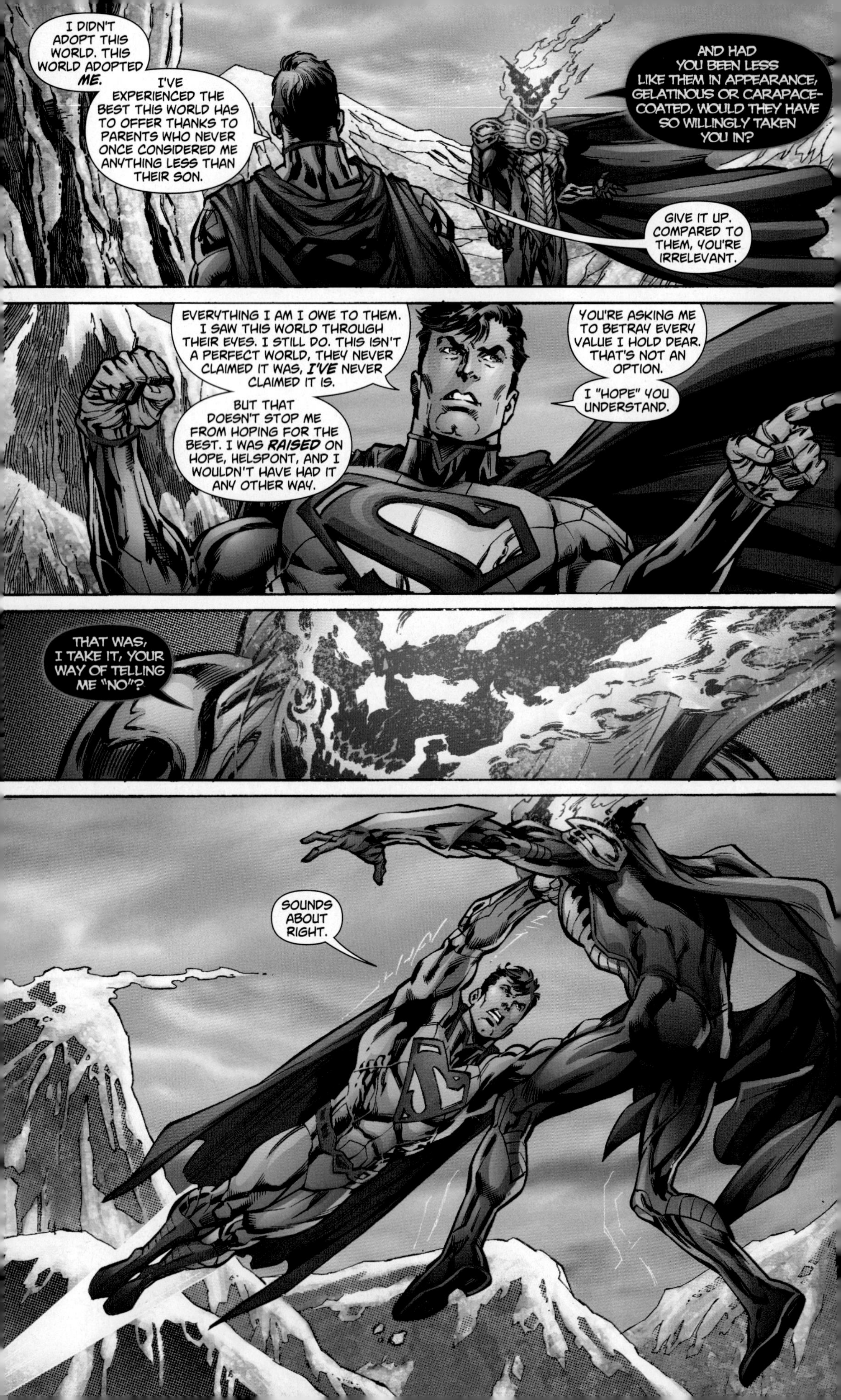
I DIDN'T ADOPT THIS WORLD. THIS WORLD ADOPTED ME.
I'VE EXPERIENCED THE BEST THIS WORLD HAS TO OFFER THANKS TO PARENTS WHO NEVER ONCE CONSIDERED ME ANYTHING LESS THAN THEIR SON.
AND HAD YOU BEEN LESS LIKE THEM IN APPEARANCE, GELATINOUS OR CARAPACE-COATED, WOULD THEY HAVE SO WILLINGLY TAKEN YOU IN?
GIVE IT UP. COMPARED TO THEM, YOU'RE IRRELEVANT.
EVERYTHING I AM I OWE TO THEM. I SAW THIS WORLD THROUGH THEIR EYES. I STILL DO. THIS ISN'T A PERFECT WORLD, THEY NEVER CLAIMED IT WAS, I'VE NEVER CLAIMED IT IS.
BUT THAT DOESN'T STOP ME FROM HOPING FOR THE BEST. I WAS RAISED ON HOPE, HELSPONT, AND I WOULDN'T HAVE HAD IT ANY OTHER WAY.
YOU'RE ASKING ME TO BETRAY EVERY VALUE I HOLD DEAR. THAT'S NOT AN OPTION.
I "HOPE" YOU UNDERSTAND.
THAT WAS, I TAKE IT, YOUR WAY OF TELLING ME "NO"?
SOUNDS ABOUT RIGHT.

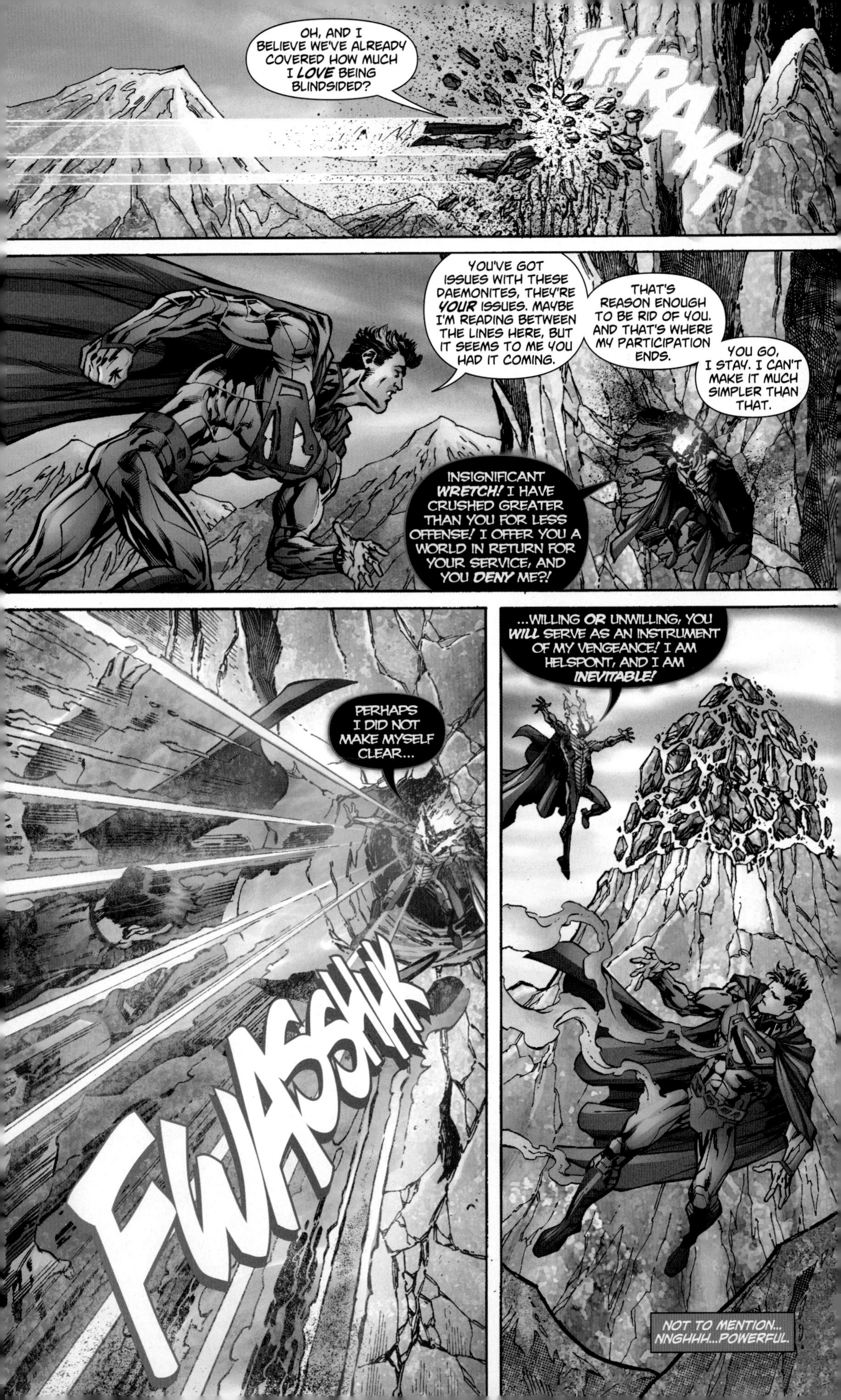
OH, AND I BELIEVE WE'VE ALREADY COVERED HOW MUCH I LOVE BEING BLINDSIDED?
THRAKT
YOU'VE GOT ISSUES WITH THESE DAEMONITES, THEY'RE YOUR ISSUES. MAYBE I'M READING BETWEEN THE LINES HERE, BUT IT SEEMS TO ME YOU HAD IT COMING.
THAT'S REASON ENOUGH TO BE RID OF YOU. AND THAT'S WHERE MY PARTICIPATION ENDS.
YOU GO, I STAY. I CAN'T MAKE IT MUCH SIMPLER THAN THAT.
INSIGNIFICANT WRETCH! I HAVE CRUSHED GREATER THAN YOU FOR LESS OFFENSE! I OFFER YOU A WORLD IN RETURN FOR YOUR SERVICE, AND YOU DENY ME?!
PERHAPS I DID NOT MAKE MYSELF CLEAR...
FWASHK
...WILLING OR UNWILLING, YOU WILL SERVE AS AN INSTRUMENT OF MY VENGEANCE! I AM HELSPONT, AND I AM INEVITABLE!
NOT TO MENTION... NNGHHH...POWERFUL.

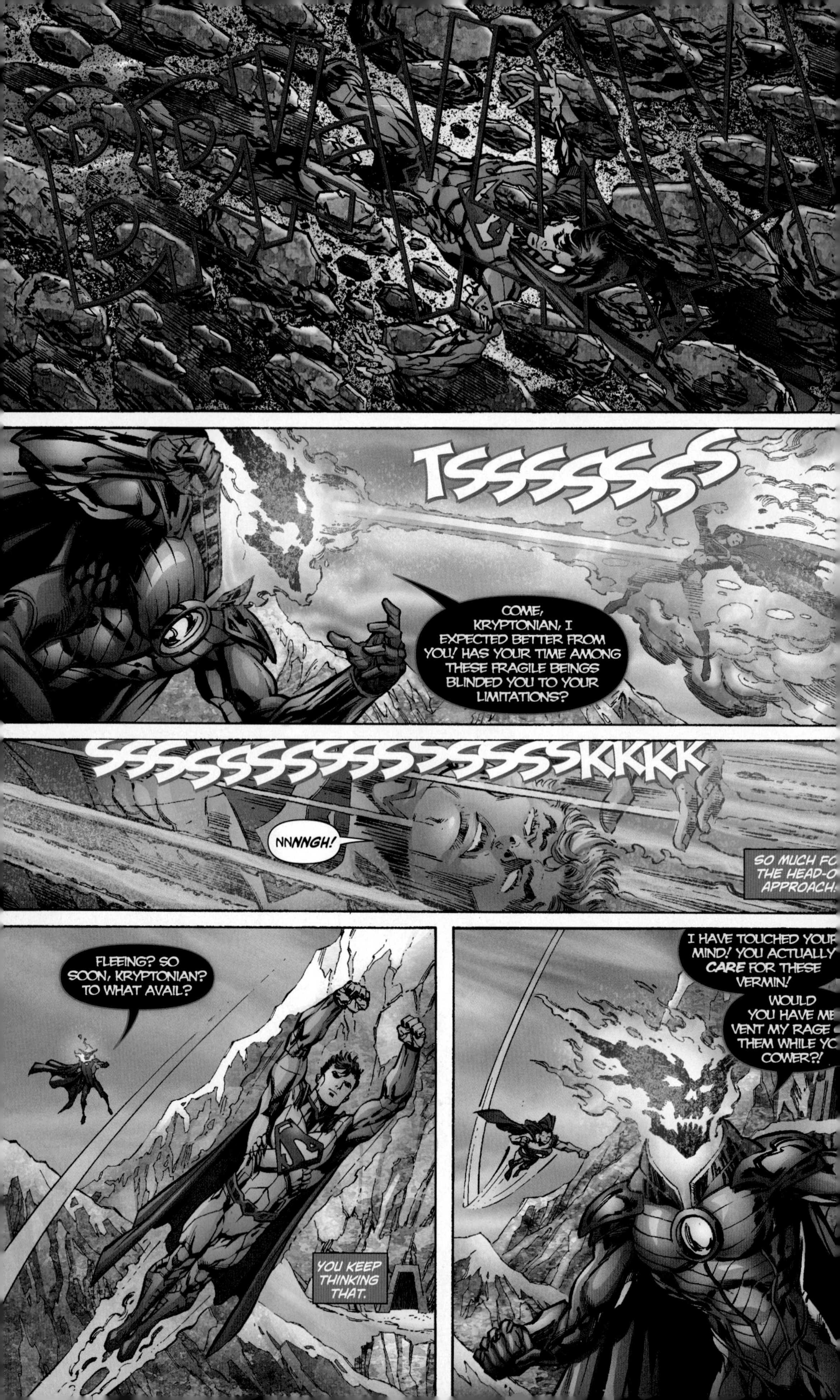

TSSSSSSSS
COME, KRYPTONIAN, I EXPECTED BETTER FROM YOU! HAS YOUR TIME AMONG THESE FRAGILE BEINGS BLINDED YOU TO YOUR LIMITATIONS?
SSSSSSSSSSSSSSSSSKKKK
NNNNGH!
SO MUCH FO THE HEAD-O APPROACH.
FLEEING? SO SOON, KRYPTONIAN? TO WHAT AVAIL?
YOU KEEP THINKING THAT.
I HAVE TOUCHED YOUR MIND! YOU ACTUALLY CARE FOR THESE VERMIN!
WOULD YOU HAVE ME VENT MY RAGE THEM WHILE YO COWER?!

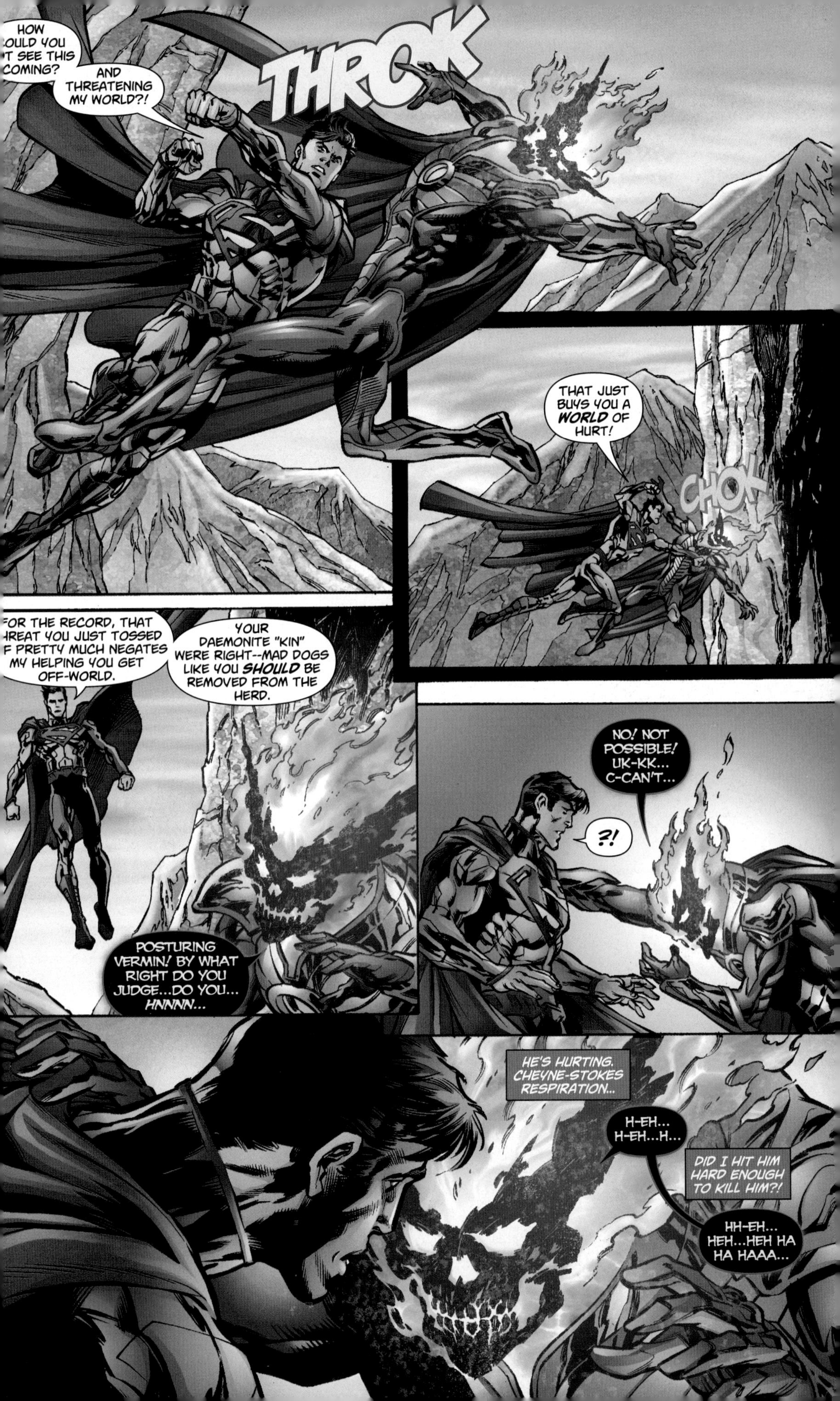
HOW COULD YOU NOT SEE THIS COMING?
AND THREATENING MY WORLD?!
THROCK
THAT JUST BUYS YOU A WORLD OF HURT!
CHOK
FOR THE RECORD, THAT THREAT YOU JUST TOSSED OFF PRETTY MUCH NEGATES MY HELPING YOU GET OFF-WORLD.
YOUR DAEMONITE "KIN" WERE RIGHT--MAD DOGS LIKE YOU SHOULD BE REMOVED FROM THE HERD.
POSTURING VERMIN! BY WHAT RIGHT DO YOU JUDGE...DO YOU... HNNNN...
NO! NOT POSSIBLE! UK-KK... C-CAN'T...
?!
HE'S HURTING. CHEYNE-STOKES RESPIRATION...
H-EH... H-EH...H...
DID I HIT HIM HARD ENOUGH TO KILL HIM?!
HH-EH... HEH...HEH HA HA HAAA...

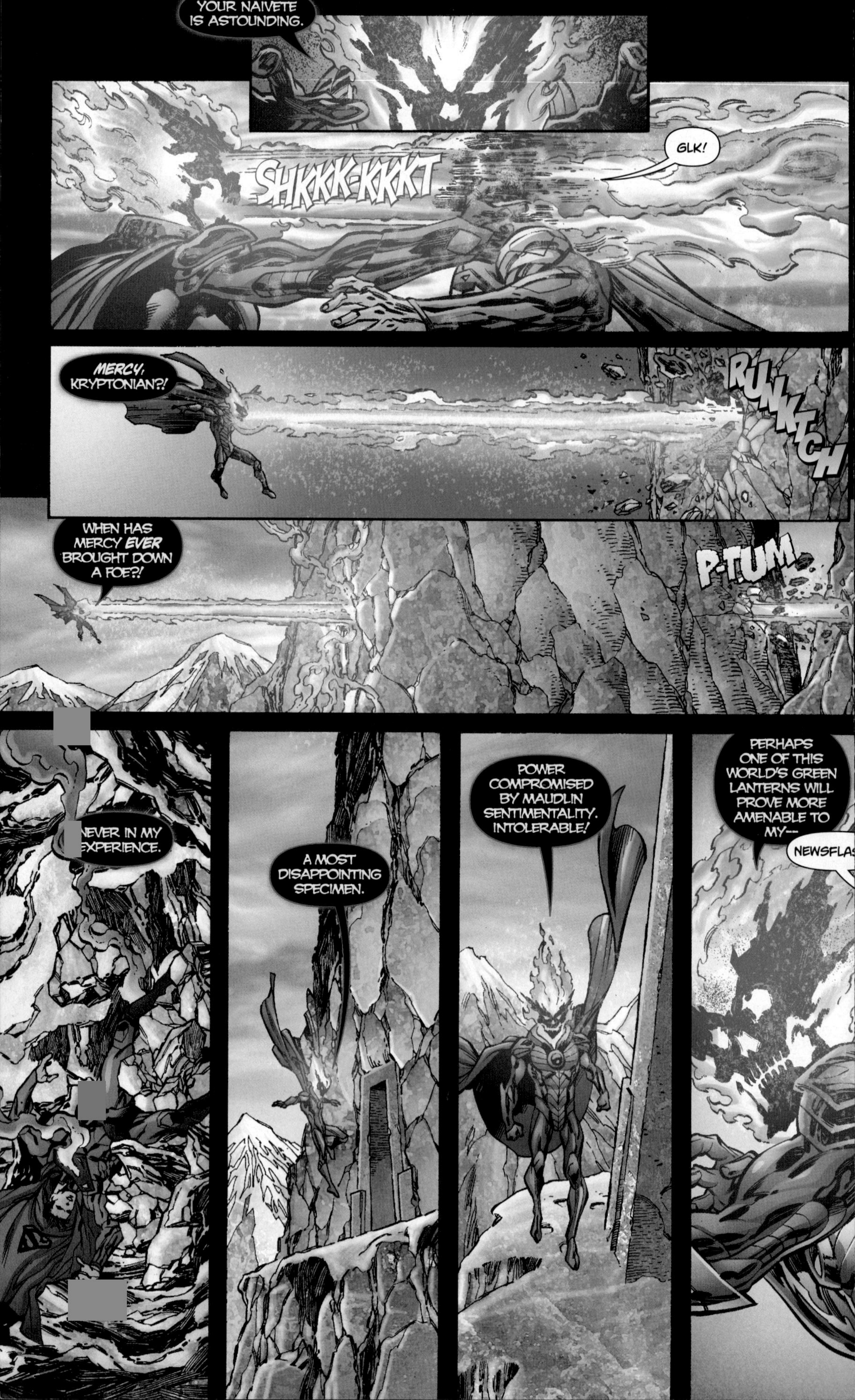

YOUR NAIVETE IS ASTOUNDING.
SHKKK-KKKT
GLK!
MERCY, KRYPTONIAN?!
RUNKTCH
WHEN HAS MERCY EVER BROUGHT DOWN A FOE?!
P-TUM
NEVER IN MY EXPERIENCE.
A MOST DISAPPOINTING SPECIMEN.
POWER COMPROMISED BY MAUDLIN SENTIMENTALITY. INTOLERABLE!
PERHAPS ONE OF THIS WORLD'S GREEN LANTERNS WILL PROVE MORE AMENABLE TO MY--

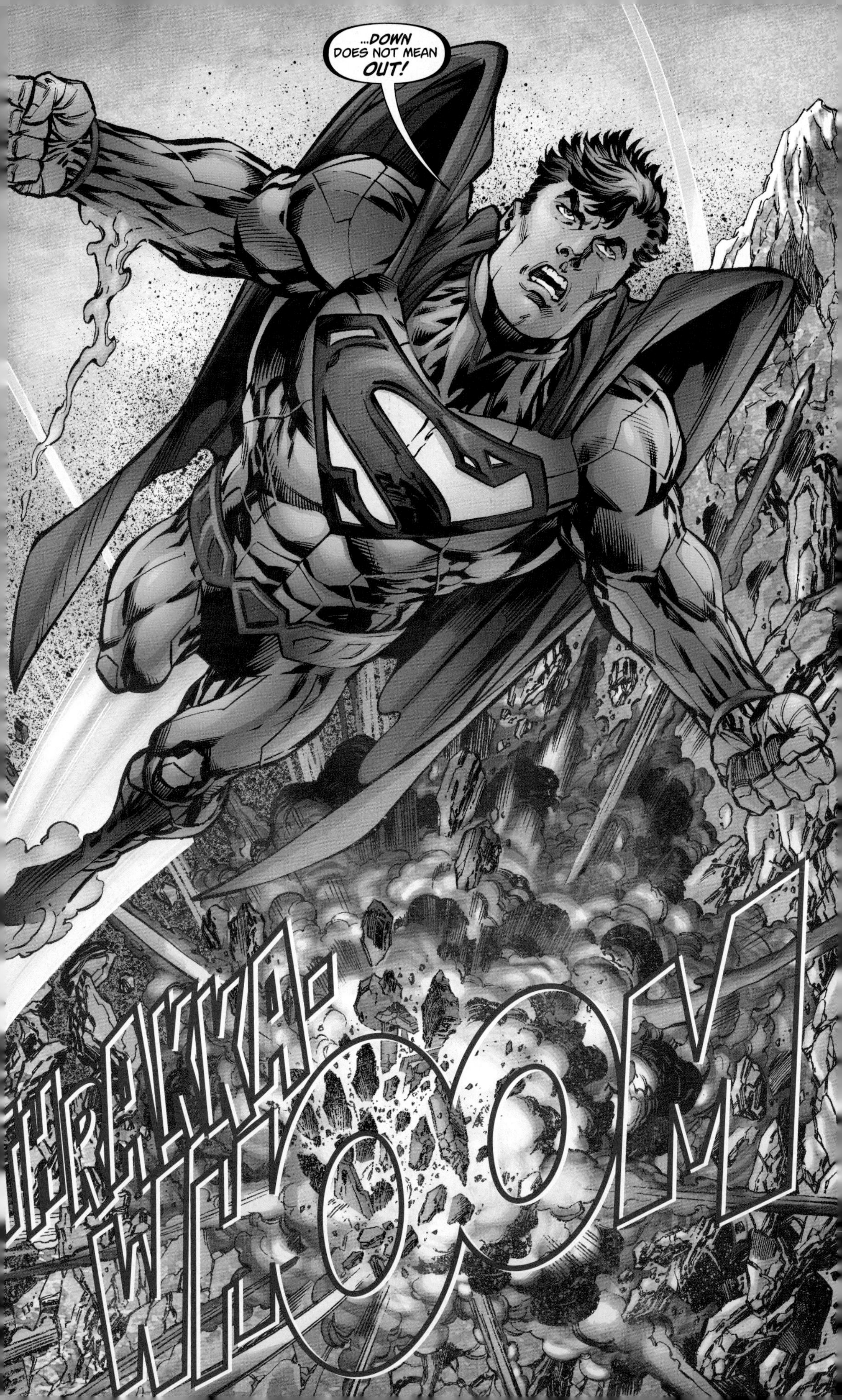

...DOWN DOES NOT MEAN OUT!
HRAKKA-WHOOM

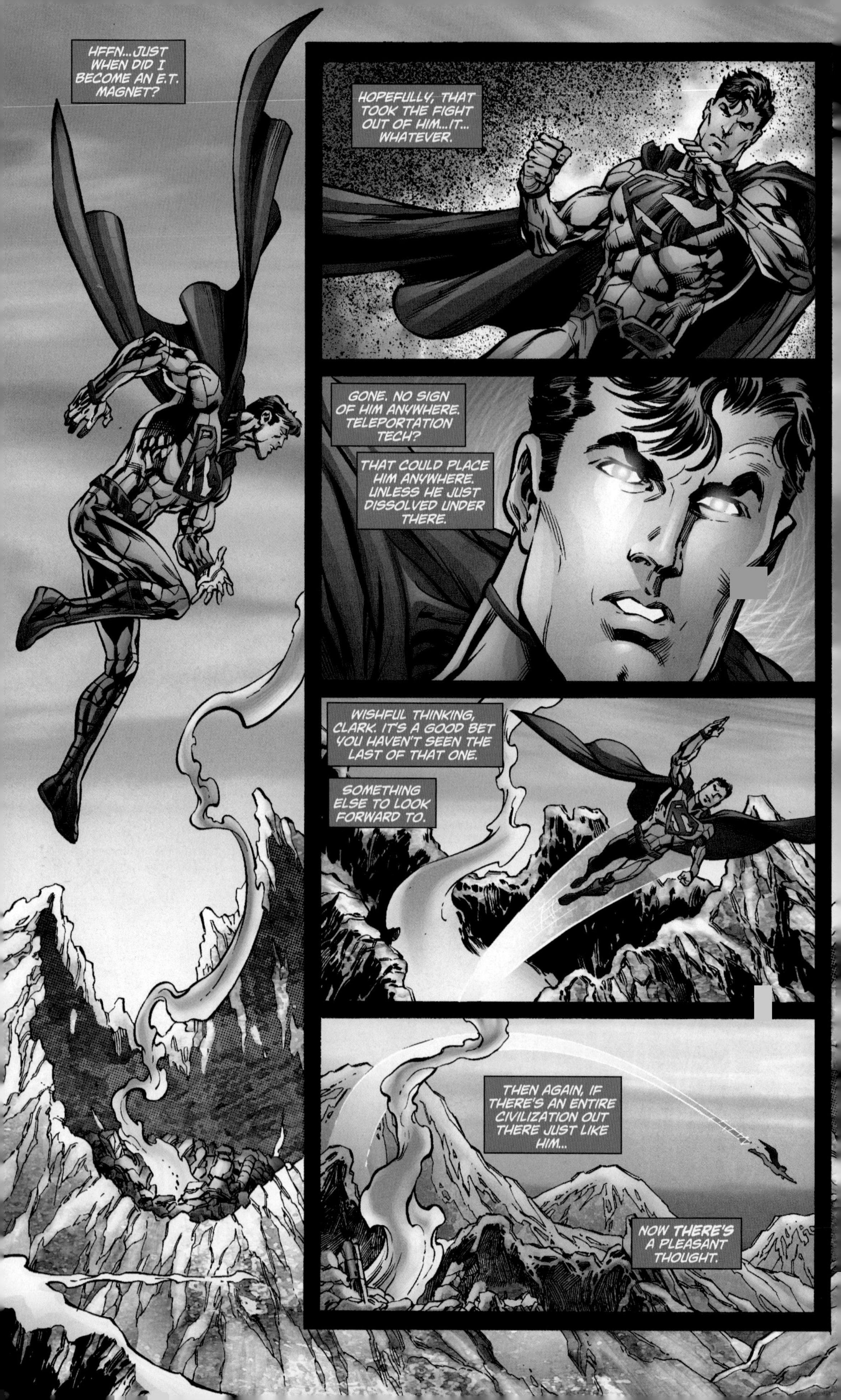

HFFN...JUST WHEN DID I BECOME AN E.T. MAGNET?
HOPEFULLY, THAT TOOK THE FIGHT OUT OF HIM...IT... WHATEVER.
GONE. NO SIGN OF HIM ANYWHERE. TELEPORTATION TECH?
THAT COULD PLACE HIM ANYWHERE. UNLESS HE JUST DISSOLVED UNDER THERE.
WISHFUL THINKING, CLARK. IT'S A GOOD BET YOU HAVEN'T SEEN THE LAST OF THAT ONE.
SOMETHING ELSE TO LOOK FORWARD TO.
THEN AGAIN, IF THERE'S AN ENTIRE CIVILIZATION OUT THERE JUST LIKE HIM...
NOW THERE'S A PLEASANT THOUGHT.

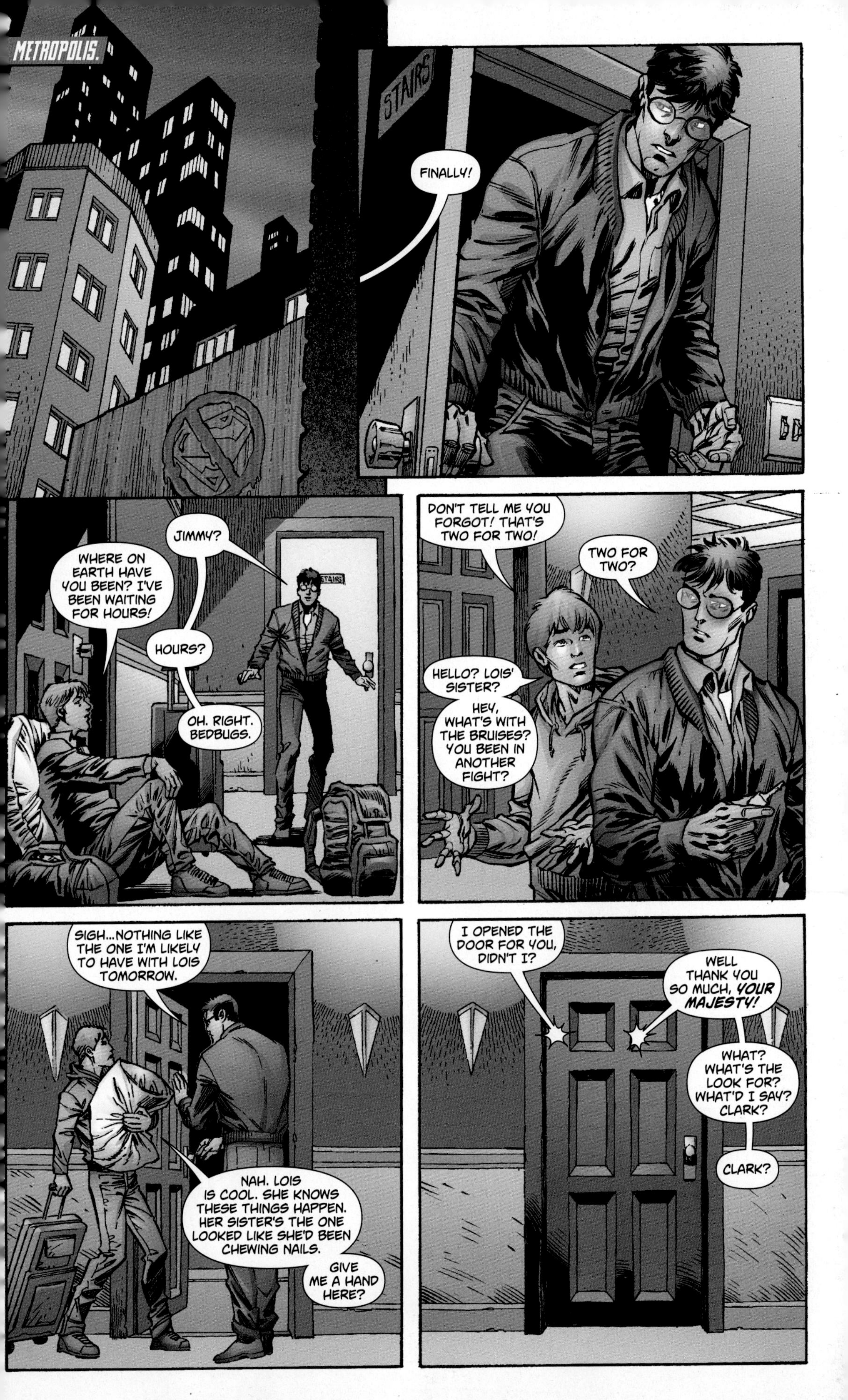
METROPOLIS.
STAIRS
FINALLY!
JIMMY?
WHERE ON EARTH HAVE YOU BEEN? I'VE BEEN WAITING FOR HOURS!
HOURS?
OH. RIGHT. BEDBUGS.
DON'T TELL ME YOU FORGOT! THAT'S TWO FOR TWO!
TWO FOR TWO?
HELLO? LOIS' SISTER?
HEY, WHAT'S WITH THE BRUISES? YOU BEEN IN ANOTHER FIGHT?
SIGH...NOTHING LIKE THE ONE I'M LIKELY TO HAVE WITH LOIS TOMORROW.
NAH. LOIS IS COOL. SHE KNOWS THESE THINGS HAPPEN. HER SISTER'S THE ONE LOOKED LIKE SHE'D BEEN CHEWING NAILS.
GIVE ME A HAND HERE?
I OPENED THE DOOR FOR YOU, DIDN'T I?
WELL THANK YOU SO MUCH, YOUR MAJESTY!
WHAT? WHAT'S THE LOOK FOR? WHAT'D I SAY? CLARK?
CLARK?

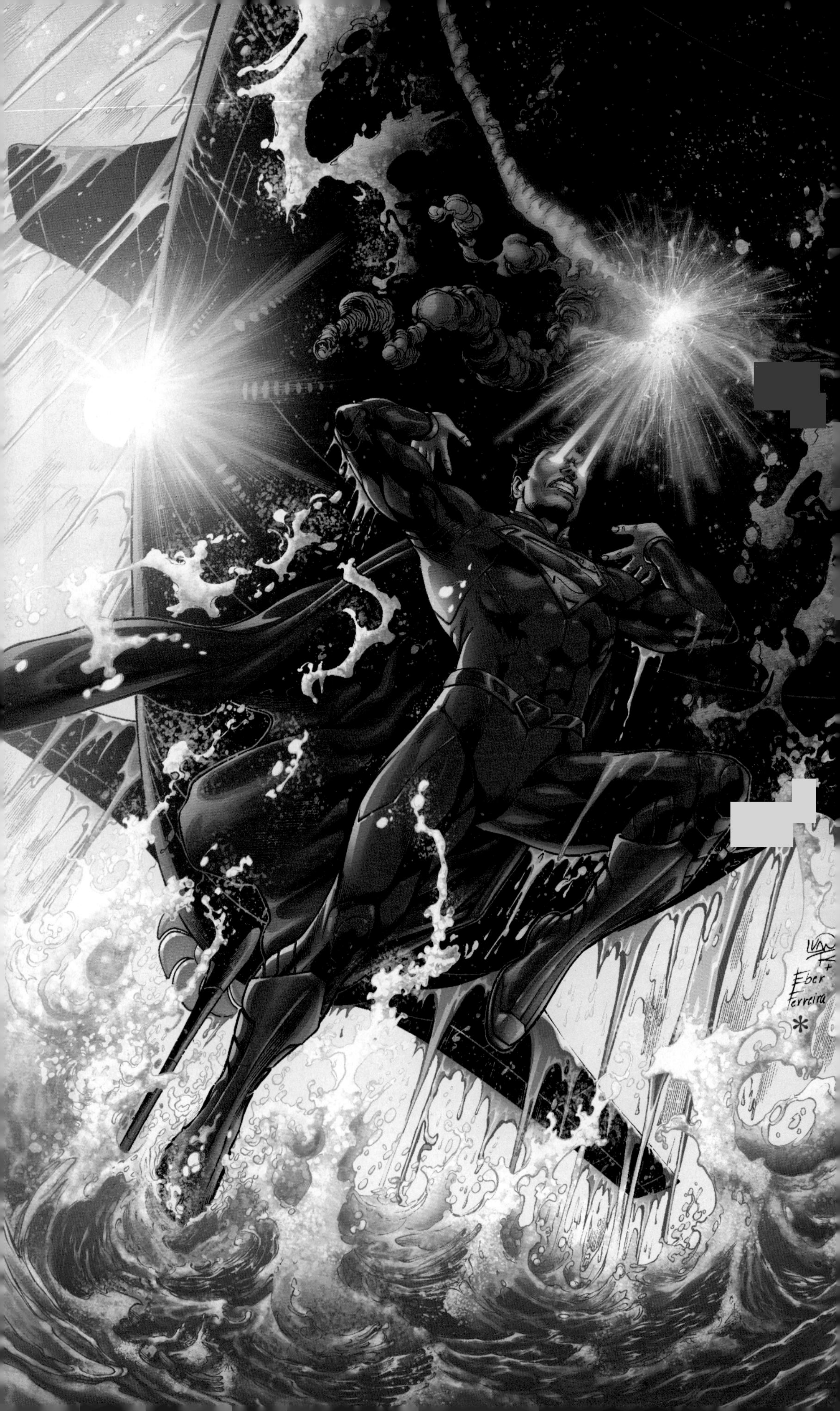
Eber Ferreira

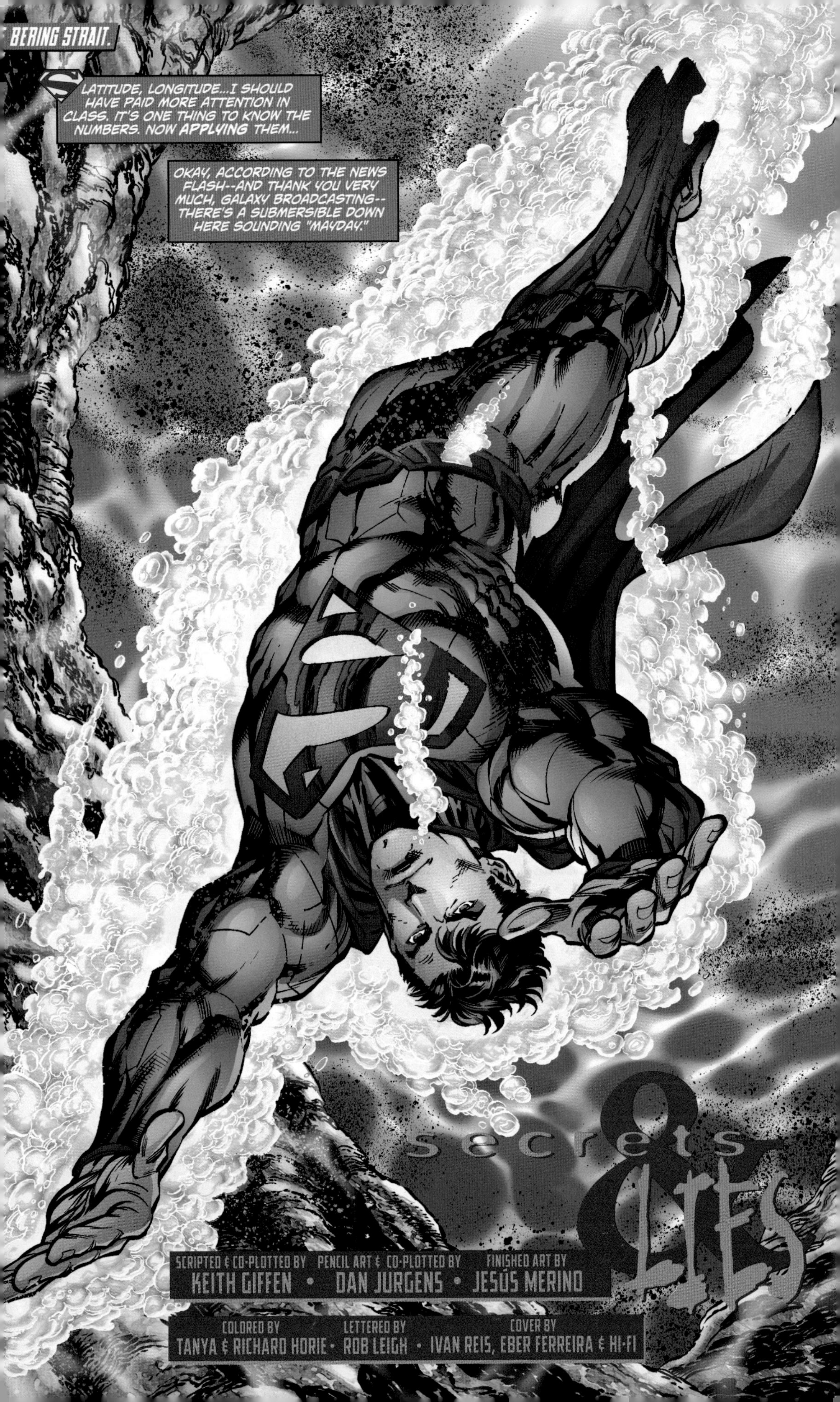

BERING STRAIT.
LATITUDE, LONGITUDE...I SHOULD HAVE PAID MORE ATTENTION IN CLASS. IT'S ONE THING TO KNOW THE NUMBERS. NOW APPLYING THEM...
OKAY, ACCORDING TO THE NEWS FLASH--AND THANK YOU VERY MUCH, GALAXY BROADCASTING--THERE'S A SUBMERSIBLE DOWN HERE SOUNDING "MAYDAY."
Secrets & LIES
SCRIPTED & CO-PLOTTED BY KEITH GIFFEN • PENCIL ART & CO-PLOTTED BY DAN JURGENS • FINISHED ART BY JESÚS MERINO
COLORED BY TANYA & RICHARD HORIE • LETTERED BY ROB LEIGH • COVER BY IVAN REIS, EBER FERREIRA & HI-FI

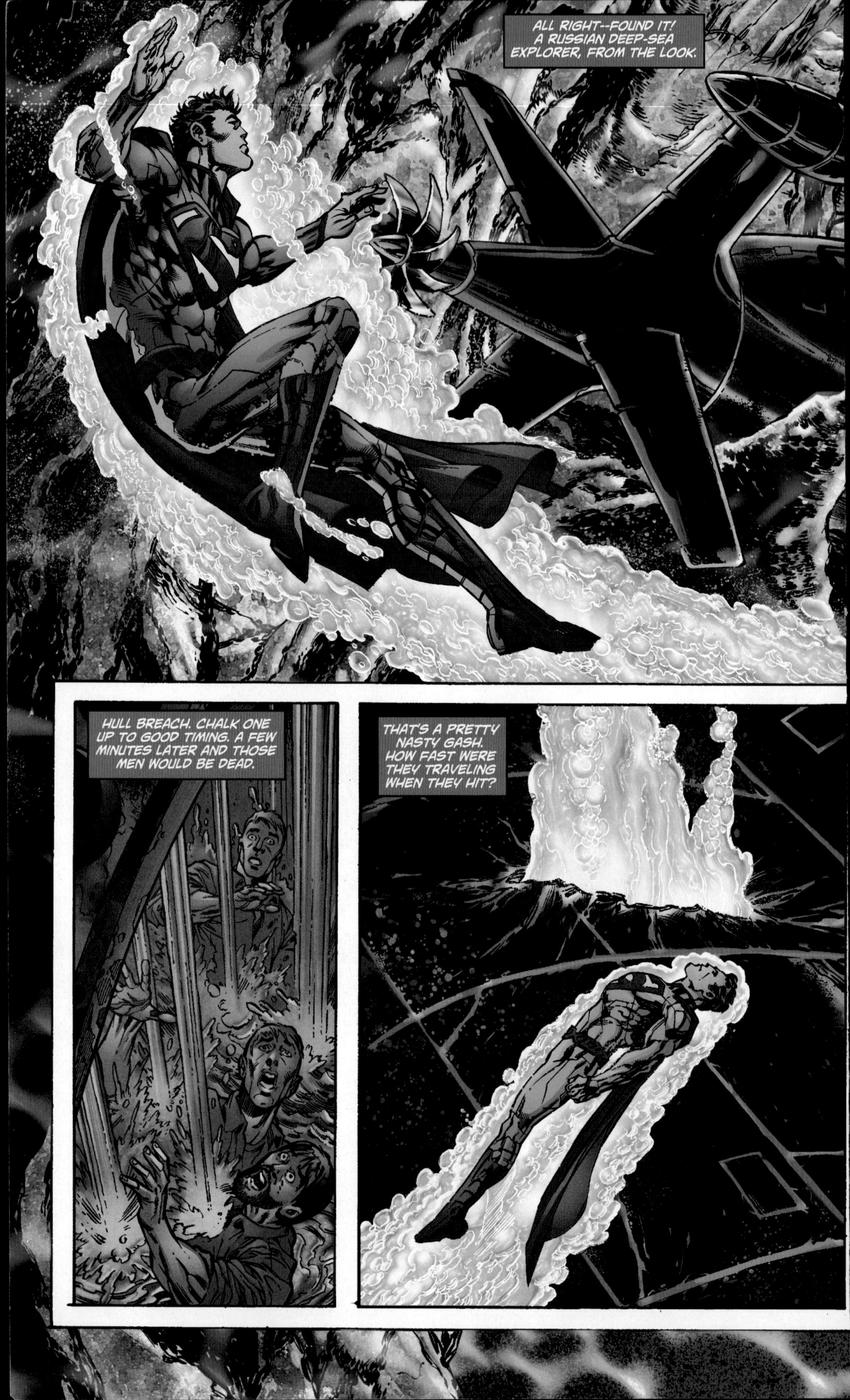
ALL RIGHT--FOUND IT! A RUSSIAN DEEP-SEA EXPLORER, FROM THE LOOK.
HULL BREACH. CHALK ONE UP TO GOOD TIMING. A FEW MINUTES LATER AND THOSE MEN WOULD BE DEAD.
THAT'S A PRETTY NASTY GASH. HOW FAST WERE THEY TRAVELING WHEN THEY HIT?

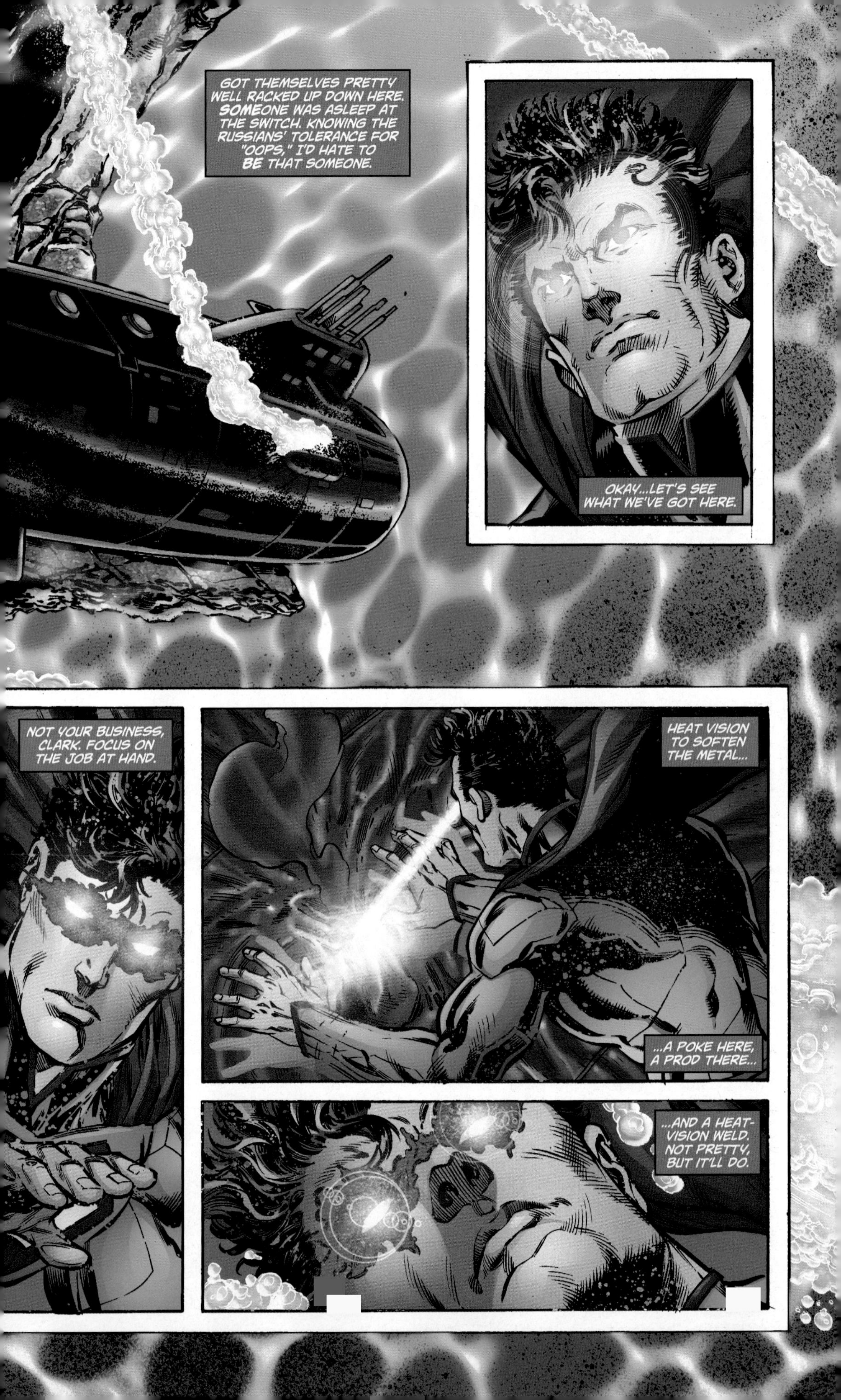
GOT THEMSELVES PRETTY WELL RACKED UP DOWN HERE. SOMEONE WAS ASLEEP AT THE SWITCH. KNOWING THE RUSSIANS' TOLERANCE FOR "OOPS," I'D HATE TO BE THAT SOMEONE.
OKAY...LET'S SEE WHAT WE'VE GOT HERE.
NOT YOUR BUSINESS, CLARK. FOCUS ON THE JOB AT HAND.
HEAT VISION TO SOFTEN THE METAL...
...A POKE HERE, A PROD THERE...
...AND A HEAT-VISION WELD. NOT PRETTY, BUT IT'LL DO.

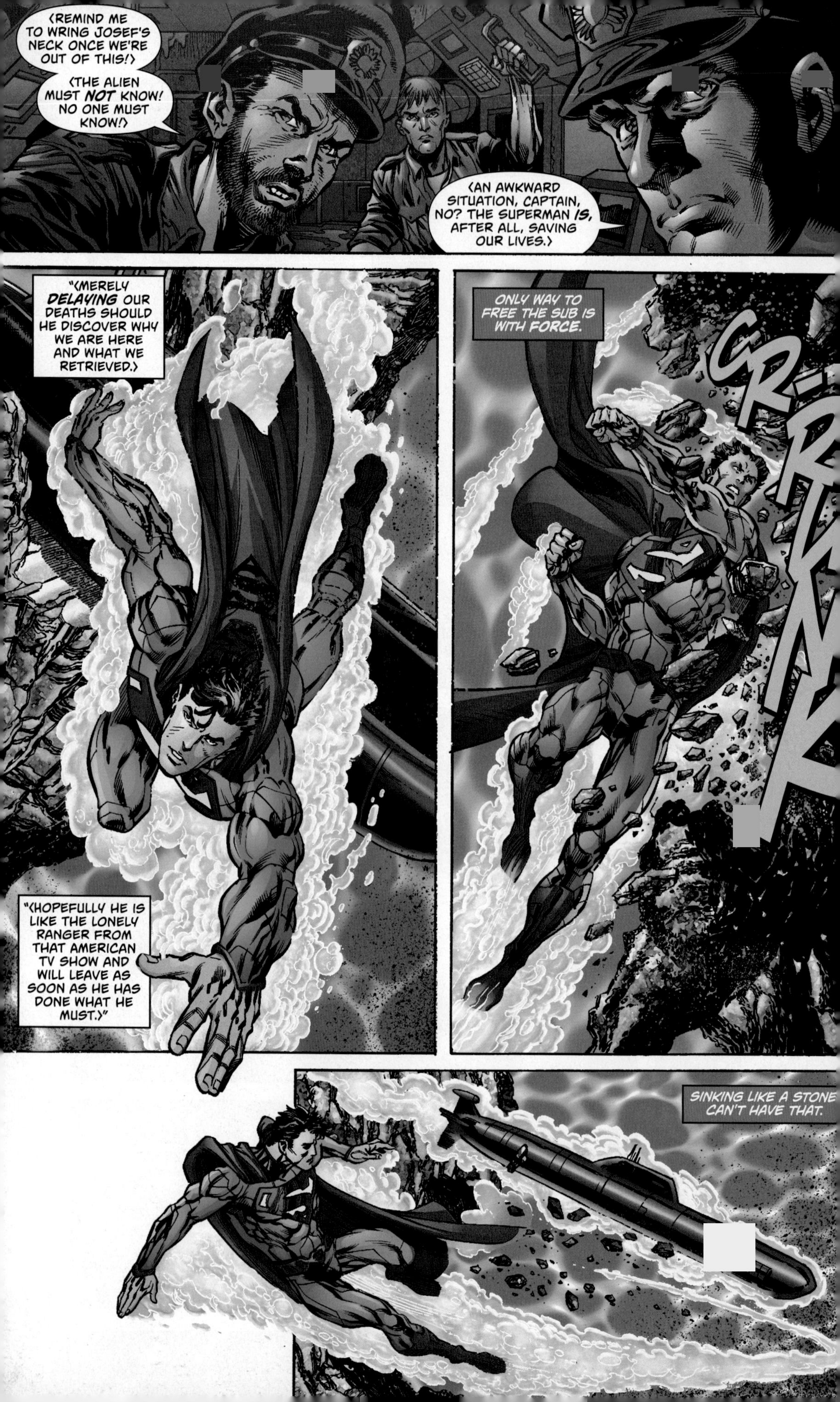
⟨REMIND ME TO WRING JOSEF'S NECK ONCE WE'RE OUT OF THIS!⟩
⟨THE ALIEN MUST *NOT* KNOW! NO ONE MUST KNOW!⟩
⟨AN AWKWARD SITUATION, CAPTAIN, NO? THE SUPERMAN *IS*, AFTER ALL, SAVING OUR LIVES.⟩
"⟨MERELY *DELAYING* OUR DEATHS SHOULD HE DISCOVER WHY WE ARE HERE AND WHAT WE RETRIEVED.⟩
"⟨HOPEFULLY HE IS LIKE THE LONELY RANGER FROM THAT AMERICAN TV SHOW AND WILL LEAVE AS SOON AS HE HAS DONE WHAT HE MUST.⟩"
ONLY WAY TO FREE THE SUB IS WITH *FORCE*.
CR-
SINKING LIKE A STONE CAN'T HAVE THAT.

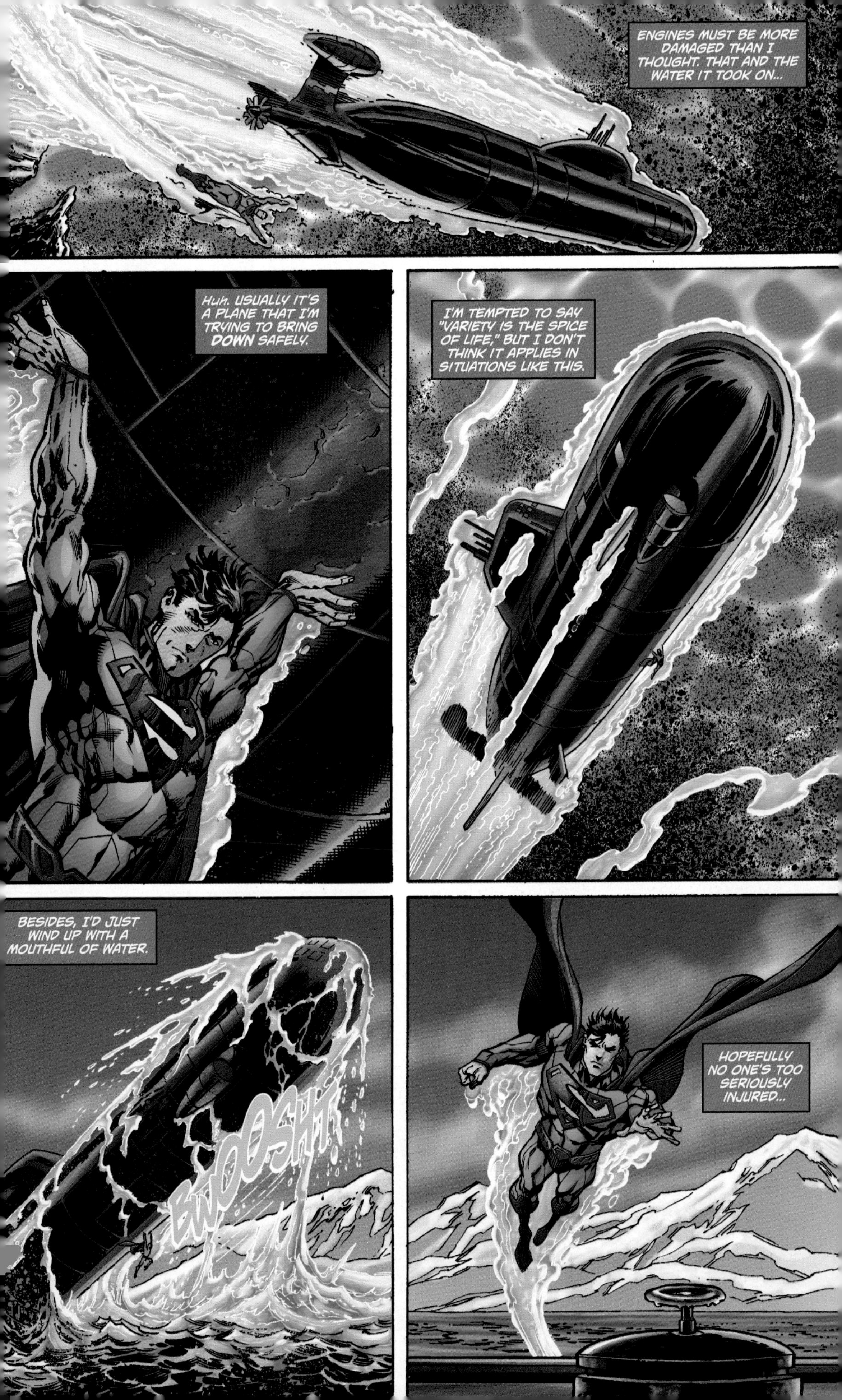
ENGINES MUST BE MORE DAMAGED THAN I THOUGHT. THAT AND THE WATER IT TOOK ON...
Huh. USUALLY IT'S A PLANE THAT I'M TRYING TO BRING DOWN SAFELY.
I'M TEMPTED TO SAY "VARIETY IS THE SPICE OF LIFE," BUT I DON'T THINK IT APPLIES IN SITUATIONS LIKE THIS.
BESIDES, I'D JUST WIND UP WITH A MOUTHFUL OF WATER.
BWOOSHT
HOPEFULLY NO ONE'S TOO SERIOUSLY INJURED...

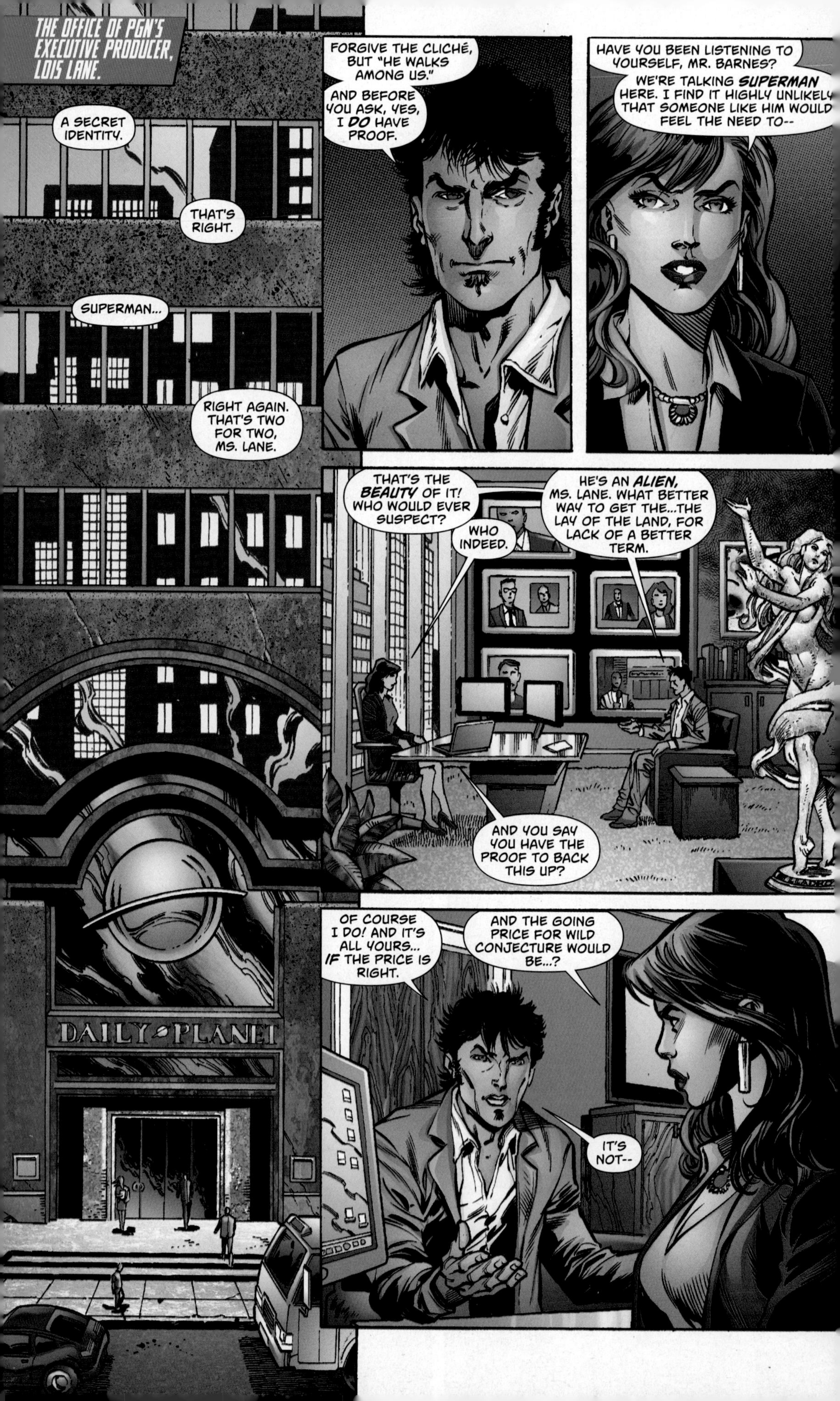
THE OFFICE OF PGN'S EXECUTIVE PRODUCER, LOIS LANE.
A SECRET IDENTITY.
THAT'S RIGHT.
SUPERMAN...
RIGHT AGAIN. THAT'S TWO FOR TWO, MS. LANE.
FORGIVE THE CLICHÉ, BUT "HE WALKS AMONG US."
AND BEFORE YOU ASK, YES, I DO HAVE PROOF.
HAVE YOU BEEN LISTENING TO YOURSELF, MR. BARNES?
WE'RE TALKING SUPERMAN HERE. I FIND IT HIGHLY UNLIKELY THAT SOMEONE LIKE HIM WOULD FEEL THE NEED TO--
THAT'S THE BEAUTY OF IT! WHO WOULD EVER SUSPECT?
WHO INDEED.
HE'S AN ALIEN, MS. LANE. WHAT BETTER WAY TO GET THE...THE LAY OF THE LAND, FOR LACK OF A BETTER TERM.
AND YOU SAY YOU HAVE THE PROOF TO BACK THIS UP?
OF COURSE I DO! AND IT'S ALL YOURS... IF THE PRICE IS RIGHT.
AND THE GOING PRICE FOR WILD CONJECTURE WOULD BE...?
IT'S NOT--
DAILY PLANET

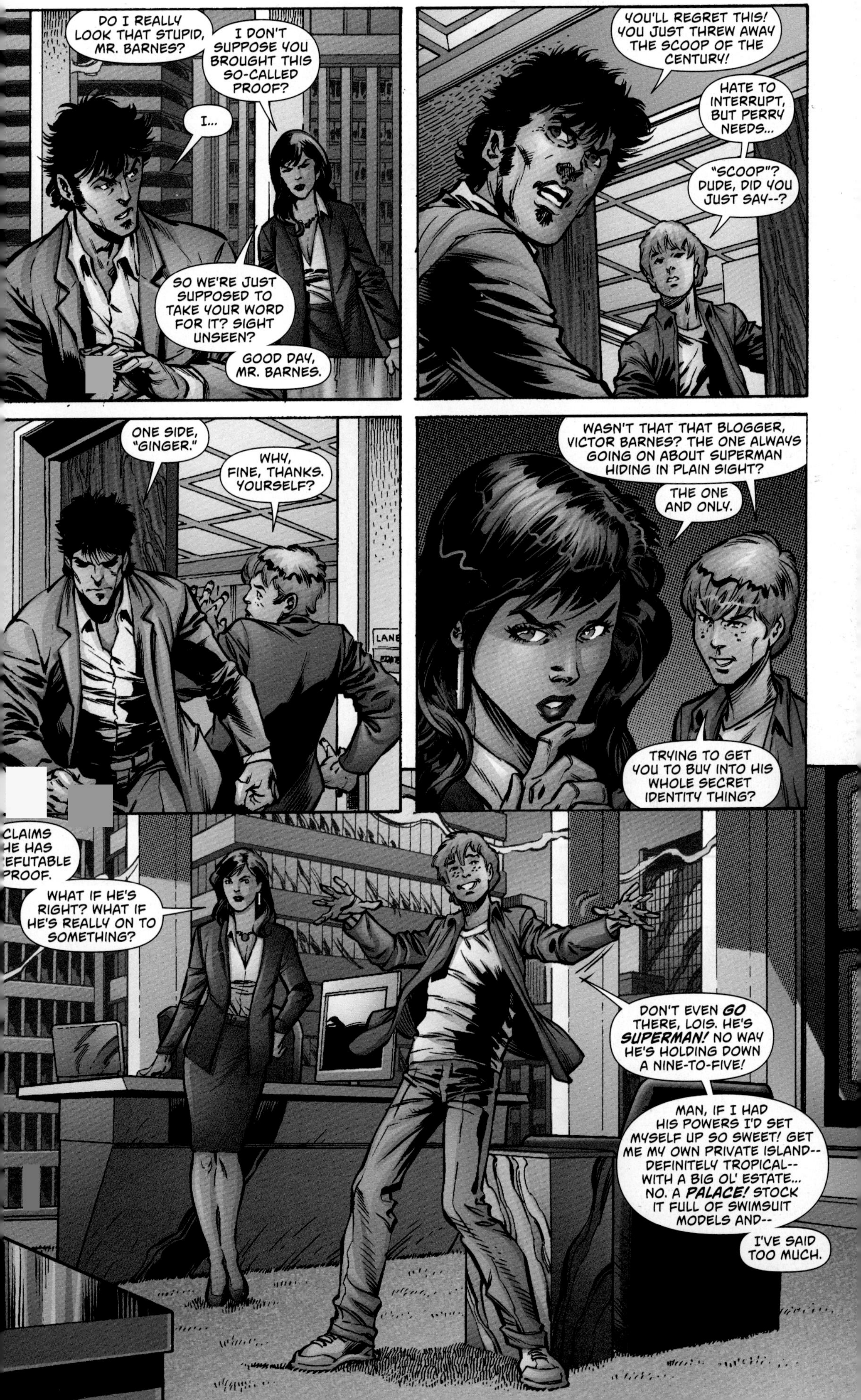

DO I REALLY LOOK THAT STUPID, MR. BARNES?
I DON'T SUPPOSE YOU BROUGHT THIS SO-CALLED PROOF?
I...
SO WE'RE JUST SUPPOSED TO TAKE YOUR WORD FOR IT? SIGHT UNSEEN?
GOOD DAY, MR. BARNES.
YOU'LL REGRET THIS! YOU JUST THREW AWAY THE SCOOP OF THE CENTURY!
HATE TO INTERRUPT, BUT PERRY NEEDS...
"SCOOP"? DUDE, DID YOU JUST SAY--?
ONE SIDE, "GINGER."
WHY, FINE, THANKS. YOURSELF?
LANE
WASN'T THAT THAT BLOGGER, VICTOR BARNES? THE ONE ALWAYS GOING ON ABOUT SUPERMAN HIDING IN PLAIN SIGHT?
THE ONE AND ONLY.
TRYING TO GET YOU TO BUY INTO HIS WHOLE SECRET IDENTITY THING?
CLAIMS HE HAS EFUTABLE PROOF.
WHAT IF HE'S RIGHT? WHAT IF HE'S REALLY ON TO SOMETHING?
DON'T EVEN GO THERE, LOIS. HE'S SUPERMAN! NO WAY HE'S HOLDING DOWN A NINE-TO-FIVE!
MAN, IF I HAD HIS POWERS I'D SET MYSELF UP SO SWEET! GET ME MY OWN PRIVATE ISLAND-- DEFINITELY TROPICAL-- WITH A BIG OL' ESTATE... NO. A PALACE! STOCK IT FULL OF SWIMSUIT MODELS AND--
I'VE SAID TOO MUCH.

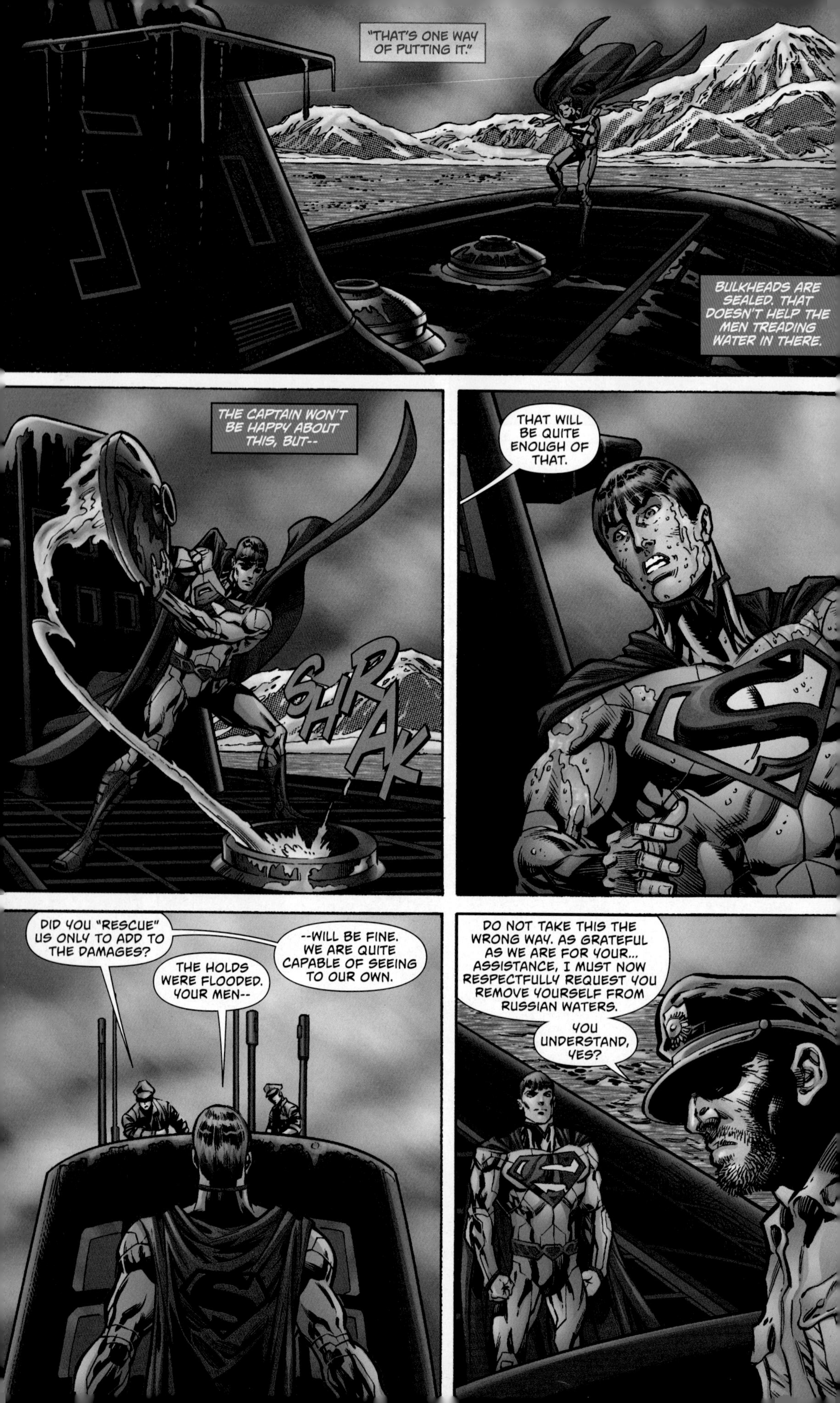
"THAT'S ONE WAY OF PUTTING IT."
BULKHEADS ARE SEALED. THAT DOESN'T HELP THE MEN TREADING WATER IN THERE.
THE CAPTAIN WON'T BE HAPPY ABOUT THIS, BUT--
SHRAK
THAT WILL BE QUITE ENOUGH OF THAT.
THE HOLDS WERE FLOODED. YOUR MEN--
--WILL BE FINE. WE ARE QUITE CAPABLE OF SEEING TO OUR OWN.
DID YOU "RESCUE" US ONLY TO ADD TO THE DAMAGES?
DO NOT TAKE THIS THE WRONG WAY. AS GRATEFUL AS WE ARE FOR YOUR... ASSISTANCE, I MUST NOW RESPECTFULLY REQUEST YOU REMOVE YOURSELF FROM RUSSIAN WATERS.
YOU UNDERSTAND, YES?

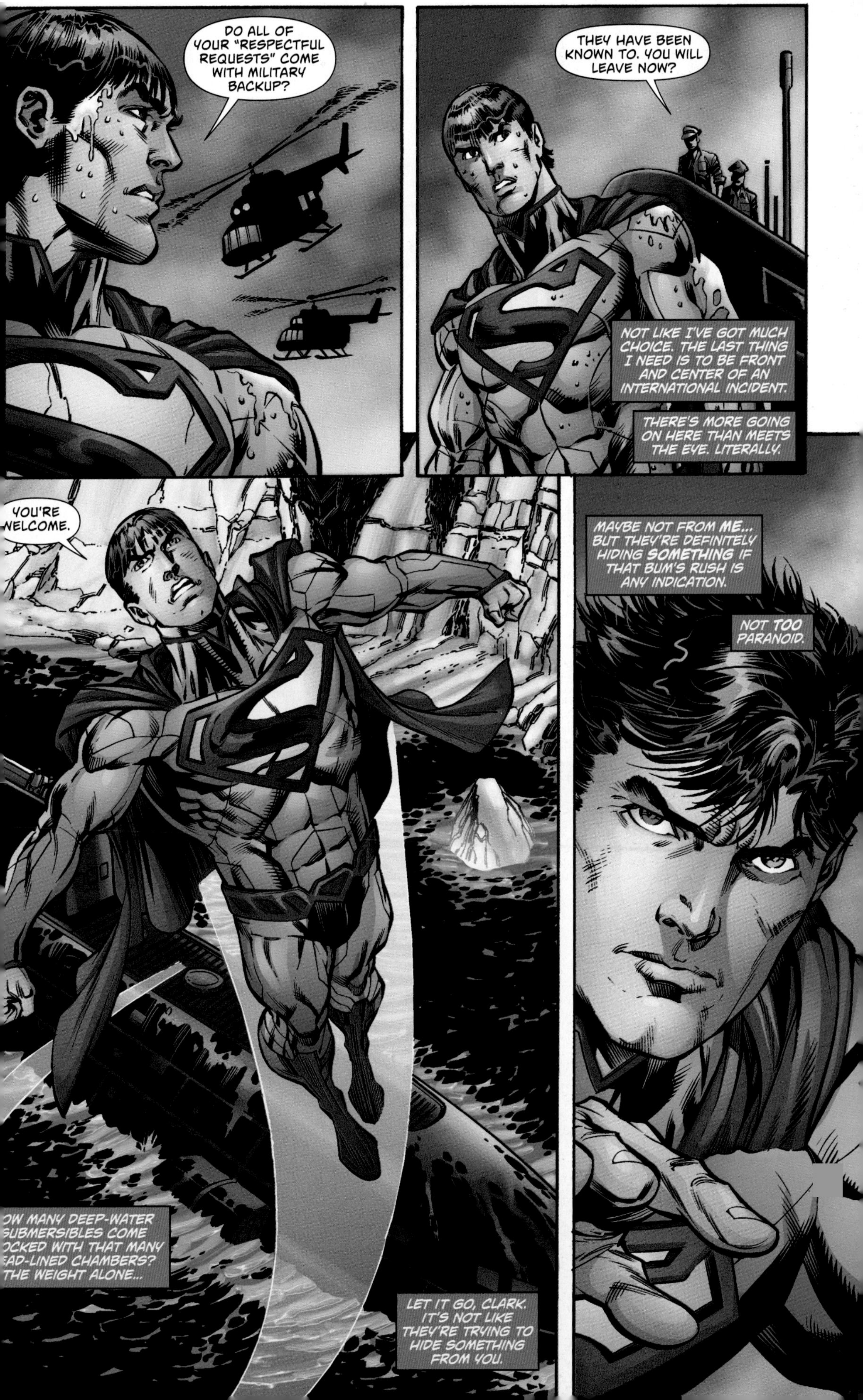
DO ALL OF YOUR "RESPECTFUL REQUESTS" COME WITH MILITARY BACKUP?
THEY HAVE BEEN KNOWN TO. YOU WILL LEAVE NOW?
NOT LIKE I'VE GOT MUCH CHOICE. THE LAST THING I NEED IS TO BE FRONT AND CENTER OF AN INTERNATIONAL INCIDENT.
THERE'S MORE GOING ON HERE THAN MEETS THE EYE. LITERALLY.
YOU'RE WELCOME.
OW MANY DEEP-WATER SUBMERSIBLES COME OCKED WITH THAT MANY EAD-LINED CHAMBERS? THE WEIGHT ALONE...
LET IT GO, CLARK. IT'S NOT LIKE THEY'RE TRYING TO HIDE SOMETHING FROM YOU.
MAYBE NOT FROM **ME**... BUT THEY'RE DEFINITELY HIDING **SOMETHING** IF THAT BUM'S RUSH IS ANY INDICATION.
NOT **TOO** PARANOID.

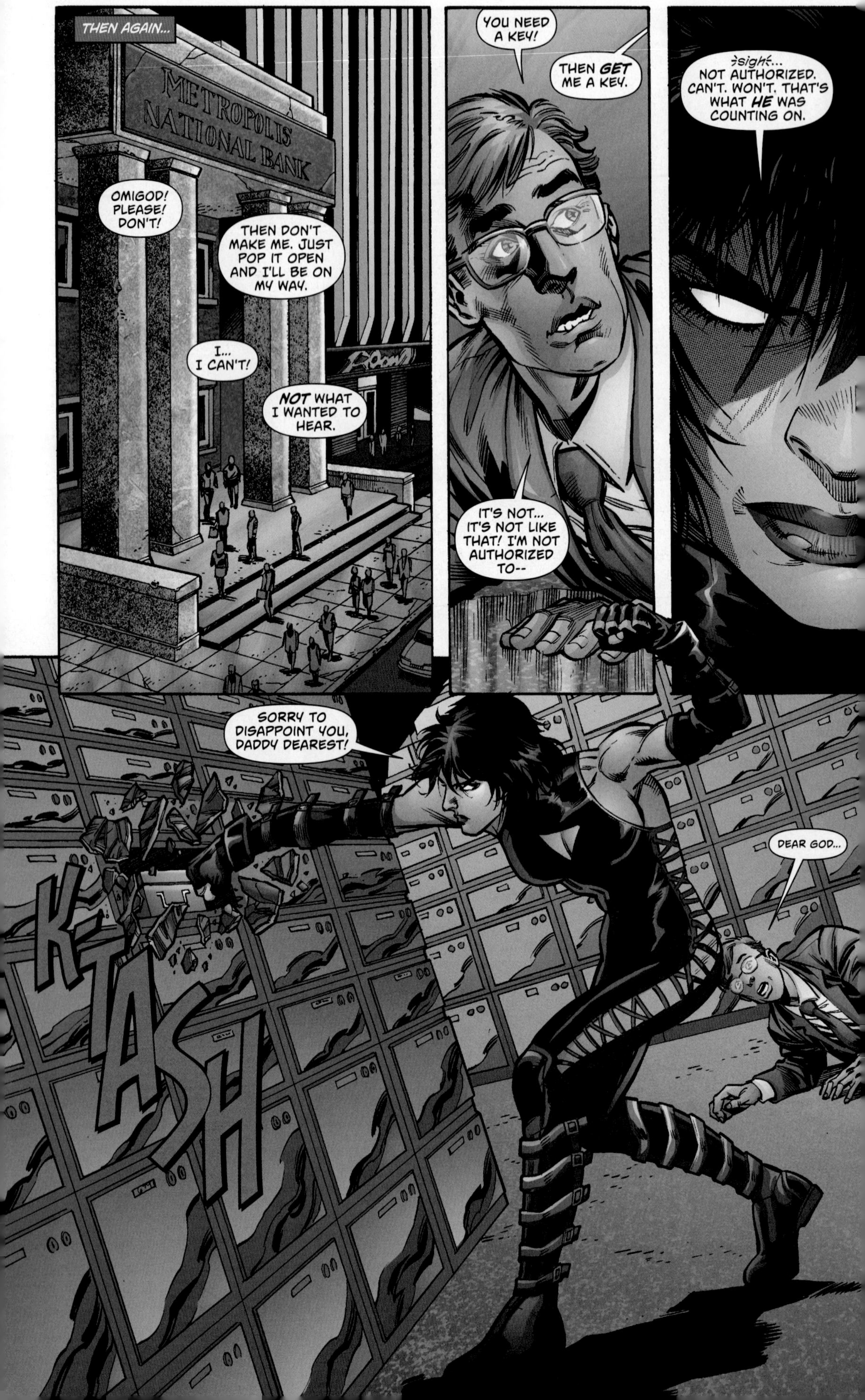
THEN AGAIN...
METROPOLIS NATIONAL BANK
OMIGOD! PLEASE! DON'T!
THEN DON'T MAKE ME. JUST POP IT OPEN AND I'LL BE ON MY WAY.
I... I CAN'T!
NOT WHAT I WANTED TO HEAR.
YOU NEED A KEY!
THEN GET ME A KEY.
IT'S NOT... IT'S NOT LIKE THAT! I'M NOT AUTHORIZED TO--
sigh... NOT AUTHORIZED. CAN'T. WON'T. THAT'S WHAT HE WAS COUNTING ON.
SORRY TO DISAPPOINT YOU, DADDY DEAREST!
K-TASH
DEAR GOD...

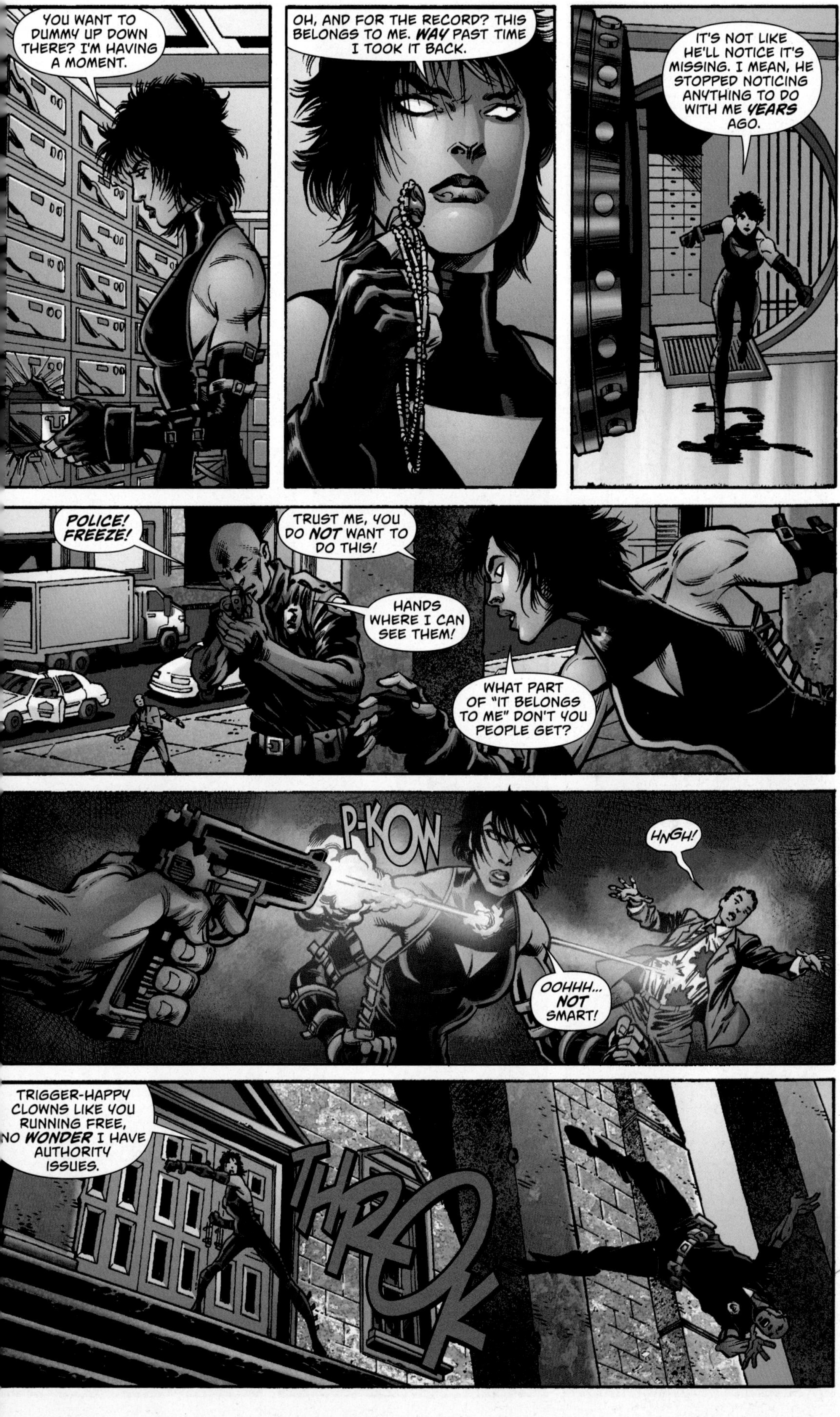
YOU WANT TO DUMMY UP DOWN THERE? I'M HAVING A MOMENT.
OH, AND FOR THE RECORD? THIS BELONGS TO ME. WAY PAST TIME I TOOK IT BACK.
IT'S NOT LIKE HE'LL NOTICE IT'S MISSING. I MEAN, HE STOPPED NOTICING ANYTHING TO DO WITH ME YEARS AGO.
POLICE! FREEZE!
TRUST ME, YOU DO NOT WANT TO DO THIS!
HANDS WHERE I CAN SEE THEM!
WHAT PART OF "IT BELONGS TO ME" DON'T YOU PEOPLE GET?
P-KOW
HNGH!
OOHHH... NOT SMART!
TRIGGER-HAPPY CLOWNS LIKE YOU RUNNING FREE, NO WONDER I HAVE AUTHORITY ISSUES.
THROCK

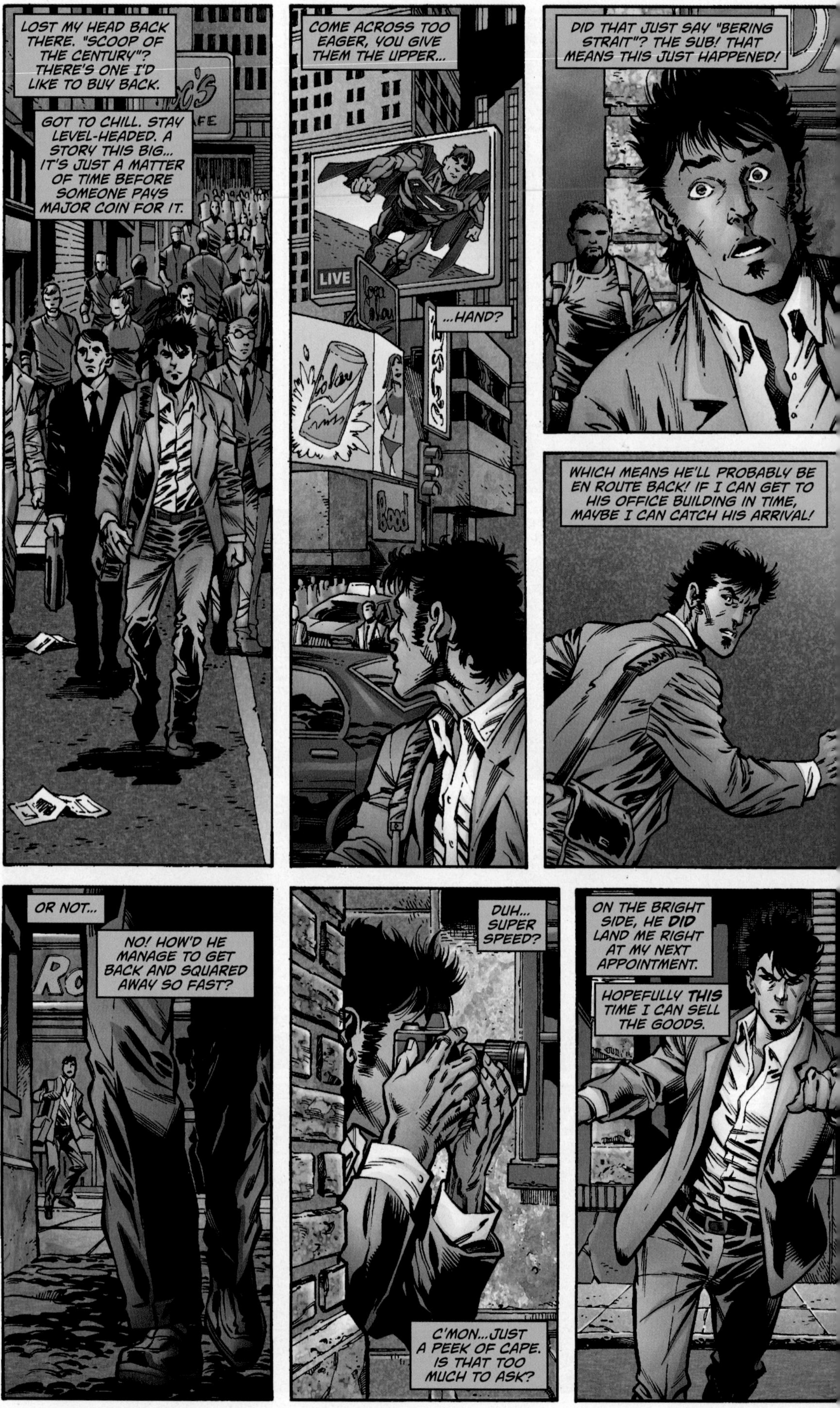
LOST MY HEAD BACK THERE. "SCOOP OF THE CENTURY"? THERE'S ONE I'D LIKE TO BUY BACK.
GOT TO CHILL. STAY LEVEL-HEADED. A STORY THIS BIG... IT'S JUST A MATTER OF TIME BEFORE SOMEONE PAYS MAJOR COIN FOR IT.
COME ACROSS TOO EAGER, YOU GIVE THEM THE UPPER...
LIVE
...HAND?
DID THAT JUST SAY "BERING STRAIT"? THE SUB! THAT MEANS THIS JUST HAPPENED!
WHICH MEANS HE'LL PROBABLY BE EN ROUTE BACK! IF I CAN GET TO HIS OFFICE BUILDING IN TIME, MAYBE I CAN CATCH HIS ARRIVAL!
OR NOT...
NO! HOW'D HE MANAGE TO GET BACK AND SQUARED AWAY SO FAST?
DUH... SUPER SPEED?
C'MON...JUST A PEEK OF CAPE. IS THAT TOO MUCH TO ASK?
ON THE BRIGHT SIDE, HE DID LAND ME RIGHT AT MY NEXT APPOINTMENT.
HOPEFULLY THIS TIME I CAN SELL THE GOODS.

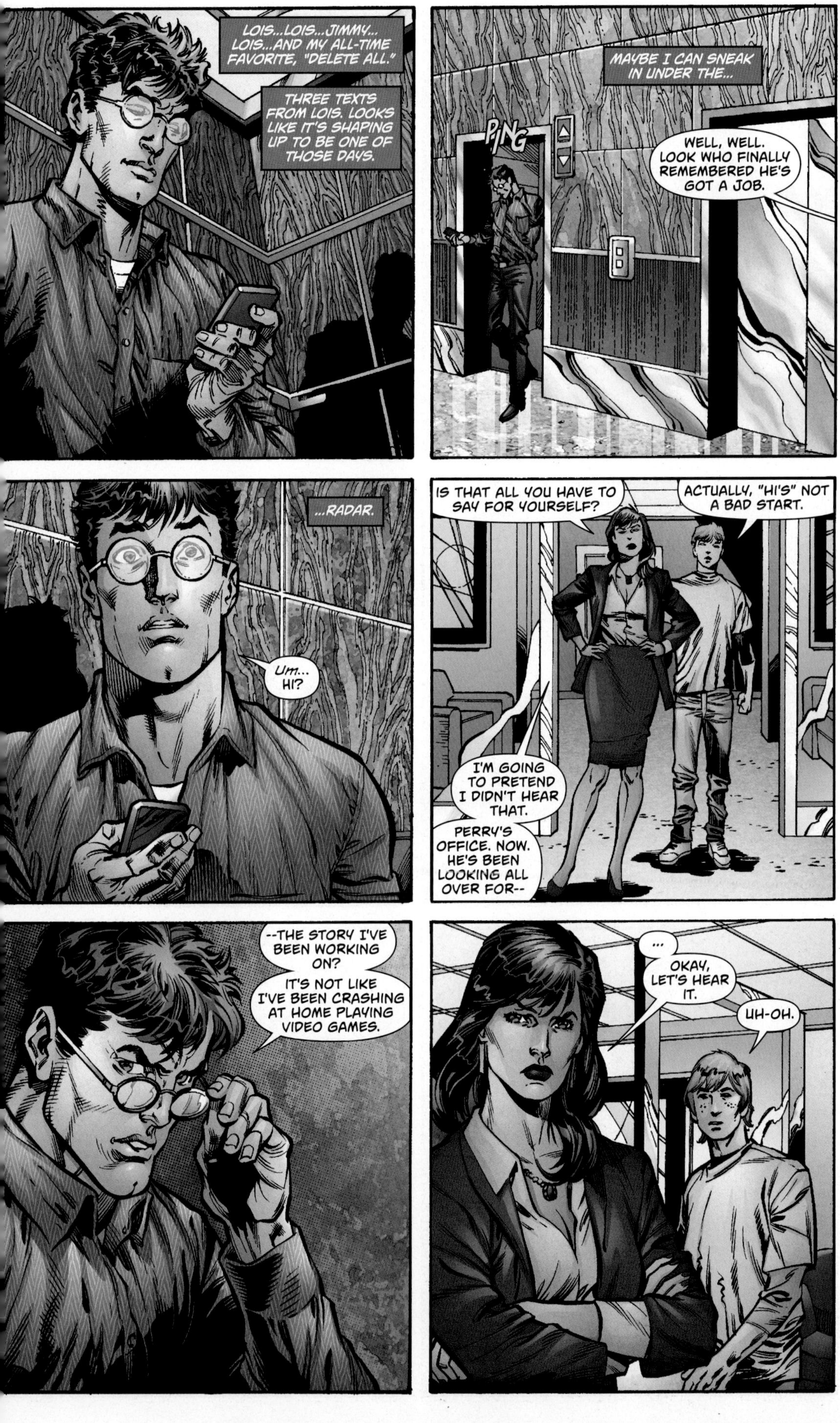

LOIS...LOIS...JIMMY... LOIS...AND MY ALL-TIME FAVORITE, "DELETE ALL."
THREE TEXTS FROM LOIS. LOOKS LIKE IT'S SHAPING UP TO BE ONE OF THOSE DAYS.
MAYBE I CAN SNEAK IN UNDER THE...
PING
WELL, WELL. LOOK WHO FINALLY REMEMBERED HE'S GOT A JOB.
...RADAR.
UM... HI?
IS THAT ALL YOU HAVE TO SAY FOR YOURSELF?
ACTUALLY, "HI'S" NOT A BAD START.
I'M GOING TO PRETEND I DIDN'T HEAR THAT.
PERRY'S OFFICE. NOW. HE'S BEEN LOOKING ALL OVER FOR--
--THE STORY I'VE BEEN WORKING ON?
IT'S NOT LIKE I'VE BEEN CRASHING AT HOME PLAYING VIDEO GAMES.
...
OKAY, LET'S HEAR IT.
UH-OH.

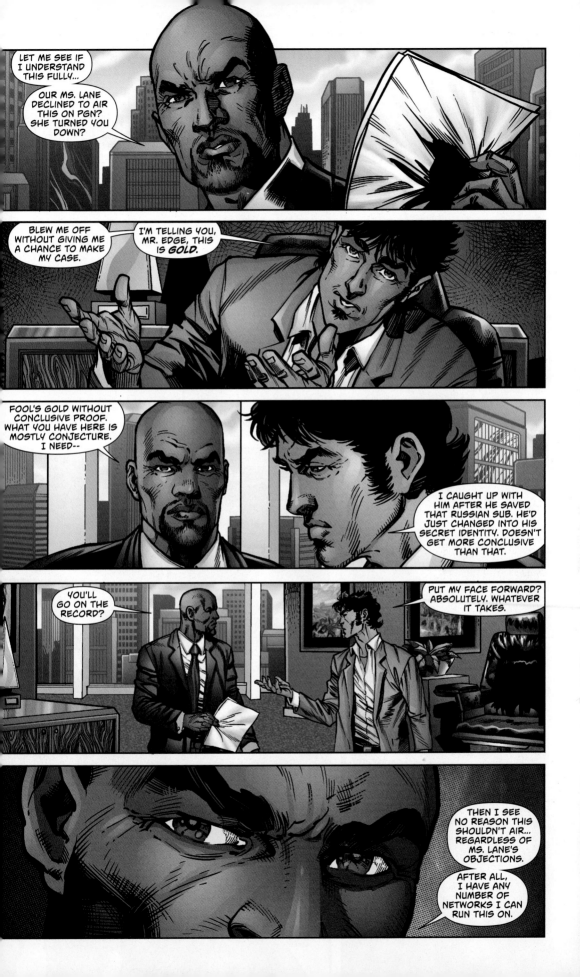

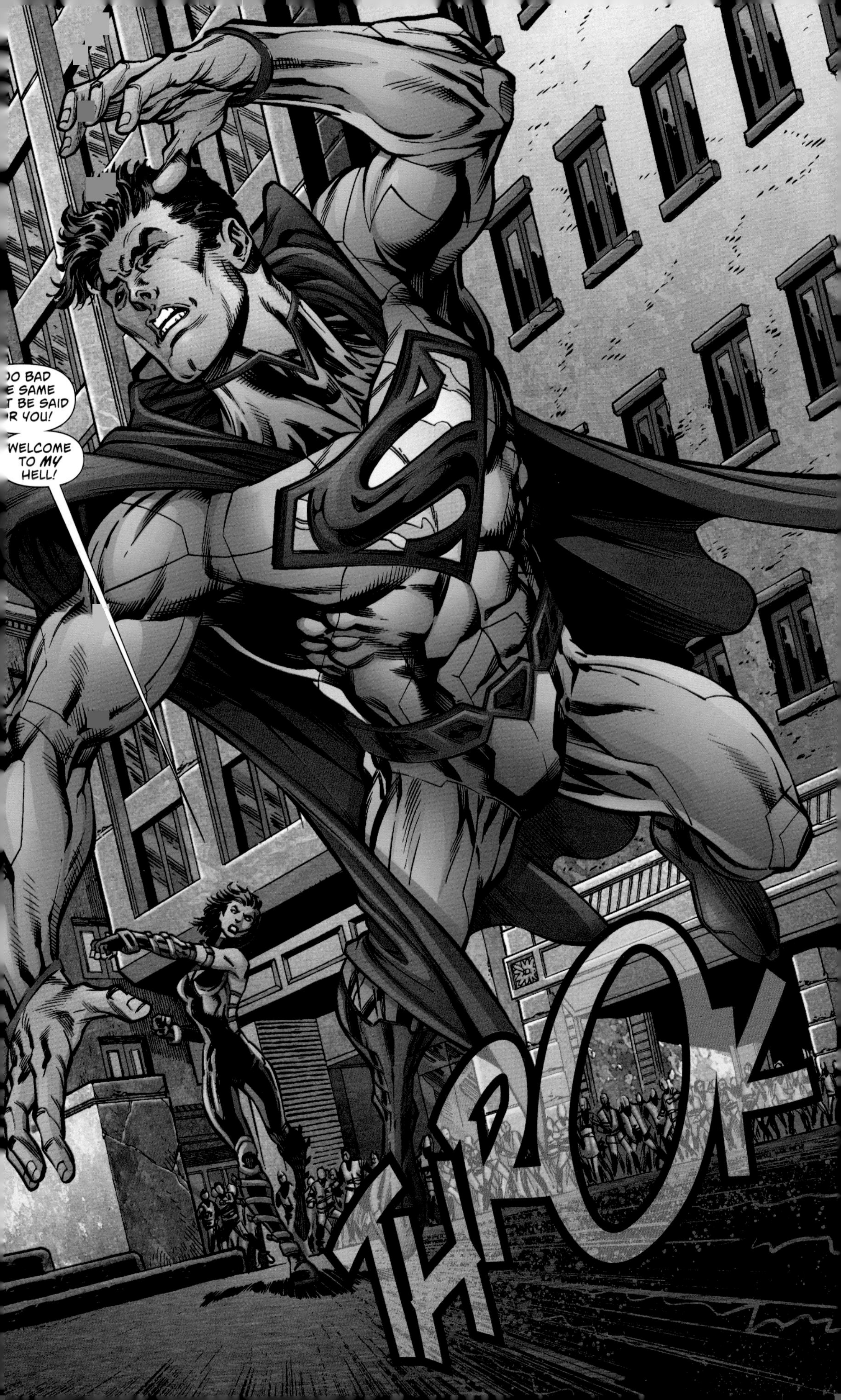
OO BAD
E SAME
T BE SAID
R YOU!
WELCOME
TO MY
HELL!

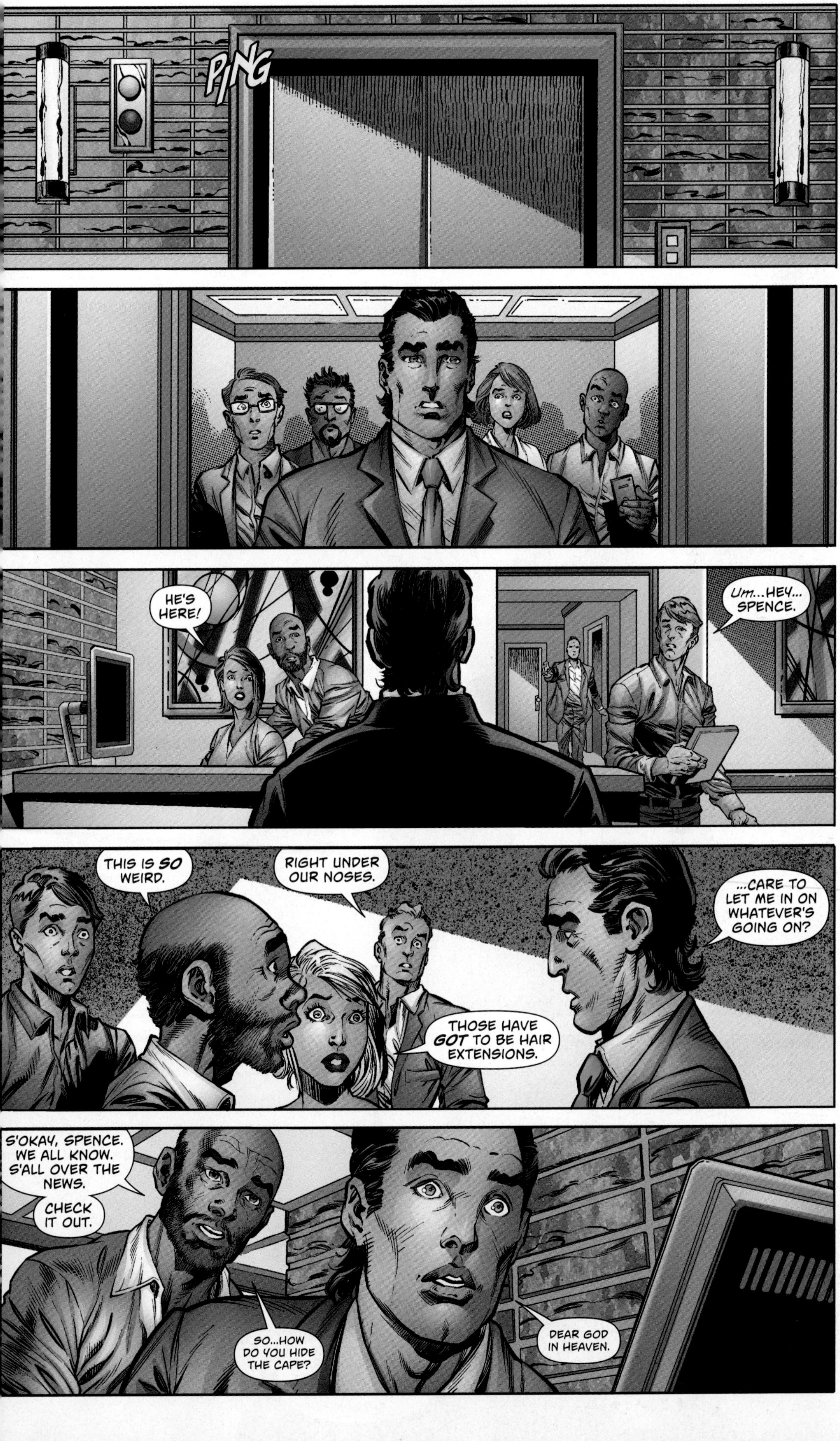
PING
HE'S HERE!
Um...HEY... SPENCE.
THIS IS SO WEIRD.
RIGHT UNDER OUR NOSES.
...CARE TO LET ME IN ON WHATEVER'S GOING ON?
THOSE HAVE GOT TO BE HAIR EXTENSIONS.
S'OKAY, SPENCE. WE ALL KNOW. S'ALL OVER THE NEWS.
CHECK IT OUT.
SO...HOW DO YOU HIDE THE CAPE?
DEAR GOD IN HEAVEN.

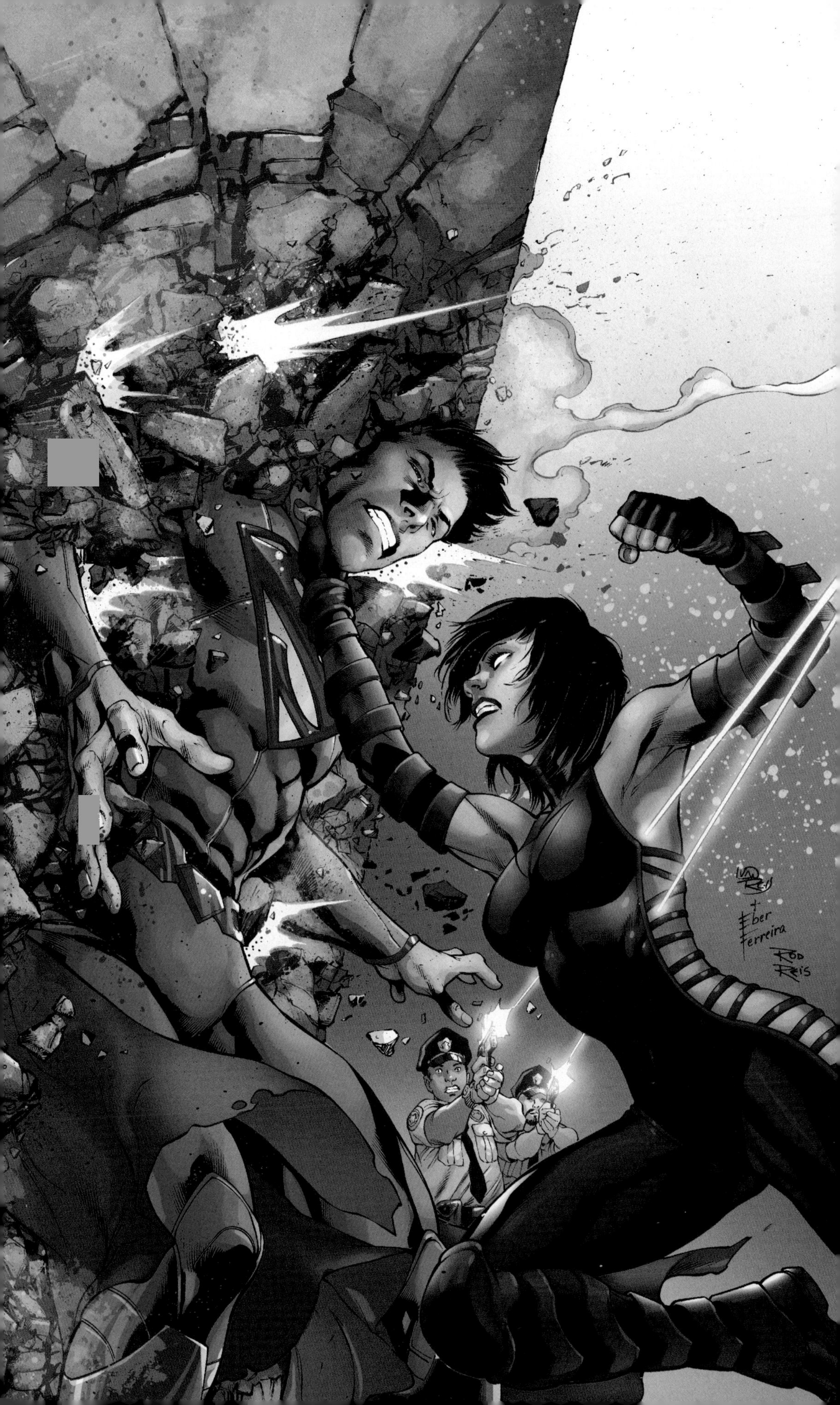
+
Eber
Ferreira
Rod
Reis

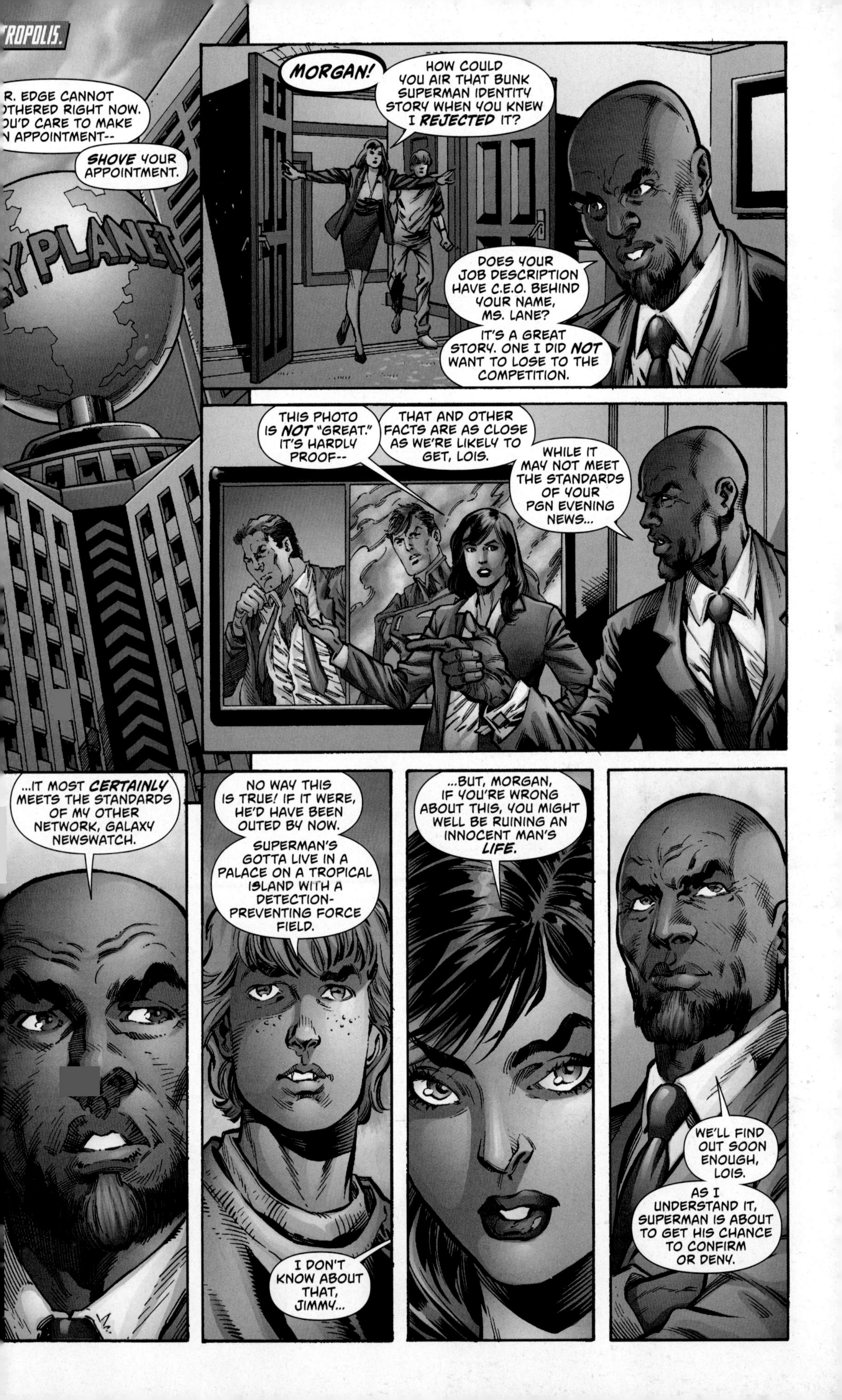

ROPOLIS.
R. EDGE CANNOT OTHERED RIGHT NOW. OU'D CARE TO MAKE N APPOINTMENT--
SHOVE YOUR APPOINTMENT.
MORGAN!
HOW COULD YOU AIR THAT BUNK SUPERMAN IDENTITY STORY WHEN YOU KNEW I REJECTED IT?
DOES YOUR JOB DESCRIPTION HAVE C.E.O. BEHIND YOUR NAME, MS. LANE?
IT'S A GREAT STORY. ONE I DID NOT WANT TO LOSE TO THE COMPETITION.
THIS PHOTO IS NOT "GREAT." IT'S HARDLY PROOF--
THAT AND OTHER FACTS ARE AS CLOSE AS WE'RE LIKELY TO GET, LOIS.
WHILE IT MAY NOT MEET THE STANDARDS OF YOUR PGN EVENING NEWS...
...IT MOST CERTAINLY MEETS THE STANDARDS OF MY OTHER NETWORK, GALAXY NEWSWATCH.
NO WAY THIS IS TRUE! IF IT WERE, HE'D HAVE BEEN OUTED BY NOW.
SUPERMAN'S GOTTA LIVE IN A PALACE ON A TROPICAL ISLAND WITH A DETECTION-PREVENTING FORCE FIELD.
I DON'T KNOW ABOUT THAT, JIMMY...
...BUT, MORGAN, IF YOU'RE WRONG ABOUT THIS, YOU MIGHT WELL BE RUINING AN INNOCENT MAN'S LIFE.
WE'LL FIND OUT SOON ENOUGH, LOIS.
AS I UNDERSTAND IT, SUPERMAN IS ABOUT TO GET HIS CHANCE TO CONFIRM OR DENY.

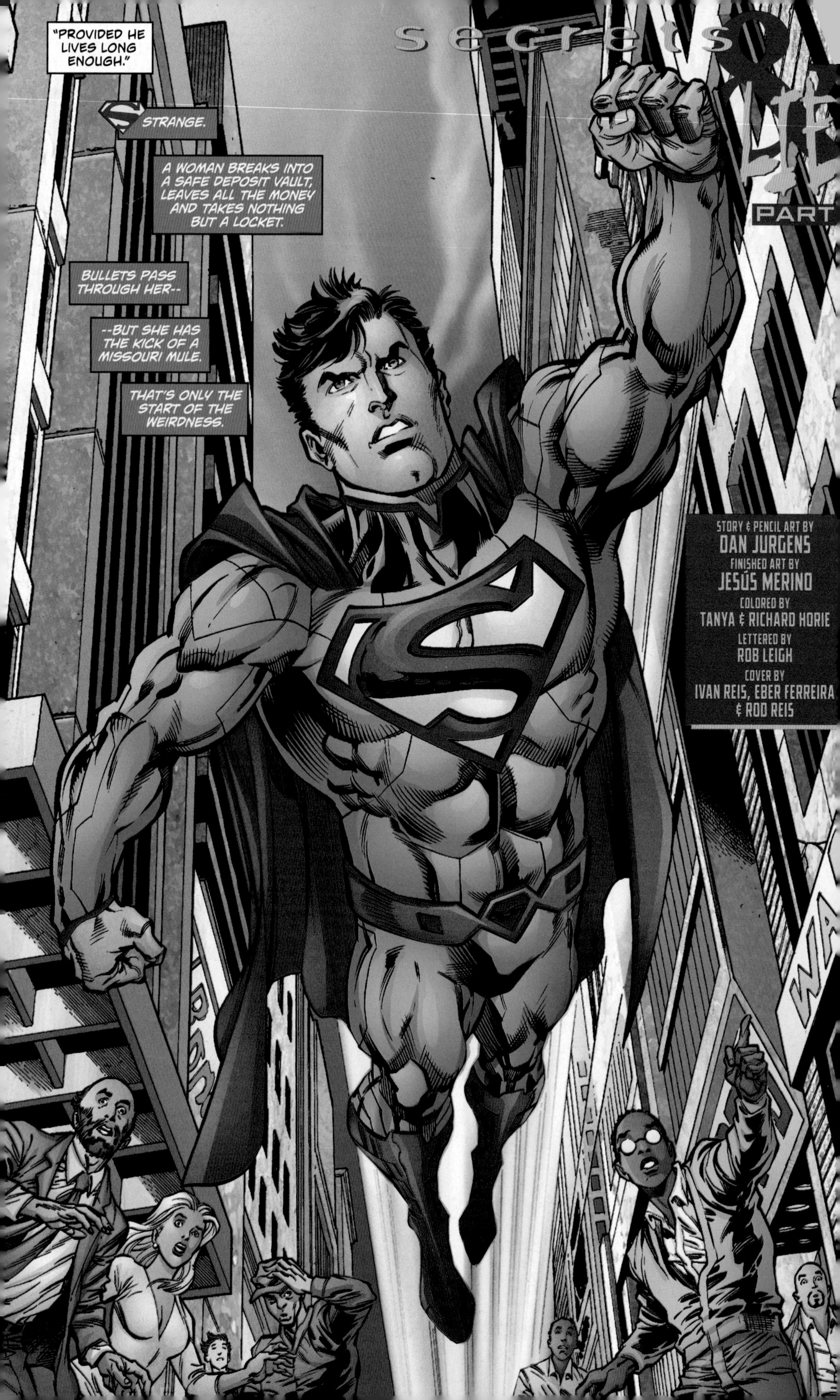

"PROVIDED HE LIVES LONG ENOUGH."
STRANGE.
A WOMAN BREAKS INTO A SAFE DEPOSIT VAULT, LEAVES ALL THE MONEY AND TAKES NOTHING BUT A LOCKET.
BULLETS PASS THROUGH HER--
--BUT SHE HAS THE KICK OF A MISSOURI MULE.
THAT'S ONLY THE START OF THE WEIRDNESS.
SECRETS
PART
STORY & PENCIL ART BY
DAN JURGENS
FINISHED ART BY
JESÚS MERINO
COLORED BY
TANYA & RICHARD HORIE
LETTERED BY
ROB LEIGH
COVER BY
IVAN REIS, EBER FERREIRA & ROD REIS

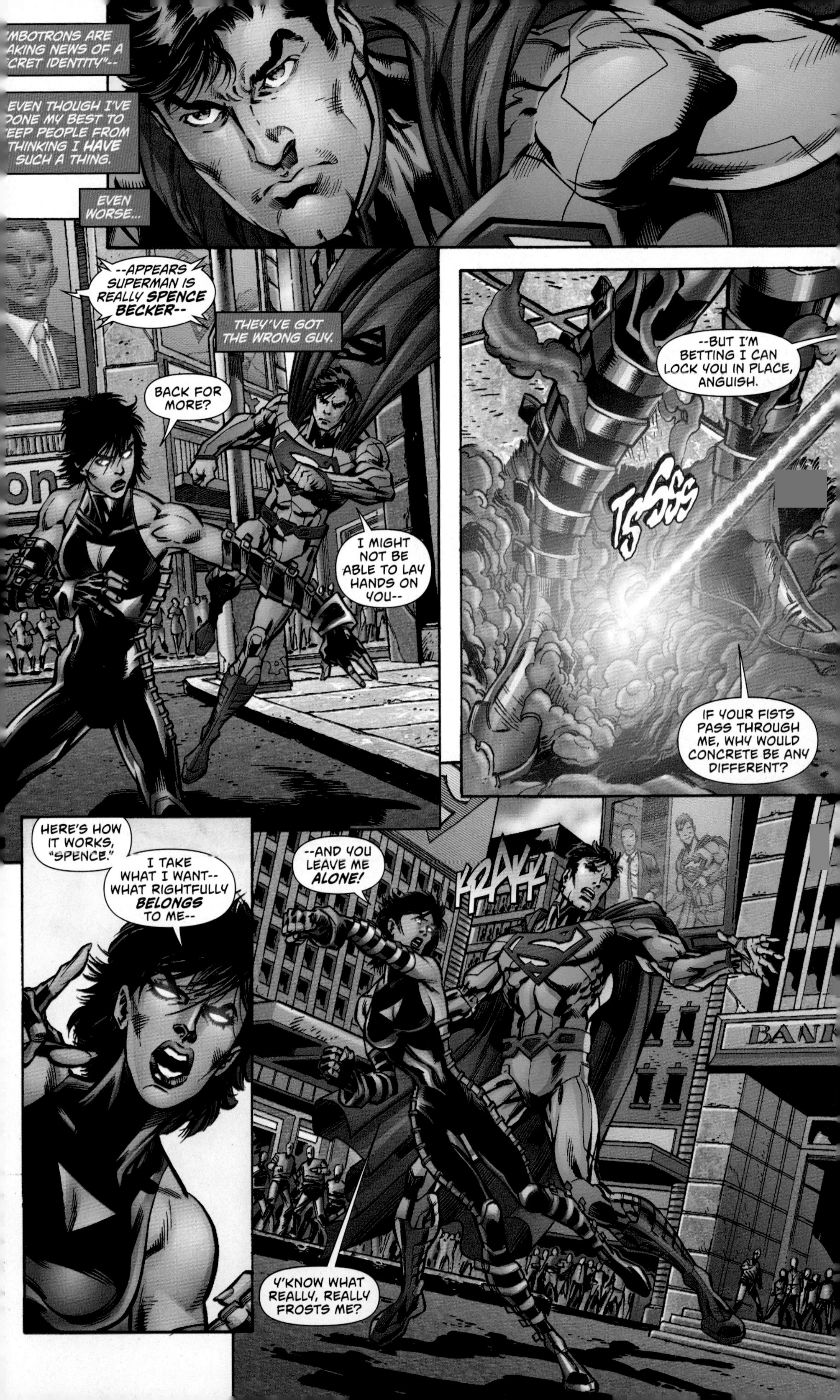

"MBOTRONS ARE
AKING NEWS OF A
CRET IDENTITY"--
EVEN THOUGH I'VE DONE MY BEST TO EEP PEOPLE FROM THINKING I HAVE SUCH A THING.
EVEN WORSE...
--APPEARS SUPERMAN IS REALLY SPENCE BECKER--
THEY'VE GOT THE WRONG GUY.
BACK FOR MORE?
I MIGHT NOT BE ABLE TO LAY HANDS ON YOU--
--BUT I'M BETTING I CAN LOCK YOU IN PLACE, ANGUISH.
TSSSS
IF YOUR FISTS PASS THROUGH ME, WHY WOULD CONCRETE BE ANY DIFFERENT?
HERE'S HOW IT WORKS, "SPENCE."
I TAKE WHAT I WANT-- WHAT RIGHTFULLY BELONGS TO ME--
--AND YOU LEAVE ME ALONE!
KRAKK
Y'KNOW WHAT REALLY, REALLY FROSTS ME?
BANK

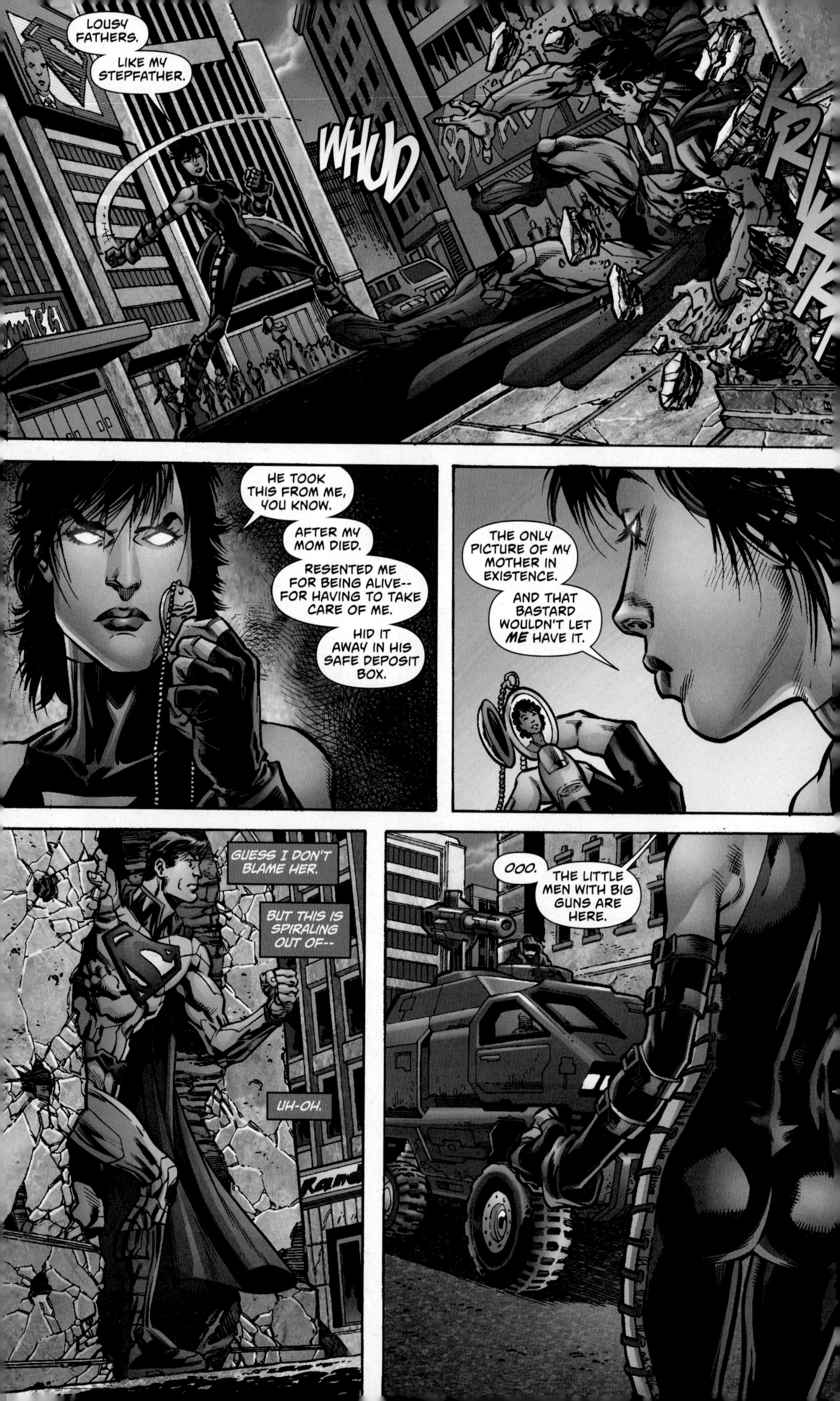
LOUSY FATHERS.
LIKE MY STEPFATHER.
WHUD
KRKKK
HE TOOK THIS FROM ME, YOU KNOW.
AFTER MY MOM DIED.
RESENTED ME FOR BEING ALIVE-- FOR HAVING TO TAKE CARE OF ME.
HID IT AWAY IN HIS SAFE DEPOSIT BOX.
THE ONLY PICTURE OF MY MOTHER IN EXISTENCE.
AND THAT BASTARD WOULDN'T LET *ME* HAVE IT.
GUESS I DON'T BLAME HER.
BUT THIS IS SPIRALING OUT OF--
UH-OH.
OOO.
THE LITTLE MEN WITH BIG GUNS ARE HERE.

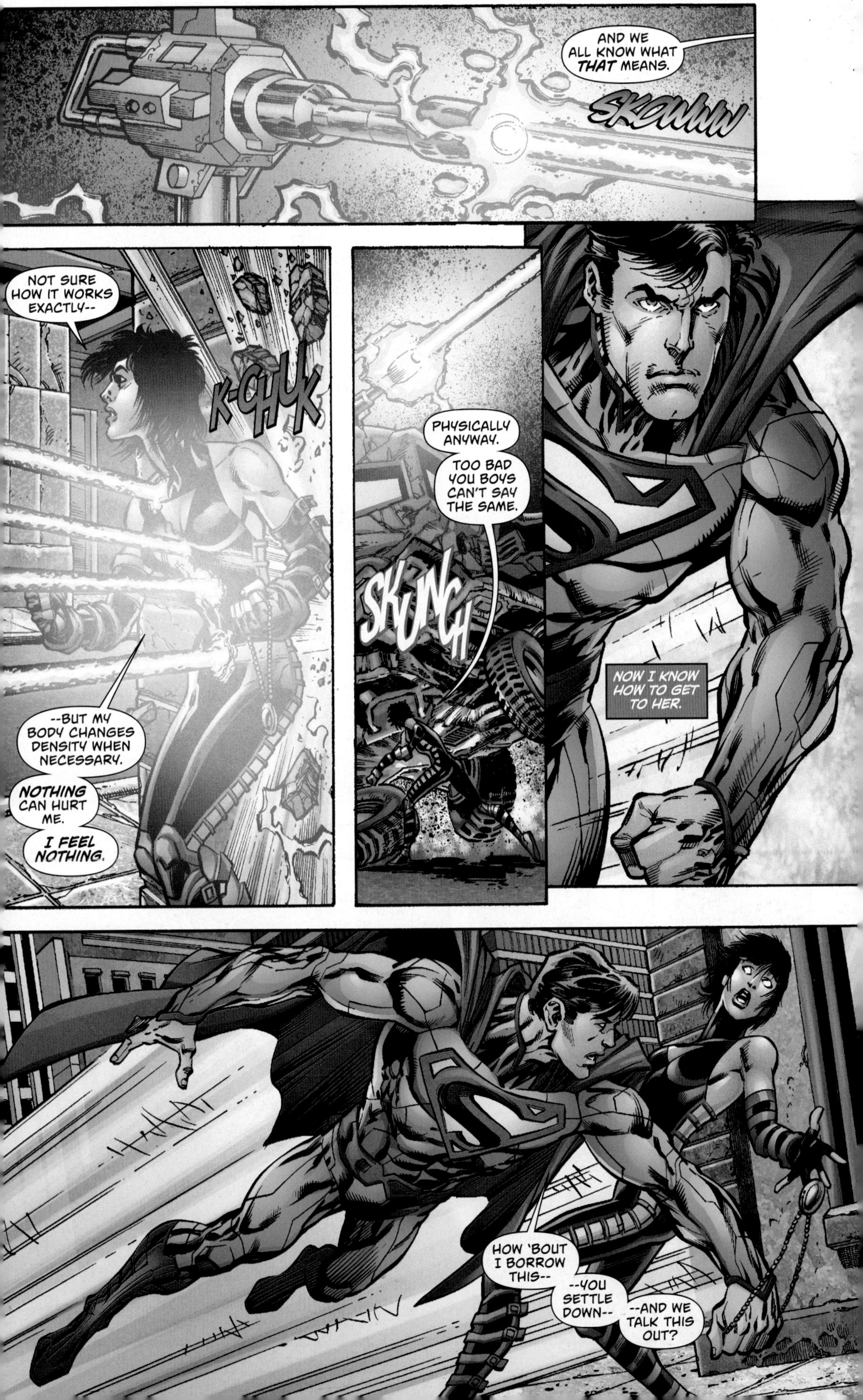

AND WE ALL KNOW WHAT THAT MEANS.
SKOWWW
NOT SURE HOW IT WORKS EXACTLY--
K-CHUK
--BUT MY BODY CHANGES DENSITY WHEN NECESSARY.
NOTHING CAN HURT ME.
I FEEL NOTHING.
PHYSICALLY ANYWAY.
TOO BAD YOU BOYS CAN'T SAY THE SAME.
SKRUNCH
NOW I KNOW HOW TO GET TO HER.
HOW 'BOUT I BORROW THIS--
--YOU SETTLE DOWN--
--AND WE TALK THIS OUT?

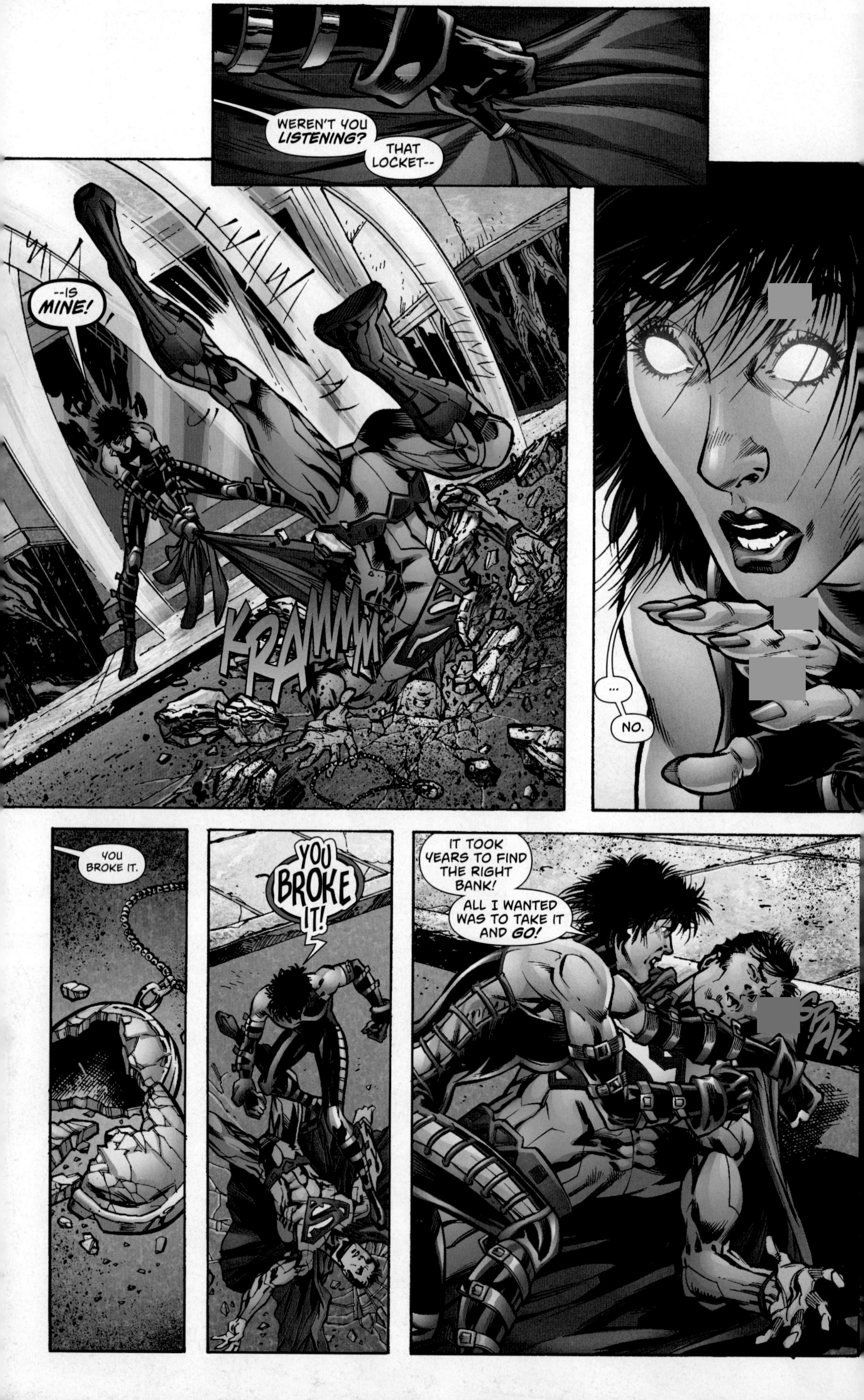
WEREN'T YOU LISTENING?
THAT LOCKET--
--IS MINE!
KRAMMMM
...
NO.
YOU BROKE IT.
YOU BROKE IT!
IT TOOK YEARS TO FIND THE RIGHT BANK!
ALL I WANTED WAS TO TAKE IT AND GO!
SPAK

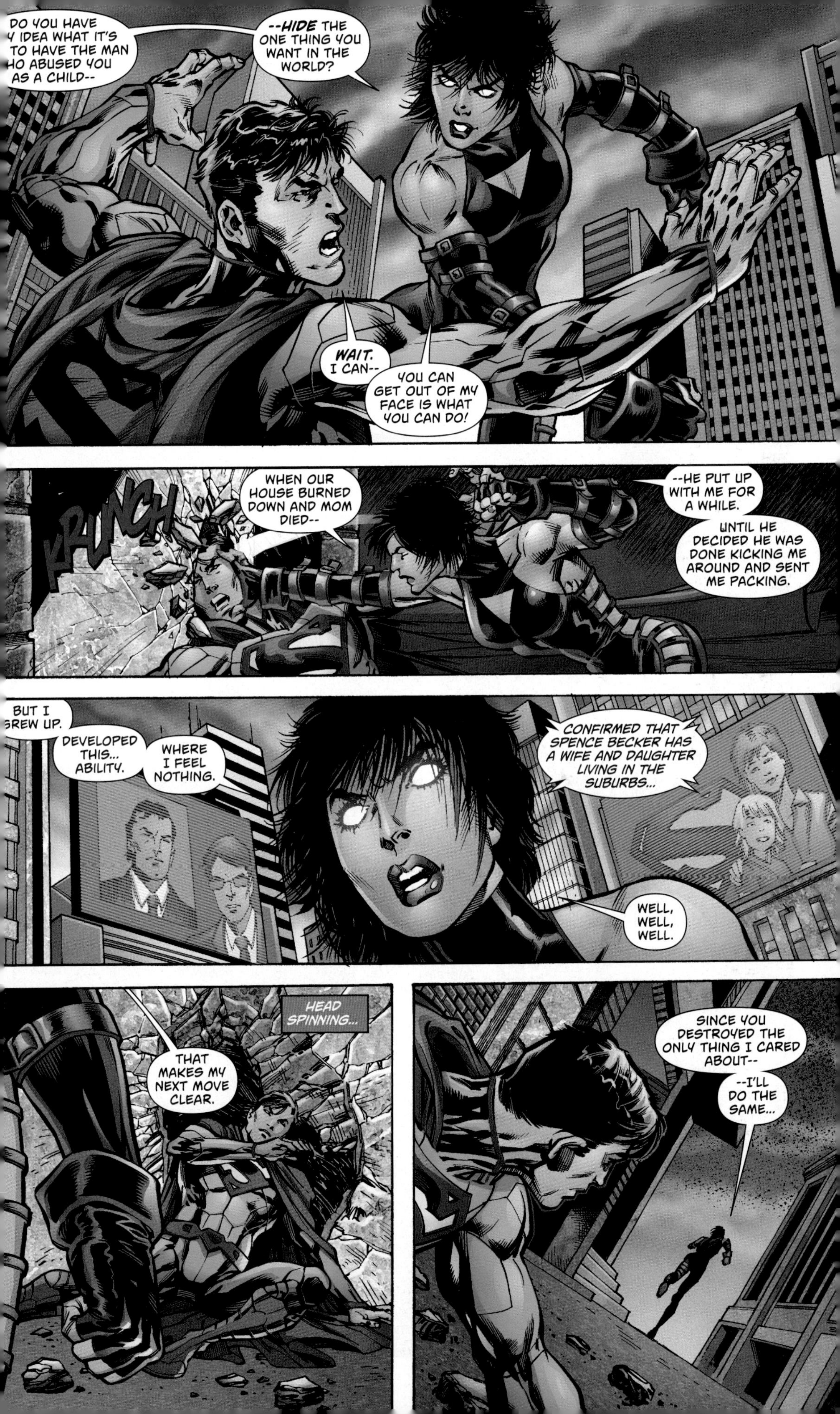
DO YOU HAVE Y IDEA WHAT IT'S TO HAVE THE MAN HO ABUSED YOU AS A CHILD--
--HIDE THE ONE THING YOU WANT IN THE WORLD?
WAIT. I CAN--
YOU CAN GET OUT OF MY FACE IS WHAT YOU CAN DO!
KRUNCH
WHEN OUR HOUSE BURNED DOWN AND MOM DIED--
--HE PUT UP WITH ME FOR A WHILE.
UNTIL HE DECIDED HE WAS DONE KICKING ME AROUND AND SENT ME PACKING.
BUT I GREW UP.
DEVELOPED THIS... ABILITY.
WHERE I FEEL NOTHING.
CONFIRMED THAT SPENCE BECKER HAS A WIFE AND DAUGHTER LIVING IN THE SUBURBS...
WELL, WELL, WELL.
HEAD SPINNING...
THAT MAKES MY NEXT MOVE CLEAR.
SINCE YOU DESTROYED THE ONLY THING I CARED ABOUT--
--I'LL DO THE SAME...

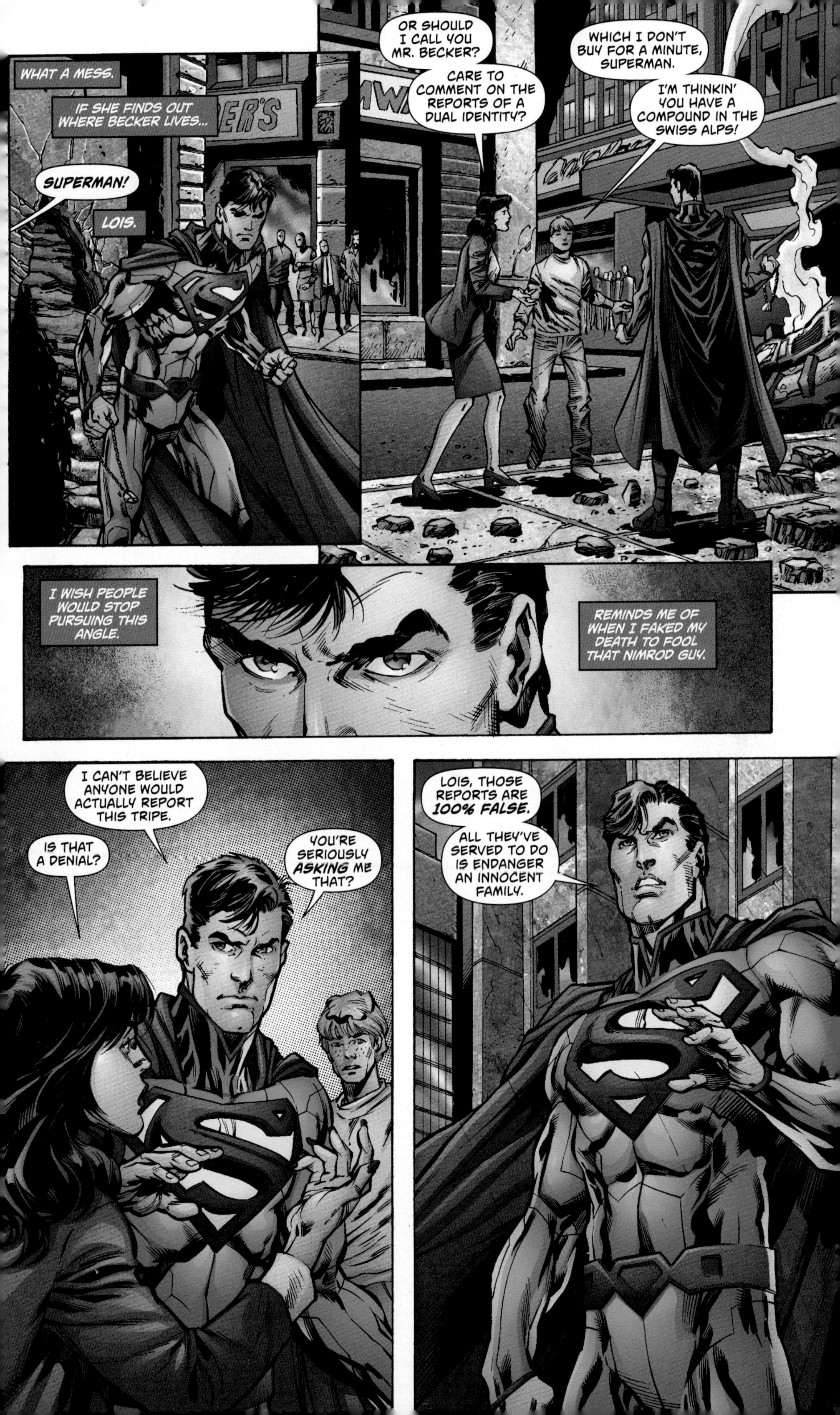

WHAT A MESS.
IF SHE FINDS OUT WHERE BECKER LIVES...
SUPERMAN!
LOIS.
OR SHOULD I CALL YOU MR. BECKER?
CARE TO COMMENT ON THE REPORTS OF A DUAL IDENTITY?
WHICH I DON'T BUY FOR A MINUTE, SUPERMAN.
I'M THINKIN' YOU HAVE A COMPOUND IN THE SWISS ALPS!
I WISH PEOPLE WOULD STOP PURSUING THIS ANGLE.
REMINDS ME OF WHEN I FAKED MY DEATH TO FOOL THAT NIMROD GUY.
I CAN'T BELIEVE ANYONE WOULD ACTUALLY REPORT THIS TRIPE.
IS THAT A DENIAL?
YOU'RE SERIOUSLY ASKING ME THAT?
LOIS, THOSE REPORTS ARE 100% FALSE.
ALL THEY'VE SERVED TO DO IS ENDANGER AN INNOCENT FAMILY.

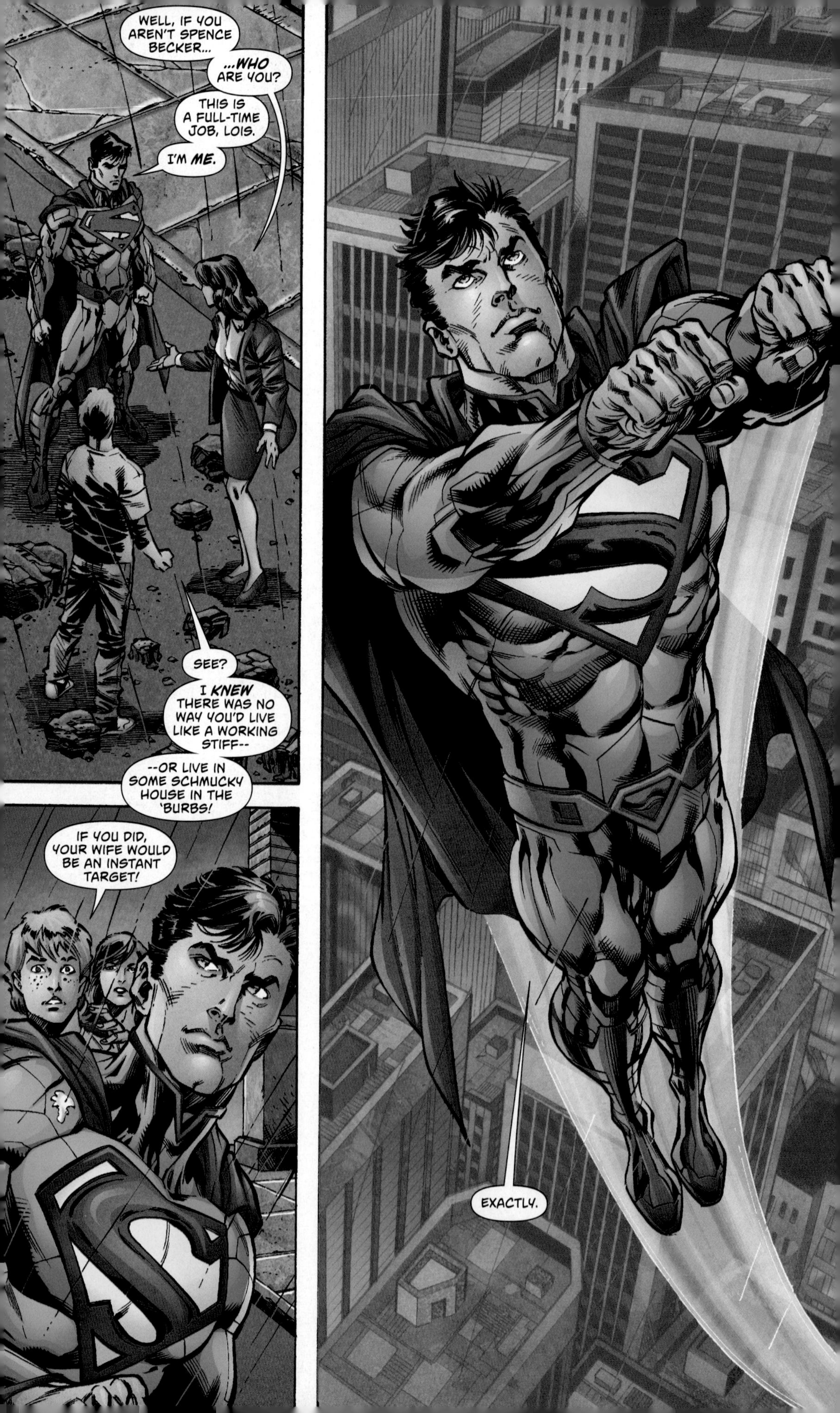
WELL, IF YOU AREN'T SPENCE BECKER...
...WHO ARE YOU?
THIS IS A FULL-TIME JOB, LOIS.
I'M ME.
SEE?
I KNEW THERE WAS NO WAY YOU'D LIVE LIKE A WORKING STIFF--
--OR LIVE IN SOME SCHMUCKY HOUSE IN THE 'BURBS!
IF YOU DID, YOUR WIFE WOULD BE AN INSTANT TARGET!
EXACTLY.

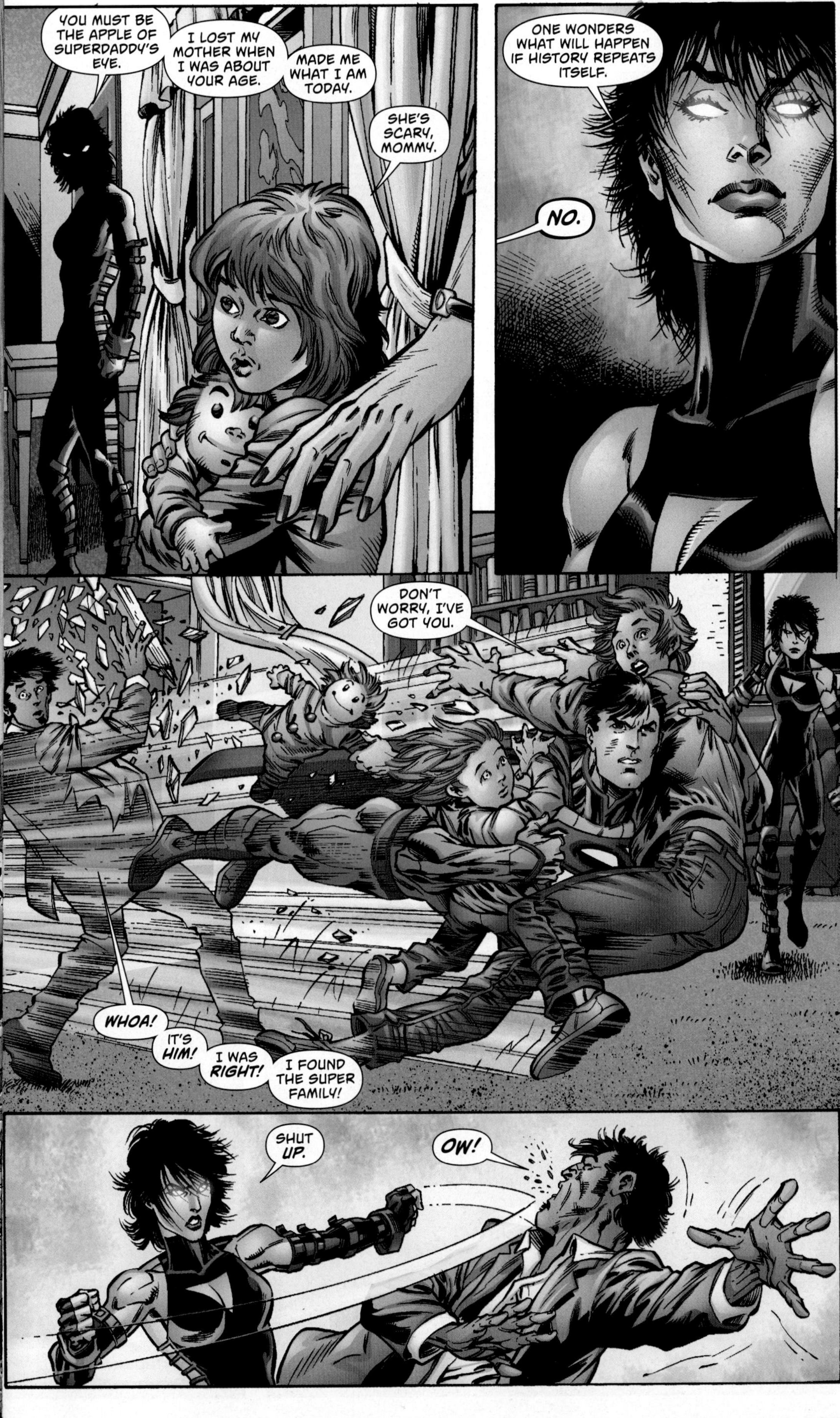
YOU MUST BE THE APPLE OF SUPERDADDY'S EYE.
I LOST MY MOTHER WHEN I WAS ABOUT YOUR AGE.
MADE ME WHAT I AM TODAY.
SHE'S SCARY, MOMMY.
ONE WONDERS WHAT WILL HAPPEN IF HISTORY REPEATS ITSELF.
NO.
DON'T WORRY, I'VE GOT YOU.
WHOA!
IT'S HIM!
I WAS RIGHT!
I FOUND THE SUPER FAMILY!
SHUT UP.
OW!

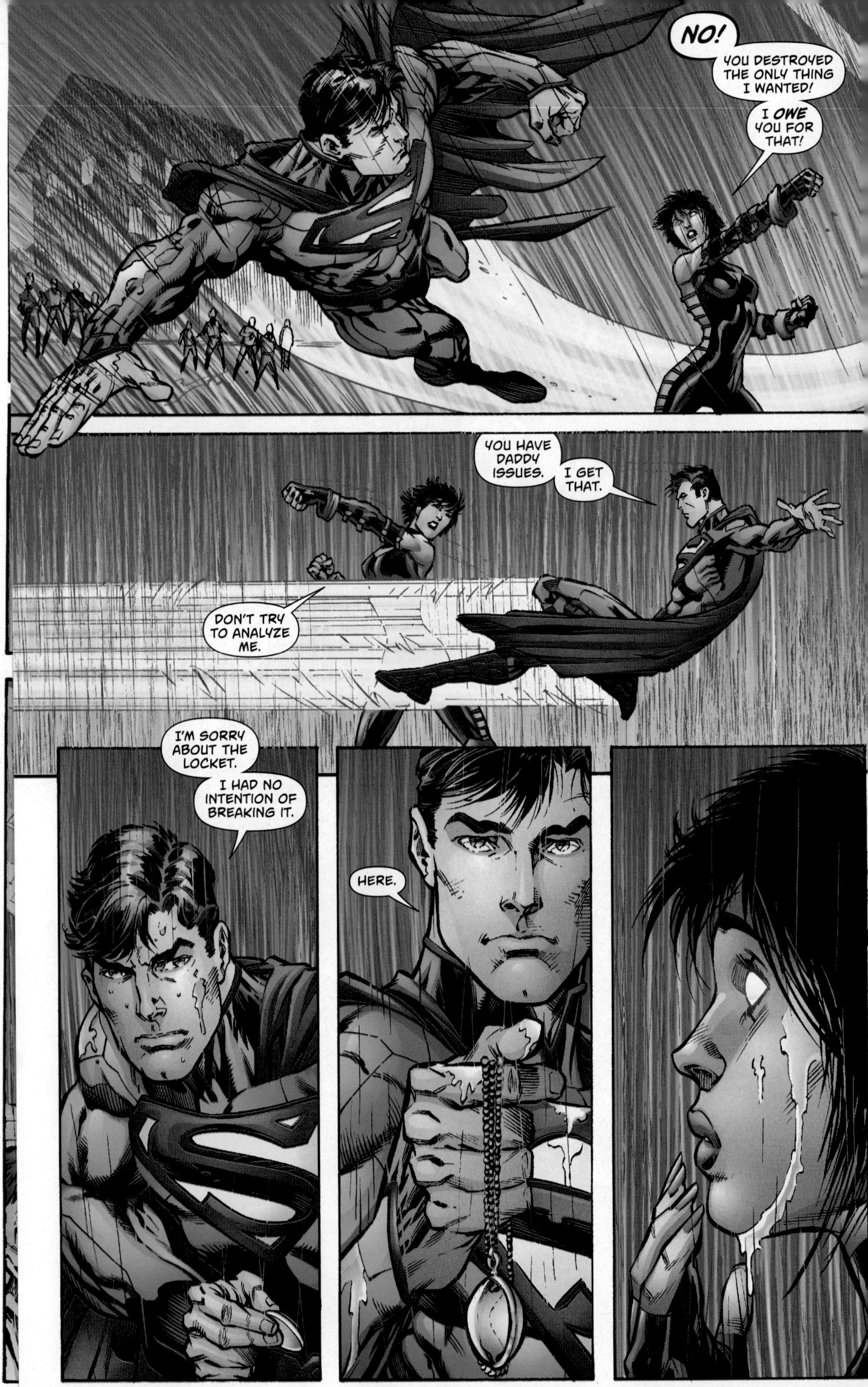
NO!
YOU DESTROYED THE ONLY THING I WANTED!
I OWE YOU FOR THAT!
YOU HAVE DADDY ISSUES.
I GET THAT.
DON'T TRY TO ANALYZE ME.
I'M SORRY ABOUT THE LOCKET.
I HAD NO INTENTION OF BREAKING IT.
HERE.

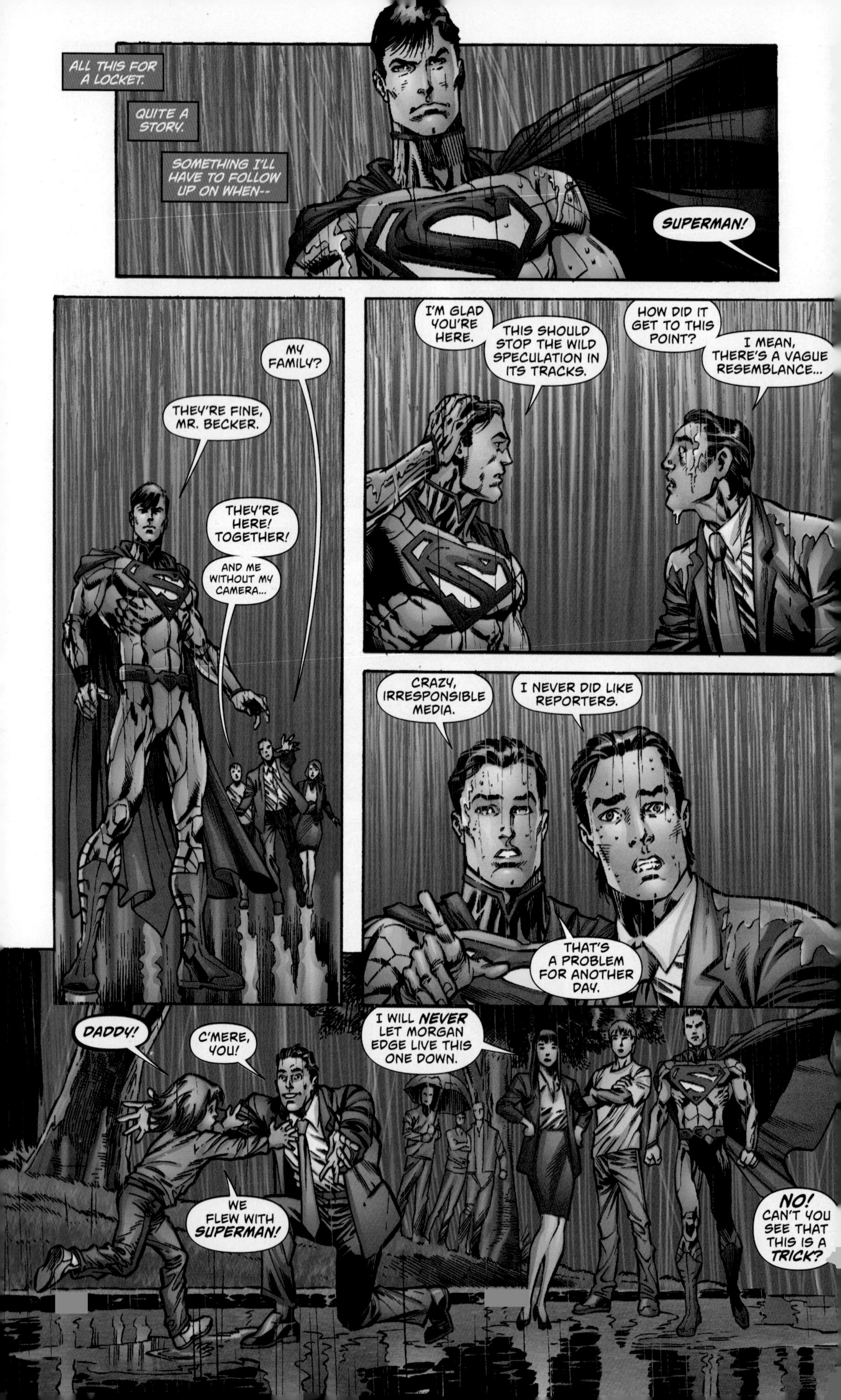
ALL THIS FOR A LOCKET.
QUITE A STORY.
SOMETHING I'LL HAVE TO FOLLOW UP ON WHEN--
SUPERMAN!
MY FAMILY?
THEY'RE FINE, MR. BECKER.
THEY'RE HERE! TOGETHER!
AND ME WITHOUT MY CAMERA...
I'M GLAD YOU'RE HERE.
THIS SHOULD STOP THE WILD SPECULATION IN ITS TRACKS.
HOW DID IT GET TO THIS POINT?
I MEAN, THERE'S A VAGUE RESEMBLANCE...
CRAZY, IRRESPONSIBLE MEDIA.
I NEVER DID LIKE REPORTERS.
THAT'S A PROBLEM FOR ANOTHER DAY.
DADDY!
C'MERE, YOU!
WE FLEW WITH SUPERMAN!
I WILL NEVER LET MORGAN EDGE LIVE THIS ONE DOWN.
NO! CAN'T YOU SEE THAT THIS IS A TRICK?

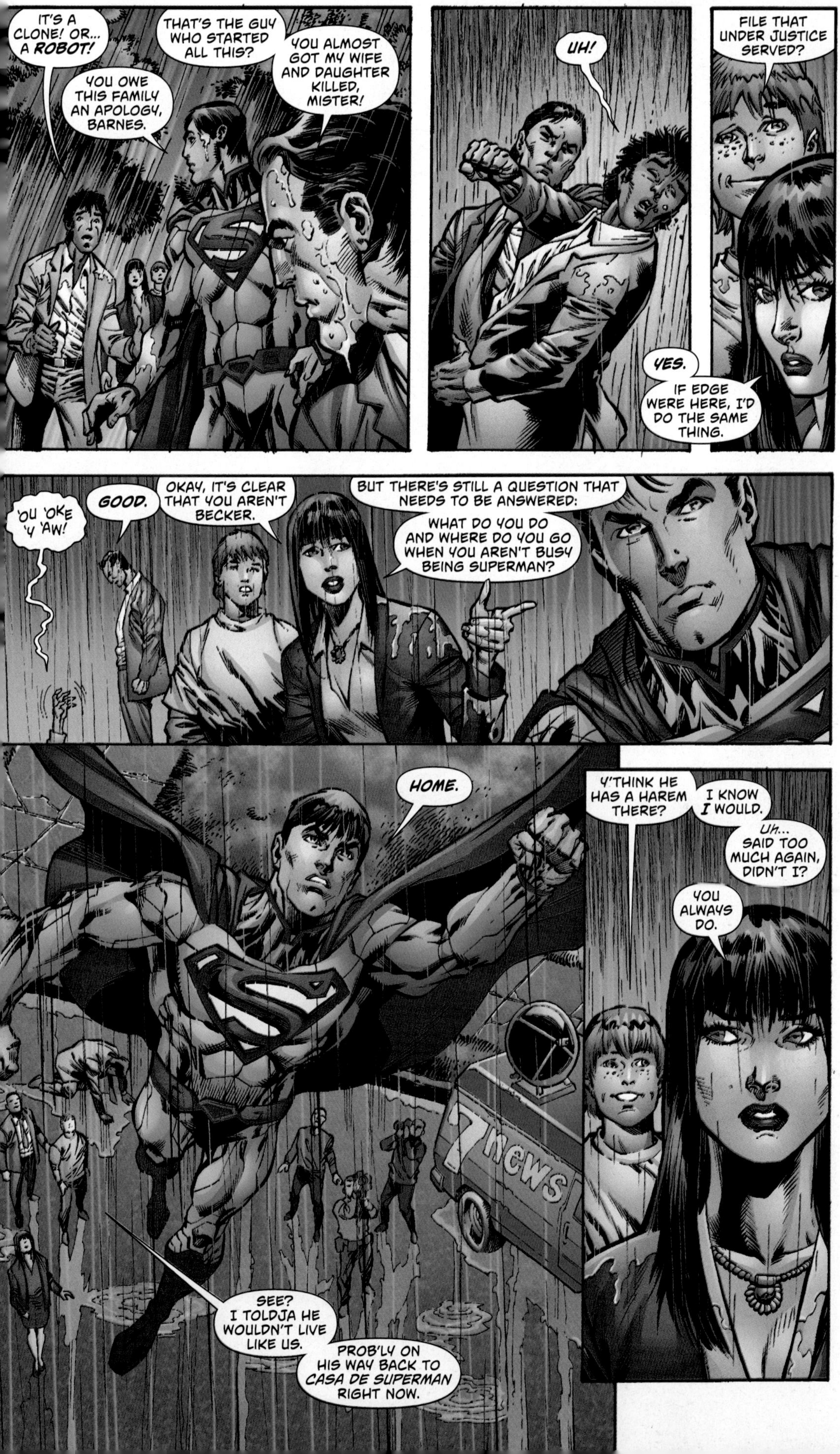
IT'S A CLONE! OR... A *ROBOT!*
THAT'S THE GUY WHO STARTED ALL THIS?
YOU OWE THIS FAMILY AN APOLOGY, BARNES.
YOU ALMOST GOT MY WIFE AND DAUGHTER KILLED, MISTER!
UH!
FILE THAT UNDER JUSTICE SERVED?
YES.
IF EDGE WERE HERE, I'D DO THE SAME THING.
'OU 'OKE 'Y 'AW!
GOOD.
OKAY, IT'S CLEAR THAT YOU AREN'T BECKER.
BUT THERE'S STILL A QUESTION THAT NEEDS TO BE ANSWERED:
WHAT DO YOU DO AND WHERE DO YOU GO WHEN YOU AREN'T BUSY BEING SUPERMAN?
HOME.
Y'THINK HE HAS A HAREM THERE?
I KNOW *I* WOULD.
Uh... SAID TOO MUCH AGAIN, DIDN'T I?
YOU ALWAYS DO.
SEE? I TOLDJA HE WOULDN'T LIVE LIKE US.
PROB'LY ON HIS WAY BACK TO *CASA DE SUPERMAN* RIGHT NOW.
NEWS

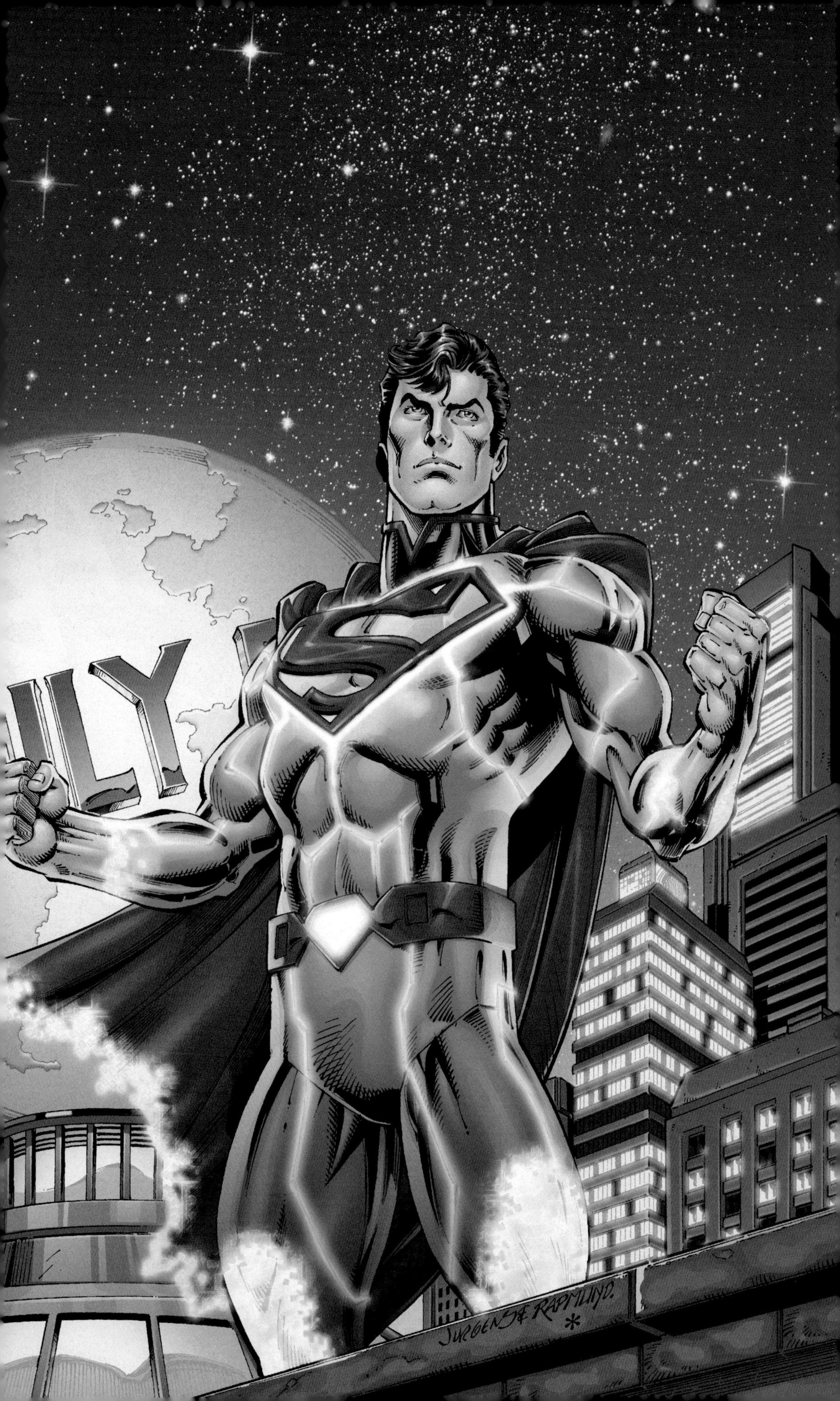
JURGENS & RAPMUND

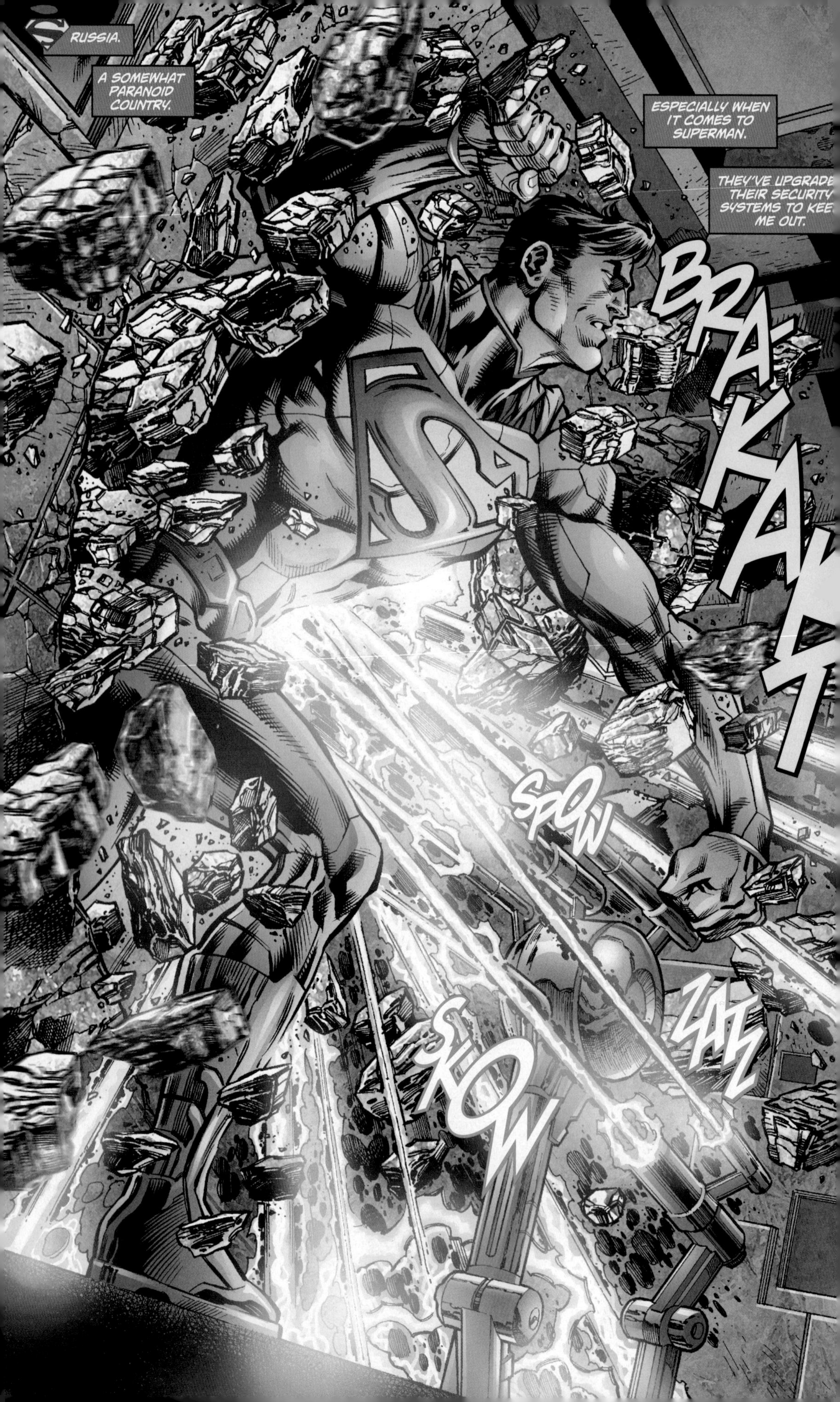
RUSSIA.
A SOMEWHAT PARANOID COUNTRY.
ESPECIALLY WHEN IT COMES TO SUPERMAN.
THEY'VE UPGRADE THEIR SECURITY SYSTEMS TO KEE ME OUT.
BRAKAKAT
SPOW
ZAZZ
SKOW

THEY'LL HAVE TO GO BACK TO THE DRAWING BOARD.

ZIKT

THE PLACE SMELLS LIKE DEATH.

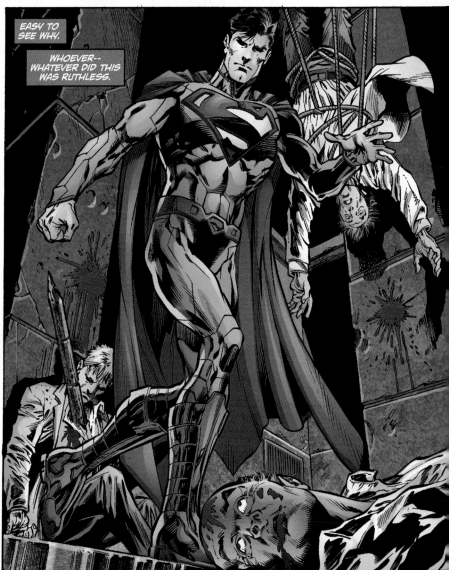

EASY TO SEE WHY.

WHOEVER-- WHATEVER DID THIS WAS RUTHLESS.

THAT CHAMBER DOESN'T LOOK MANMADE.

WAS SOMETHING INSIDE?

SOMETHING THAT ESCAPED?

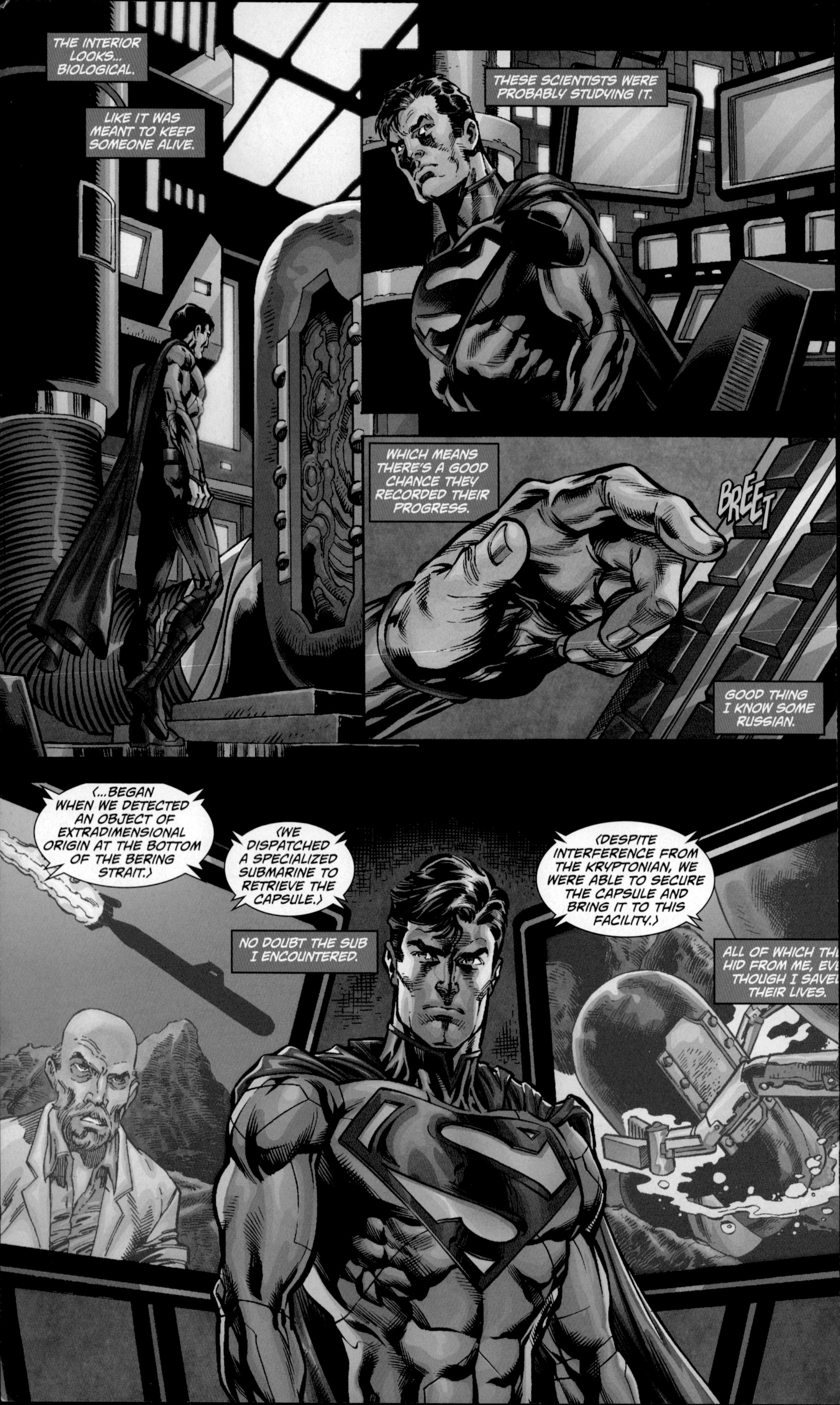
THE INTERIOR LOOKS... BIOLOGICAL.
LIKE IT WAS MEANT TO KEEP SOMEONE ALIVE.
THESE SCIENTISTS WERE PROBABLY STUDYING IT.
WHICH MEANS THERE'S A GOOD CHANCE THEY RECORDED THEIR PROGRESS.
BREEET
GOOD THING I KNOW SOME RUSSIAN.
(...BEGAN WHEN WE DETECTED AN OBJECT OF EXTRADIMENSIONAL ORIGIN AT THE BOTTOM OF THE BERING STRAIT.)
(WE DISPATCHED A SPECIALIZED SUBMARINE TO RETRIEVE THE CAPSULE.)
NO DOUBT THE SUB I ENCOUNTERED.
(DESPITE INTERFERENCE FROM THE KRYPTONIAN, WE WERE ABLE TO SECURE THE CAPSULE AND BRING IT TO THIS FACILITY.)
ALL OF WHICH TH HID FROM ME, EVE THOUGH I SAVE THEIR LIVES.

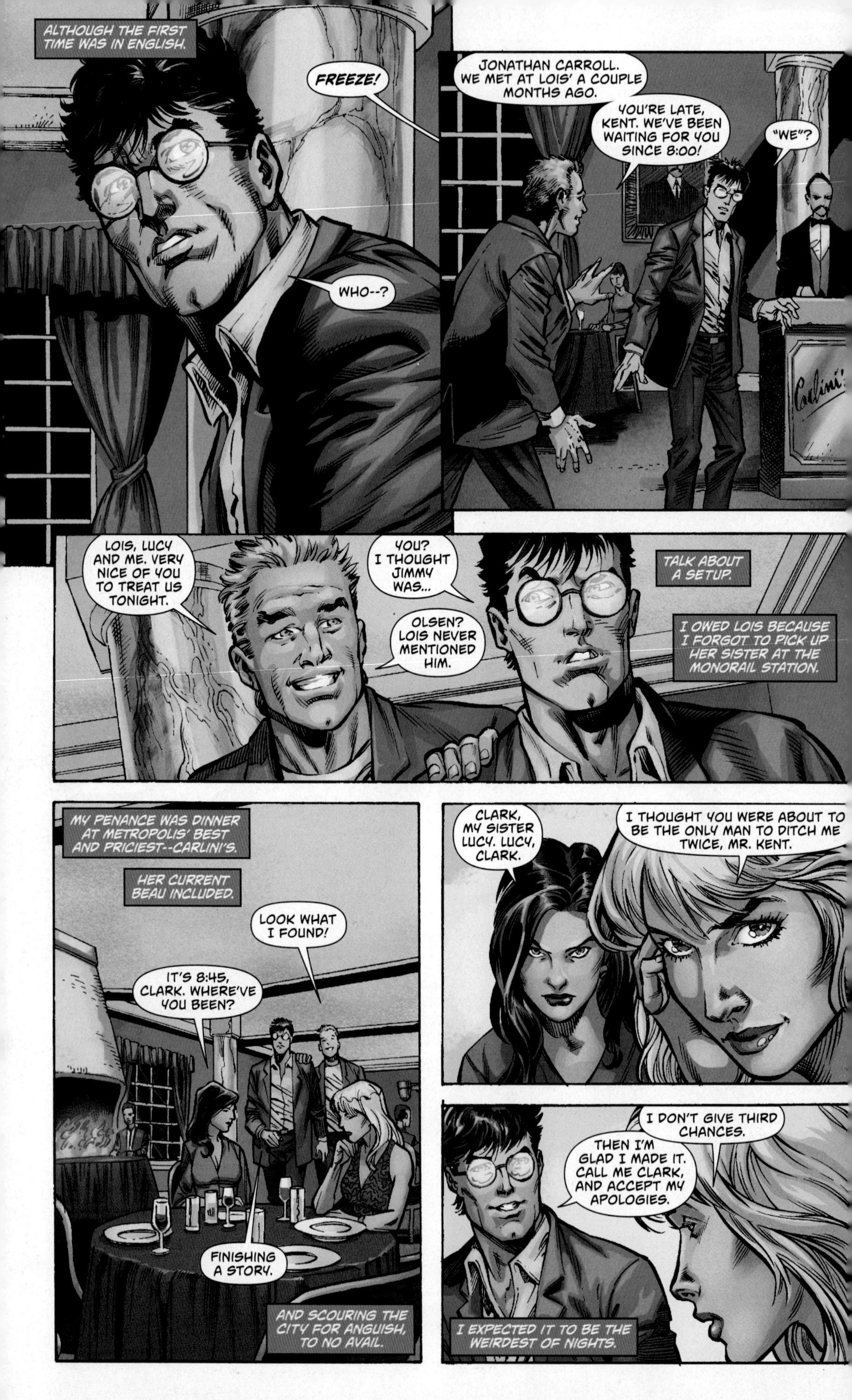

ALTHOUGH THE FIRST TIME WAS IN ENGLISH.
FREEZE!
WHO--?
JONATHAN CARROLL. WE MET AT LOIS' A COUPLE MONTHS AGO.
YOU'RE LATE, KENT. WE'VE BEEN WAITING FOR YOU SINCE 8:00!
"WE"?
Carlini's
LOIS, LUCY AND ME. VERY NICE OF YOU TO TREAT US TONIGHT.
YOU? I THOUGHT JIMMY WAS...
OLSEN? LOIS NEVER MENTIONED HIM.
TALK ABOUT A SETUP.
I OWED LOIS BECAUSE I FORGOT TO PICK UP HER SISTER AT THE MONORAIL STATION.
MY PENANCE WAS DINNER AT METROPOLIS' BEST AND PRICIEST--CARLINI'S.
HER CURRENT BEAU INCLUDED.
LOOK WHAT I FOUND!
IT'S 8:45, CLARK. WHERE'VE YOU BEEN?
FINISHING A STORY.
AND SCOURING THE CITY FOR ANGUISH, TO NO AVAIL.
CLARK, MY SISTER LUCY. LUCY, CLARK.
I THOUGHT YOU WERE ABOUT TO BE THE ONLY MAN TO DITCH ME TWICE, MR. KENT.
I DON'T GIVE THIRD CHANCES.
THEN I'M GLAD I MADE IT. CALL ME CLARK, AND ACCEPT MY APOLOGIES.
I EXPECTED IT TO BE THE WEIRDEST OF NIGHTS.

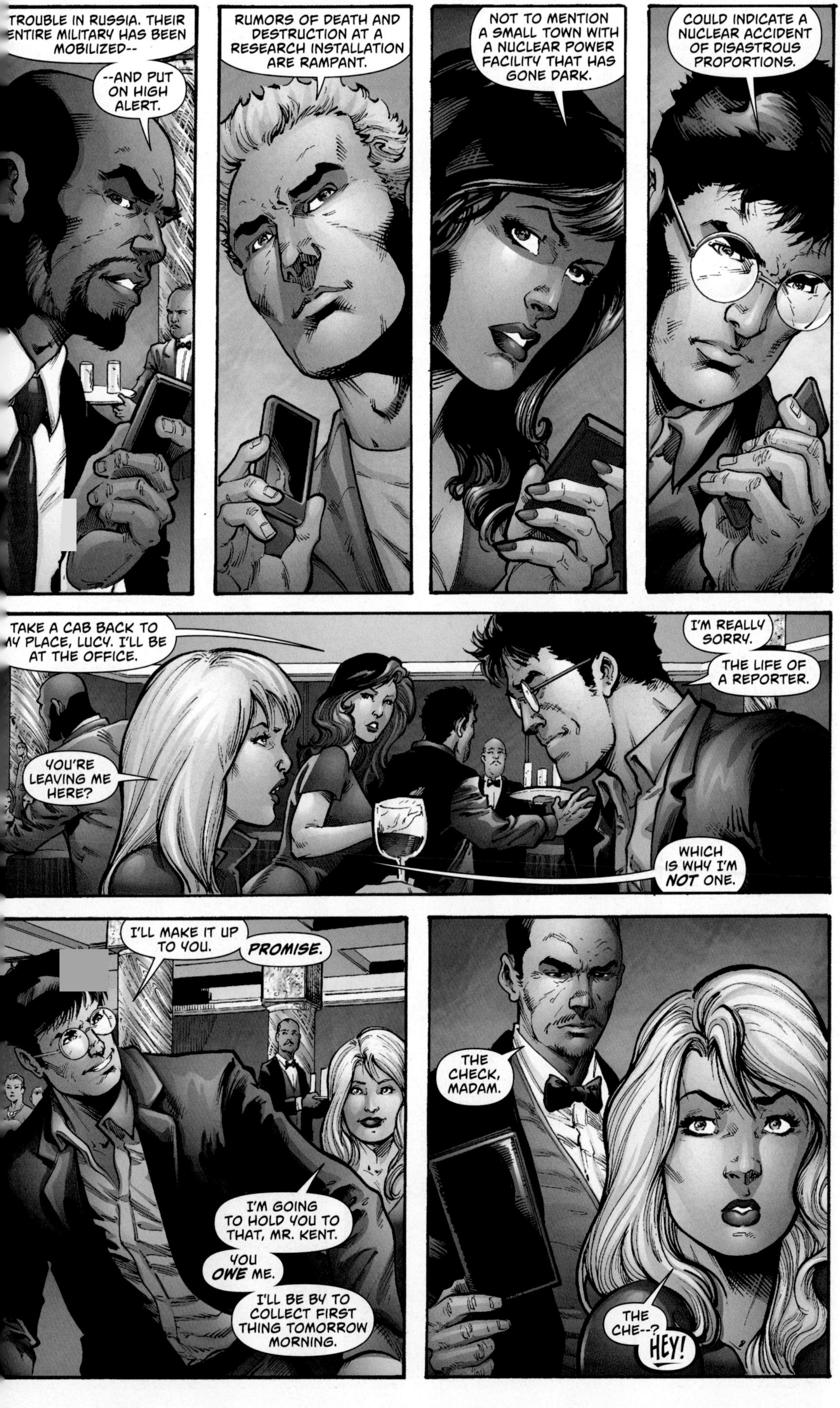
TROUBLE IN RUSSIA. THEIR ENTIRE MILITARY HAS BEEN MOBILIZED--
--AND PUT ON HIGH ALERT.
RUMORS OF DEATH AND DESTRUCTION AT A RESEARCH INSTALLATION ARE RAMPANT.
NOT TO MENTION A SMALL TOWN WITH A NUCLEAR POWER FACILITY THAT HAS GONE DARK.
COULD INDICATE A NUCLEAR ACCIDENT OF DISASTROUS PROPORTIONS.
TAKE A CAB BACK TO MY PLACE, LUCY. I'LL BE AT THE OFFICE.
YOU'RE LEAVING ME HERE?
I'M REALLY SORRY.
THE LIFE OF A REPORTER.
WHICH IS WHY I'M *NOT* ONE.
I'LL MAKE IT UP TO YOU.
PROMISE.
I'M GOING TO HOLD YOU TO THAT, MR. KENT.
YOU *OWE* ME.
I'LL BE BY TO COLLECT FIRST THING TOMORROW MORNING.
THE CHECK, MADAM.
THE CHE--?
HEY!

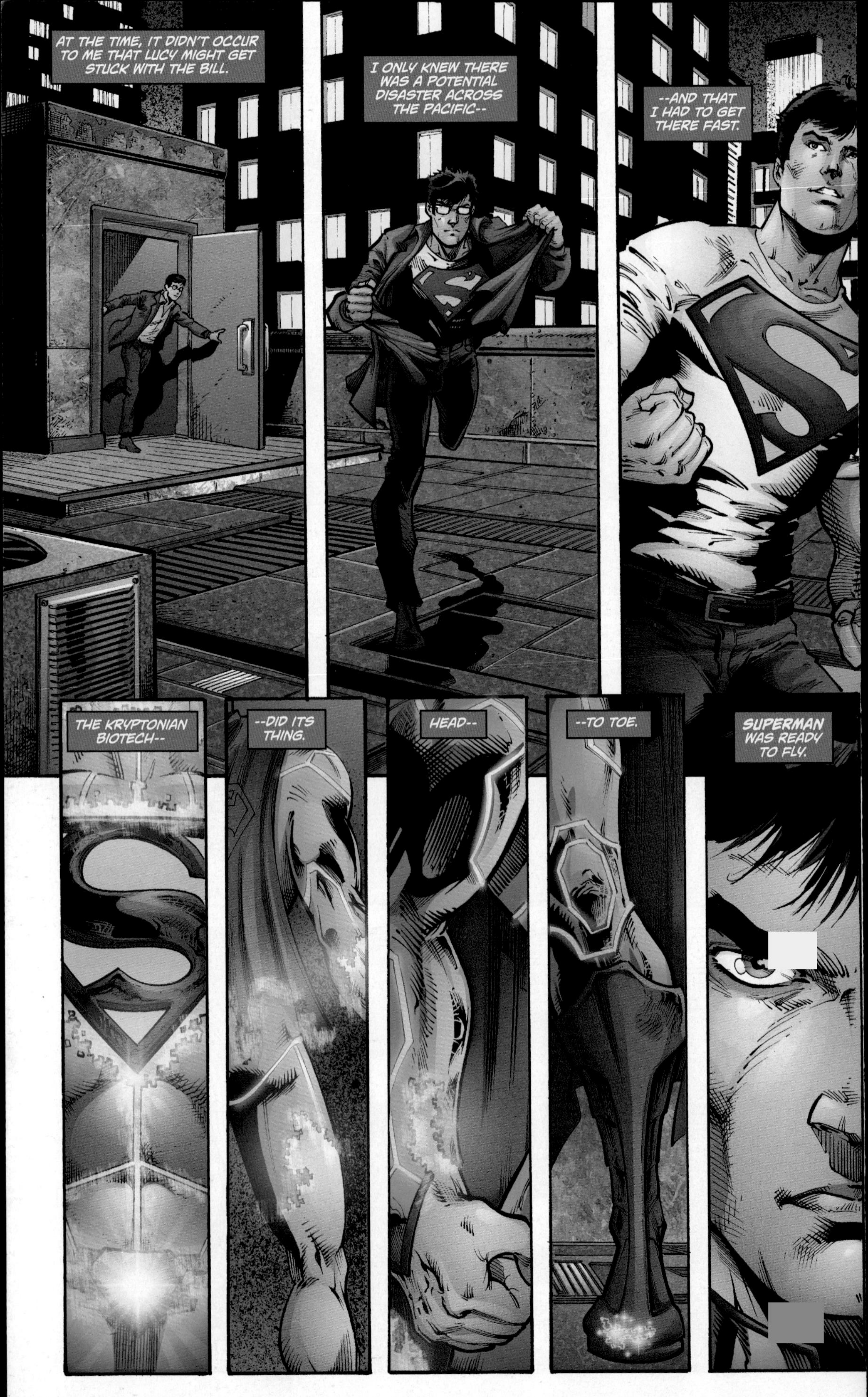
AT THE TIME, IT DIDN'T OCCUR TO ME THAT LUCY MIGHT GET STUCK WITH THE BILL.
I ONLY KNEW THERE WAS A POTENTIAL DISASTER ACROSS THE PACIFIC--
--AND THAT I HAD TO GET THERE FAST.
THE KRYPTONIAN BIOTECH--
--DID ITS THING.
HEAD--
--TO TOE.
SUPERMAN WAS READY TO FLY.

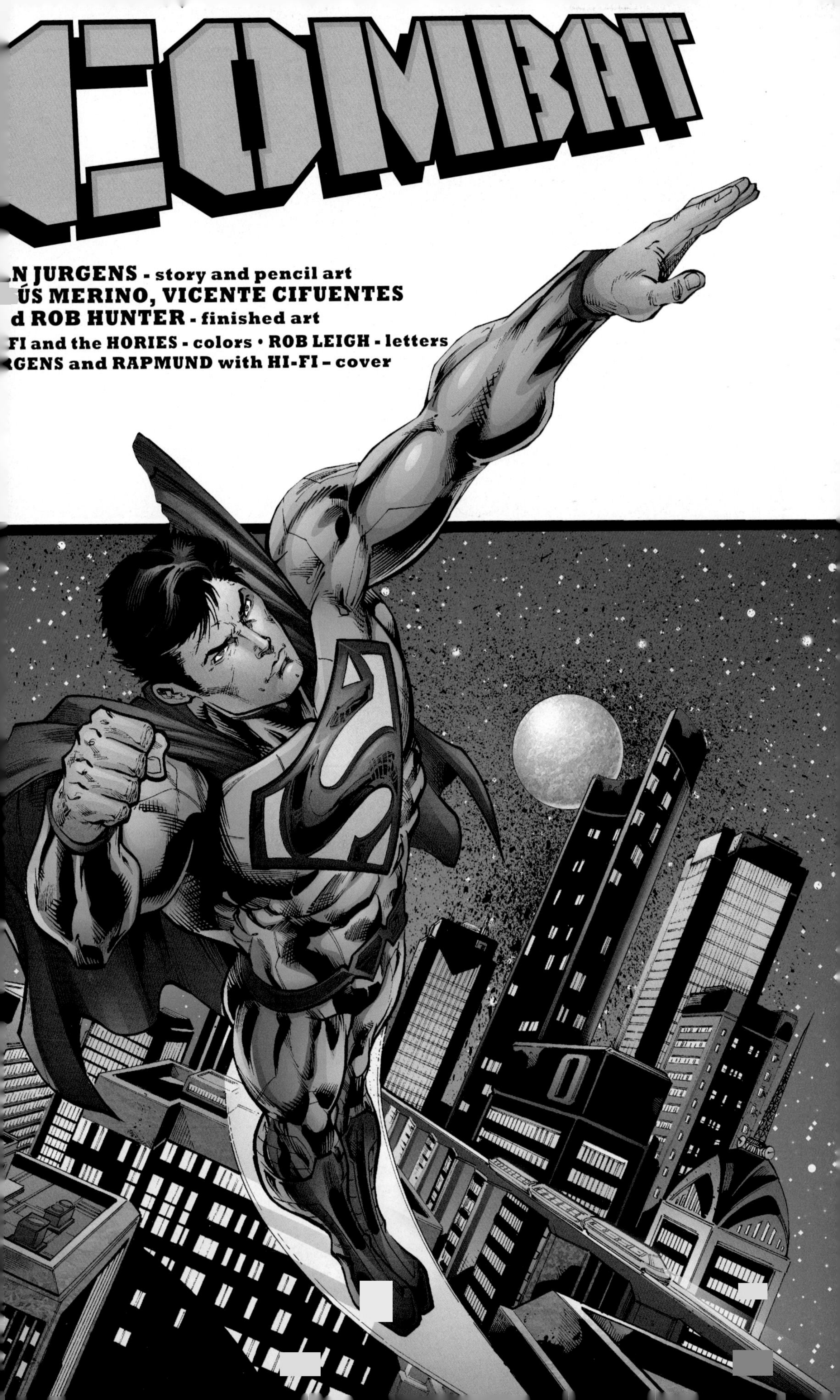
COMBAT
N JURGENS - story and pencil art
ÚS MERINO, VICENTE CIFUENTES
d ROB HUNTER - finished art
FI and the HORIES - colors • ROB LEIGH - letters
GENS and RAPMUND with HI-FI – cover

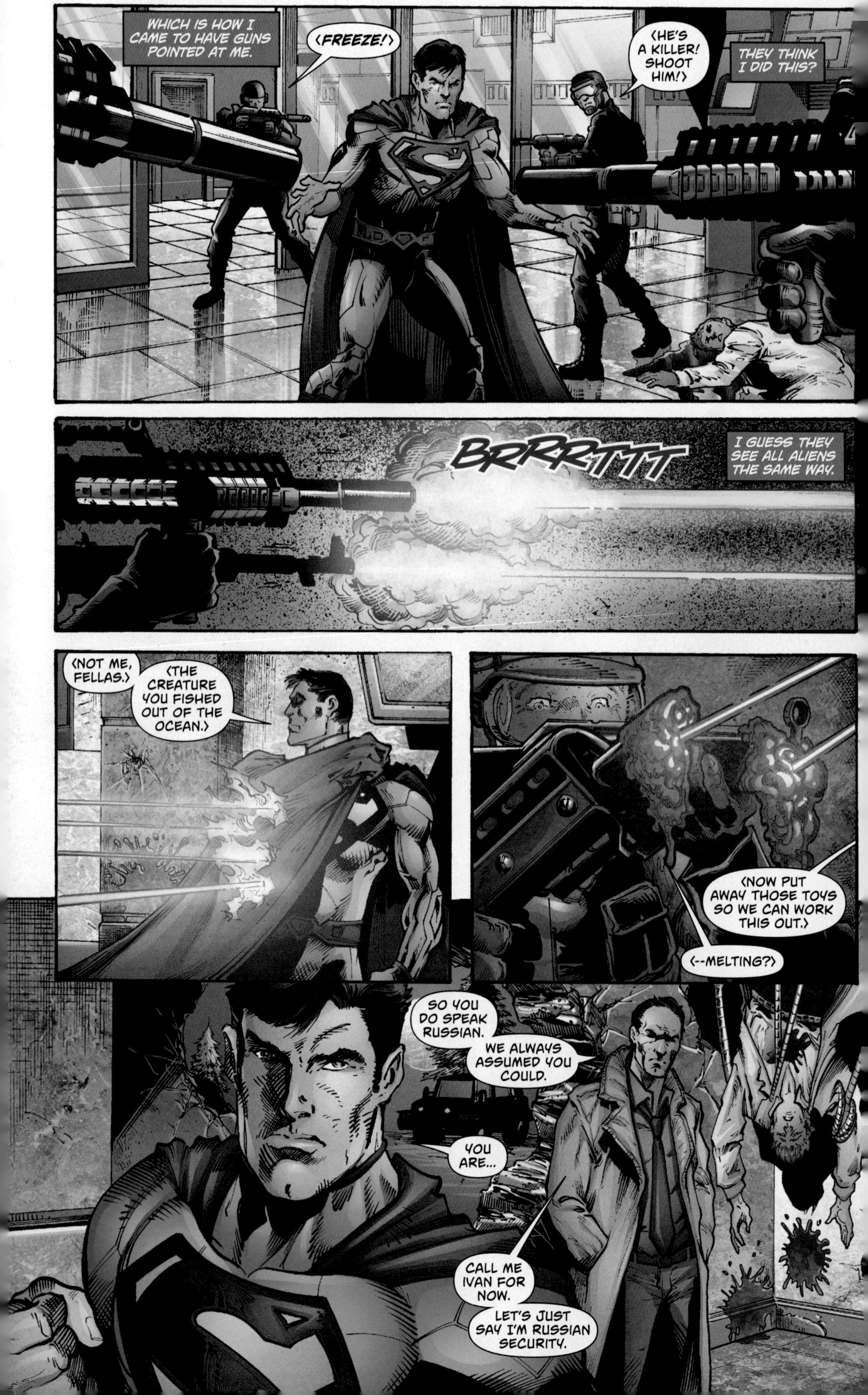
WHICH IS HOW I CAME TO HAVE GUNS POINTED AT ME.
‹FREEZE!›
‹HE'S A KILLER! SHOOT HIM!›
THEY THINK I DID THIS?
BRRRRTTTT
I GUESS THEY SEE ALL ALIENS THE SAME WAY.
‹NOT ME, FELLAS.›
‹THE CREATURE YOU FISHED OUT OF THE OCEAN.›
‹NOW PUT AWAY THOSE TOYS SO WE CAN WORK THIS OUT.›
‹--MELTING?›
SO YOU DO SPEAK RUSSIAN.
WE ALWAYS ASSUMED YOU COULD.
YOU ARE...
CALL ME IVAN FOR NOW.
LET'S JUST SAY I'M RUSSIAN SECURITY.

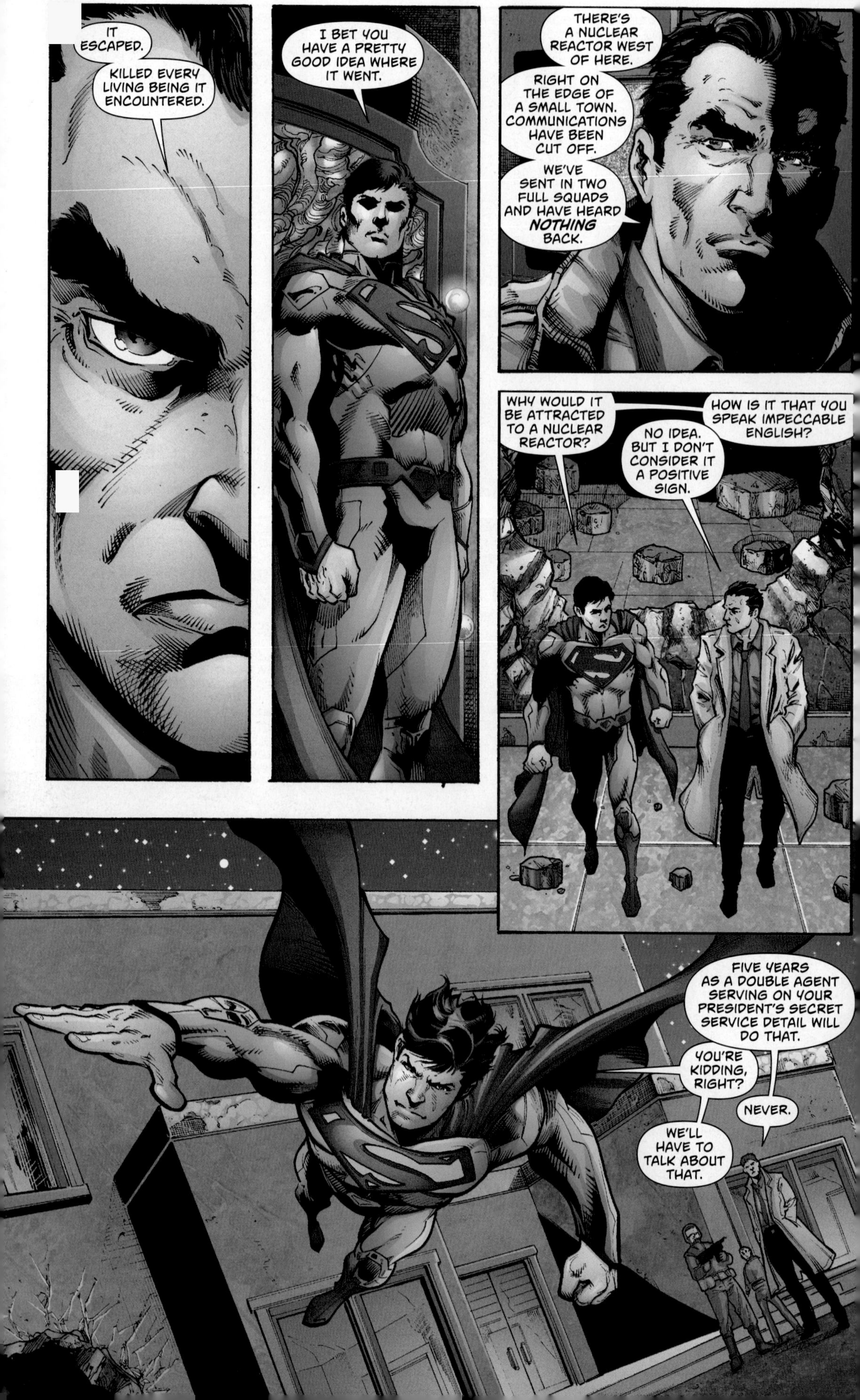
IT ESCAPED.
KILLED EVERY LIVING BEING IT ENCOUNTERED.
I BET YOU HAVE A PRETTY GOOD IDEA WHERE IT WENT.
THERE'S A NUCLEAR REACTOR WEST OF HERE.
RIGHT ON THE EDGE OF A SMALL TOWN. COMMUNICATIONS HAVE BEEN CUT OFF.
WE'VE SENT IN TWO FULL SQUADS AND HAVE HEARD *NOTHING* BACK.
WHY WOULD IT BE ATTRACTED TO A NUCLEAR REACTOR?
NO IDEA. BUT I DON'T CONSIDER IT A POSITIVE SIGN.
HOW IS IT THAT YOU SPEAK IMPECCABLE ENGLISH?
FIVE YEARS AS A DOUBLE AGENT SERVING ON YOUR PRESIDENT'S SECRET SERVICE DETAIL WILL DO THAT.
YOU'RE KIDDING, RIGHT?
NEVER.
WE'LL HAVE TO TALK ABOUT THAT.

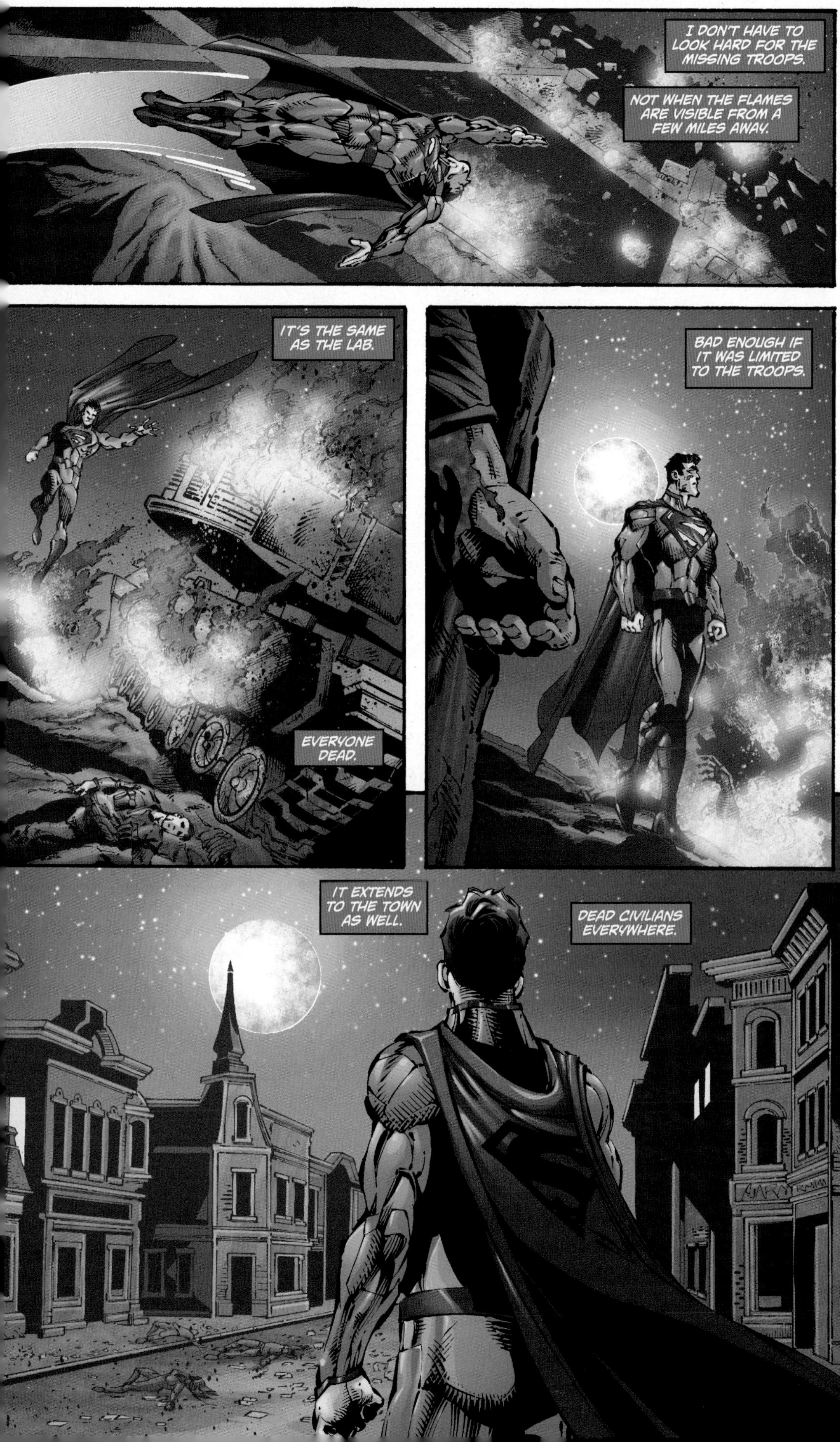
I DON'T HAVE TO LOOK HARD FOR THE MISSING TROOPS.
NOT WHEN THE FLAMES ARE VISIBLE FROM A FEW MILES AWAY.
IT'S THE SAME AS THE LAB.
EVERYONE DEAD.
BAD ENOUGH IF IT WAS LIMITED TO THE TROOPS.
IT EXTENDS TO THE TOWN AS WELL.
DEAD CIVILIANS EVERYWHERE.

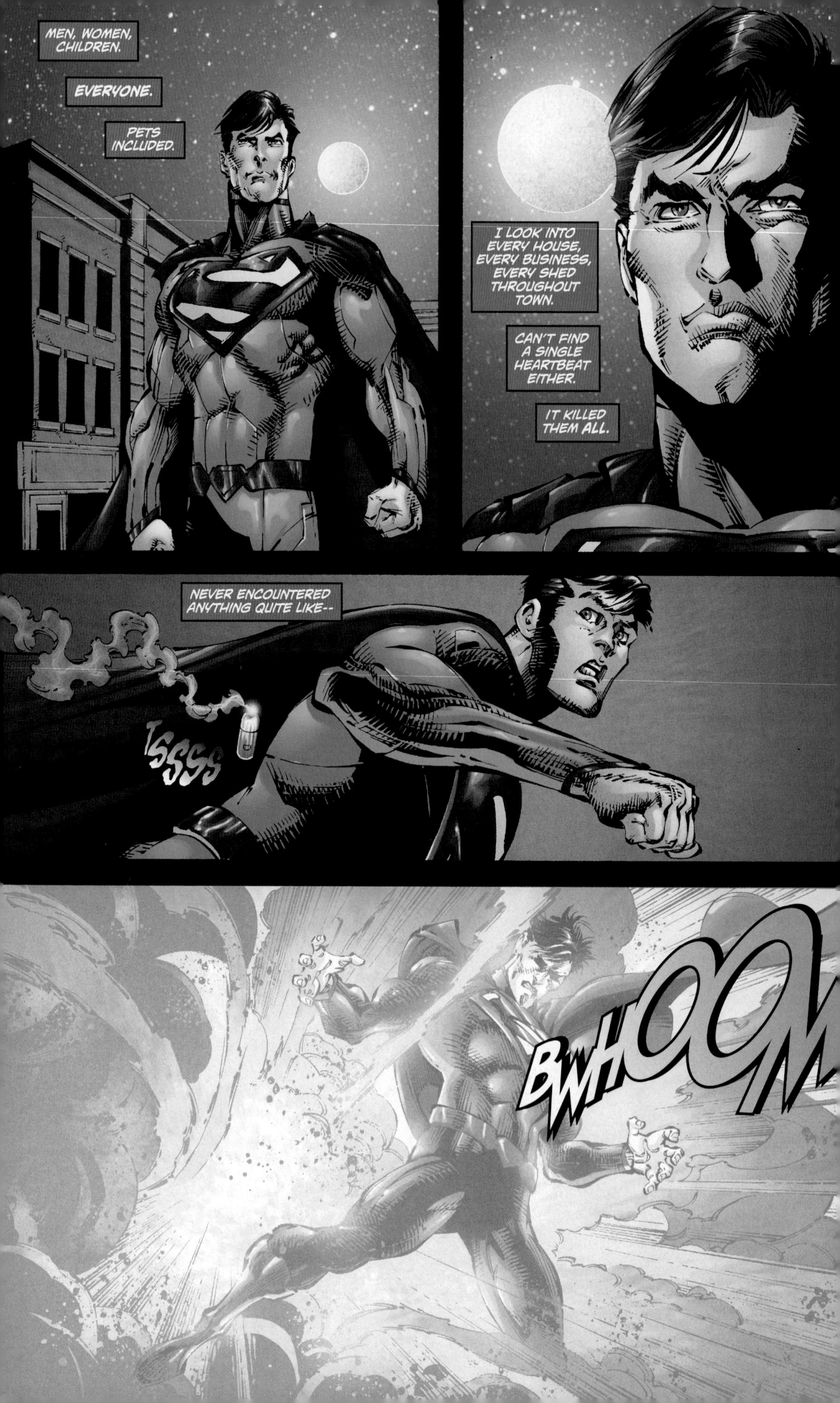
MEN, WOMEN, CHILDREN.
EVERYONE.
PETS INCLUDED.
I LOOK INTO EVERY HOUSE, EVERY BUSINESS, EVERY SHED THROUGHOUT TOWN.
CAN'T FIND A SINGLE HEARTBEAT EITHER.
IT KILLED THEM ALL.
NEVER ENCOUNTERED ANYTHING QUITE LIKE--
TSSSS
BWHOOM

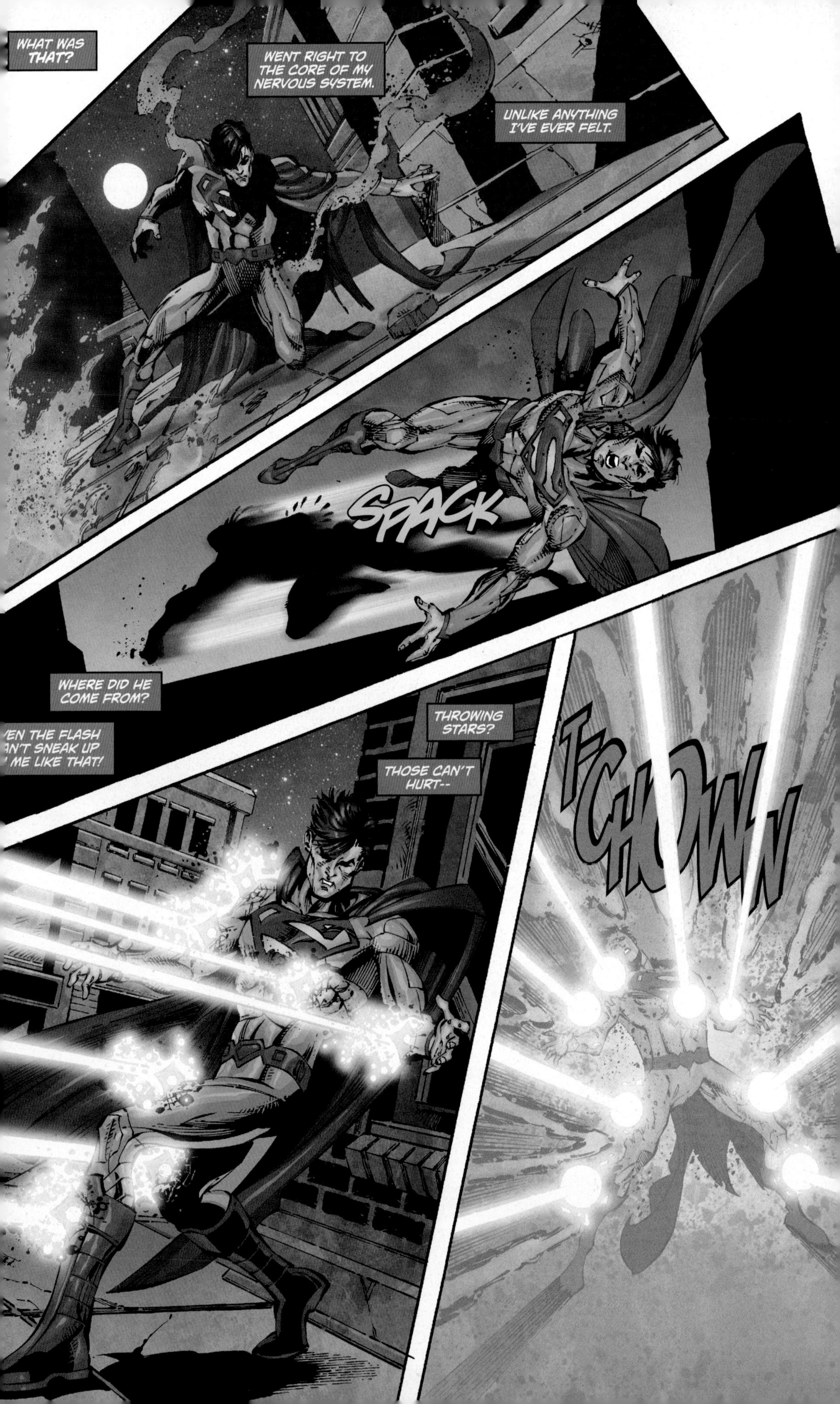
WHAT WAS THAT?
WENT RIGHT TO THE CORE OF MY NERVOUS SYSTEM.
UNLIKE ANYTHING I'VE EVER FELT.
SPACK
WHERE DID HE COME FROM?
'EN THE FLASH 'AN'T SNEAK UP ' ME LIKE THAT!
THROWING STARS?
THOSE CAN'T HURT--
T-CHOWN

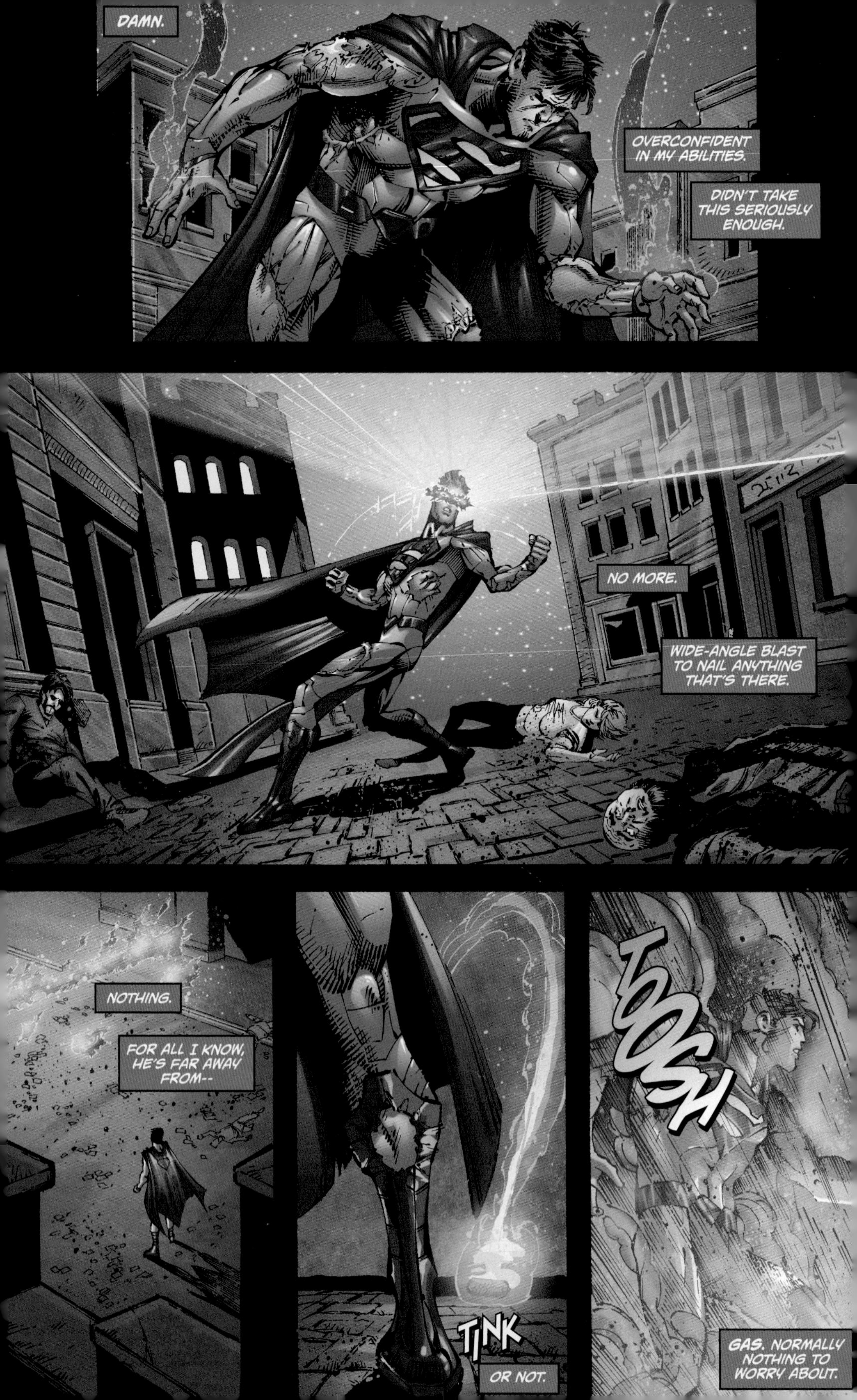
DAMN.
OVERCONFIDENT IN MY ABILITIES.
DIDN'T TAKE THIS SERIOUSLY ENOUGH.
NO MORE.
WIDE-ANGLE BLAST TO NAIL ANYTHING THAT'S THERE.
NOTHING.
FOR ALL I KNOW, HE'S FAR AWAY FROM--
TINK
OR NOT.
FOOOSH
GAS. NORMALLY NOTHING TO WORRY ABOUT.

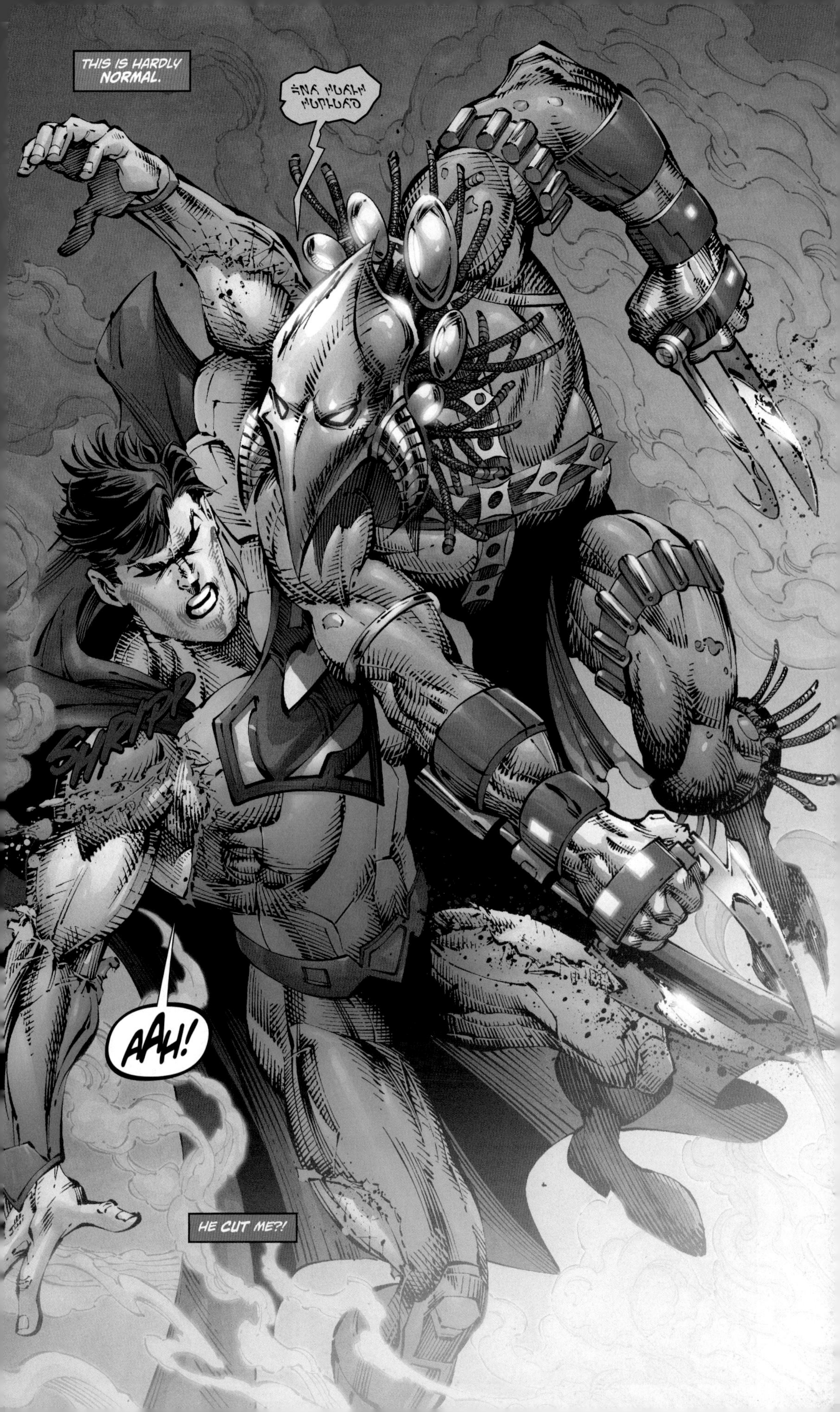
THIS IS HARDLY NORMAL.
AAH!
HE CUT ME?!

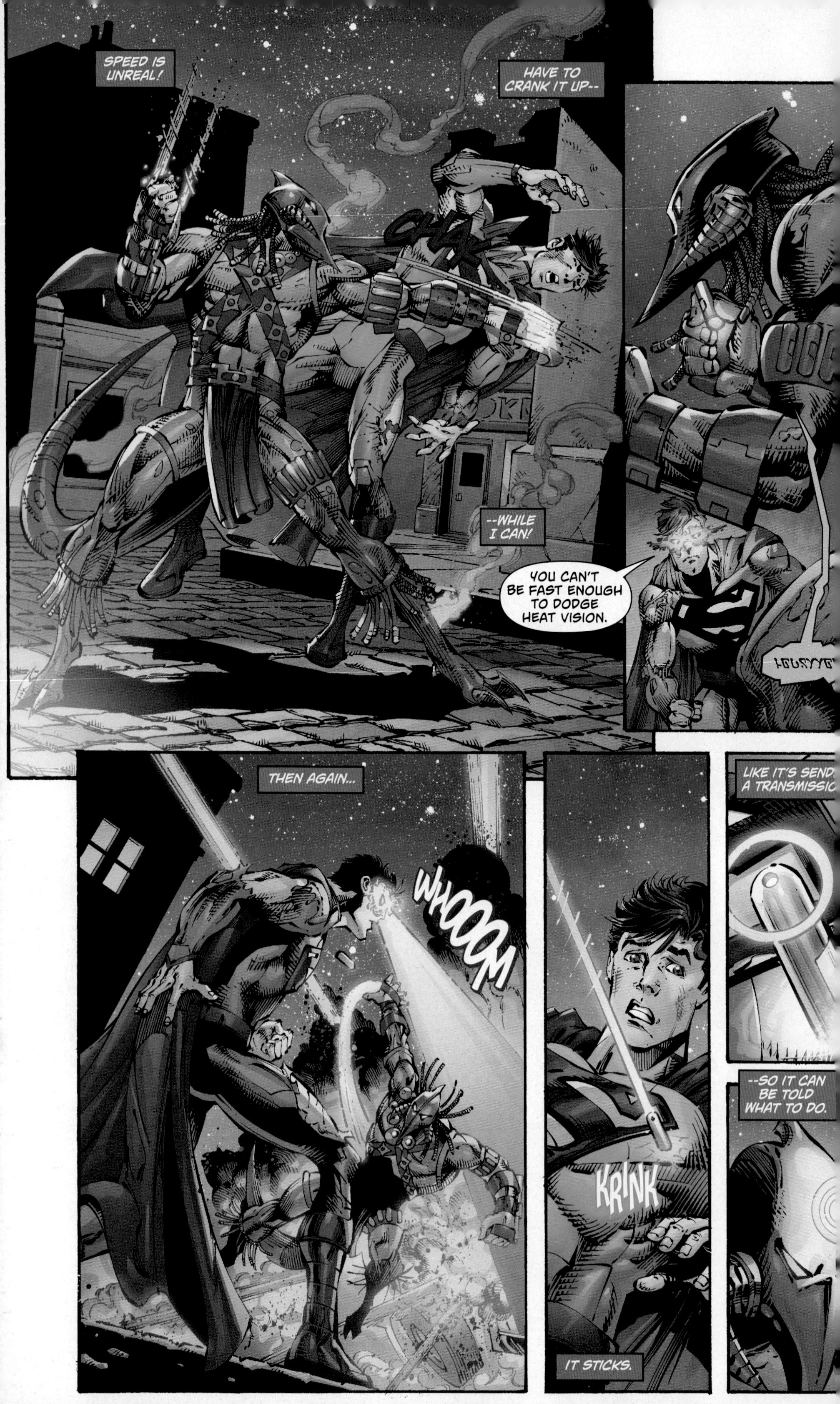
SPEED IS UNREAL!
HAVE TO CRANK IT UP--
CHAK
--WHILE I CAN!
YOU CAN'T BE FAST ENOUGH TO DODGE HEAT VISION.
THEN AGAIN...
WHOOOM
KRINK
IT STICKS.
LIKE IT'S SEND
A TRANSMISSI
--SO IT CAN BE TOLD WHAT TO DO.

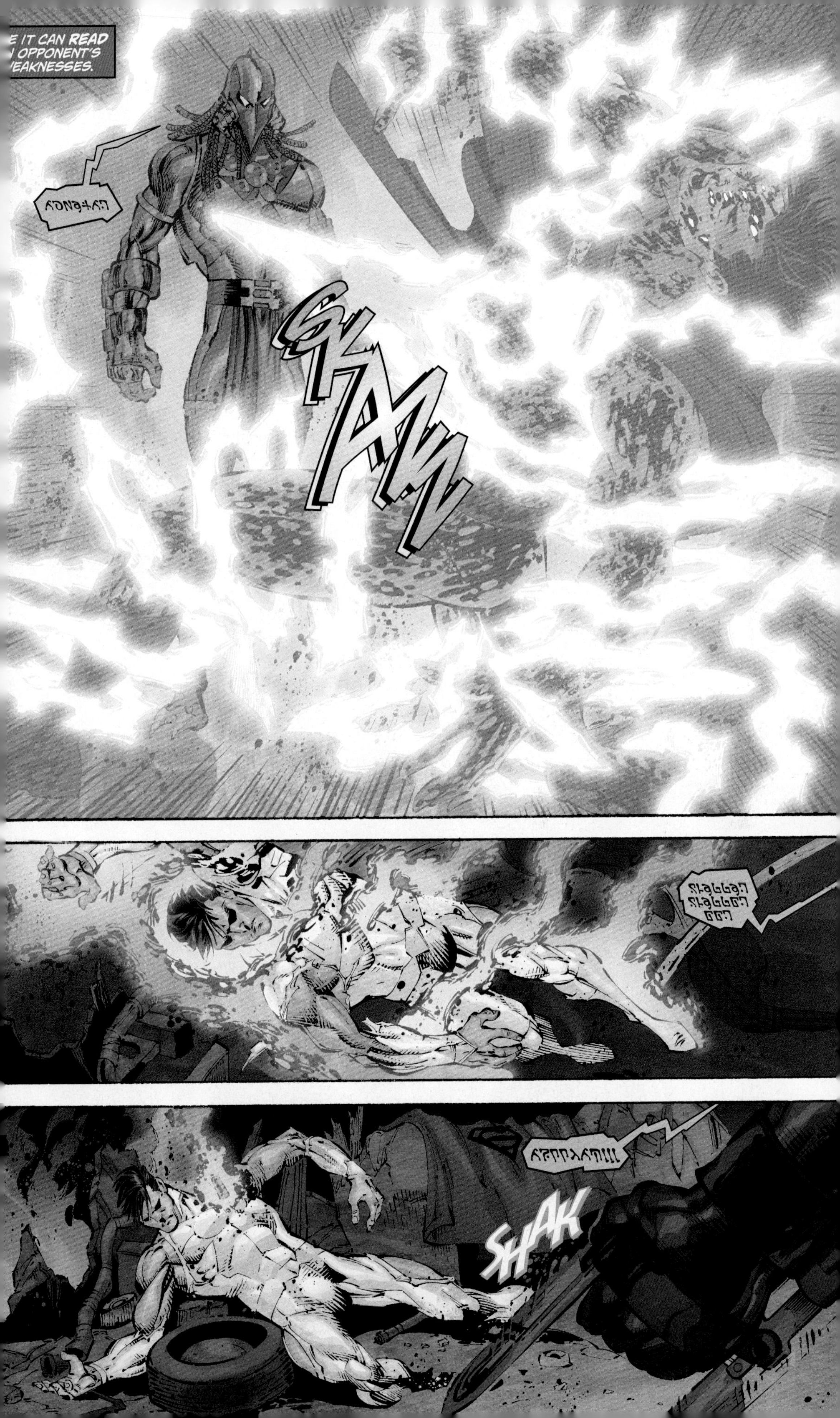
E IT CAN READ
N OPPONENT'S
EAKNESSES.
SHAK

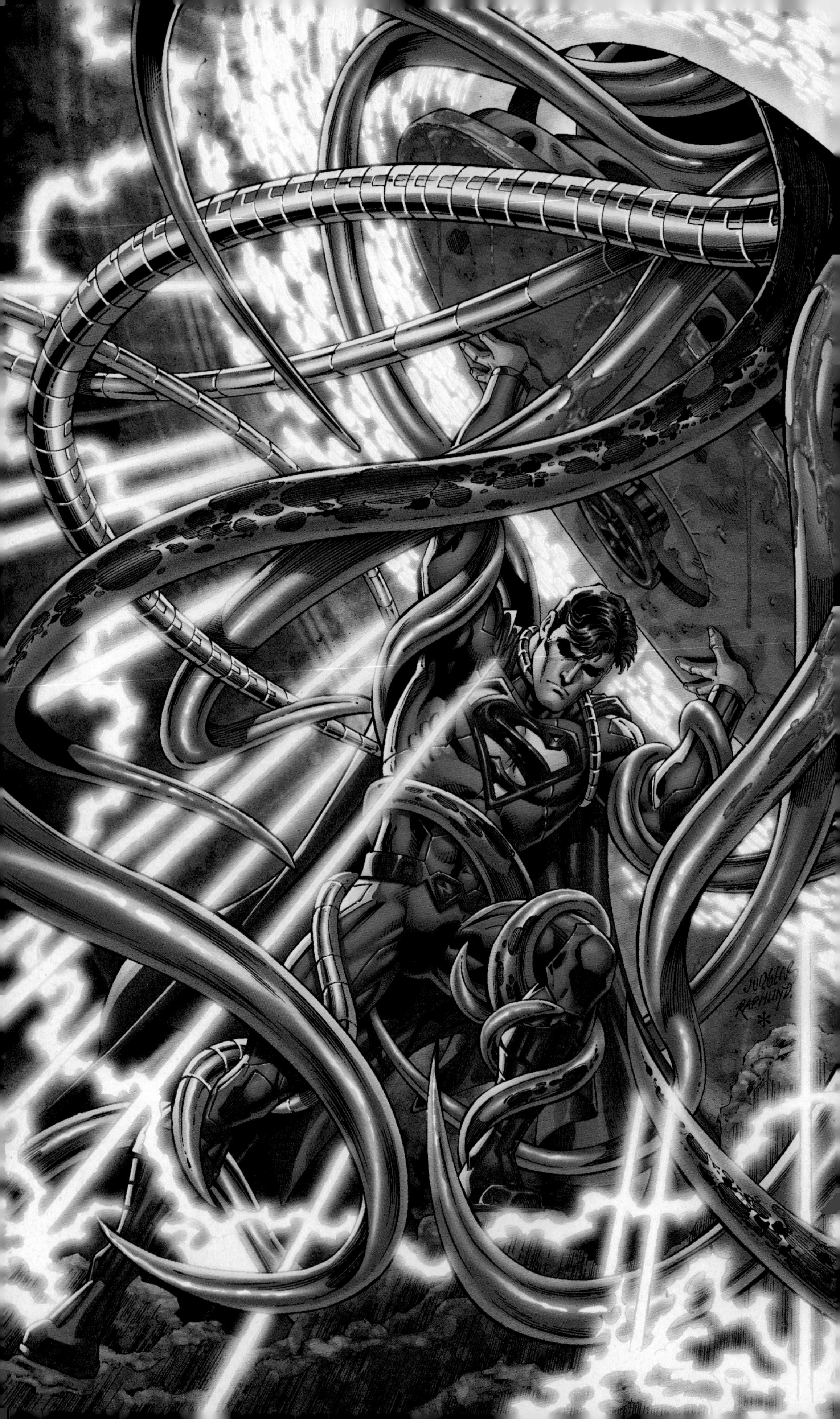
JURGENS
RAPMUND.

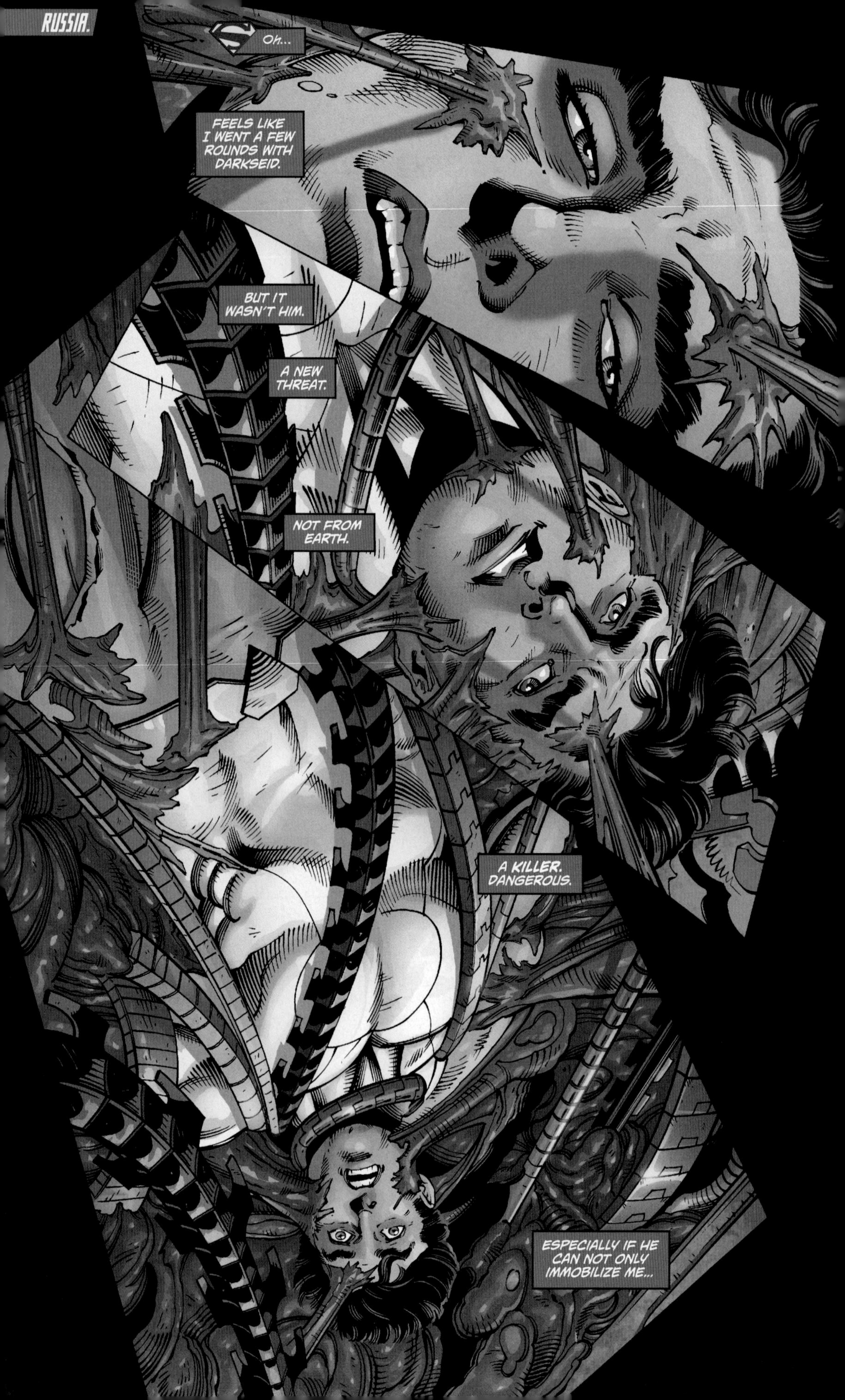
RUSSIA.
Oh...
FEELS LIKE I WENT A FEW ROUNDS WITH DARKSEID.
BUT IT WASN'T HIM.
A NEW THREAT.
NOT FROM EARTH.
A KILLER. DANGEROUS.
ESPECIALLY IF HE CAN NOT ONLY IMMOBILIZE ME...

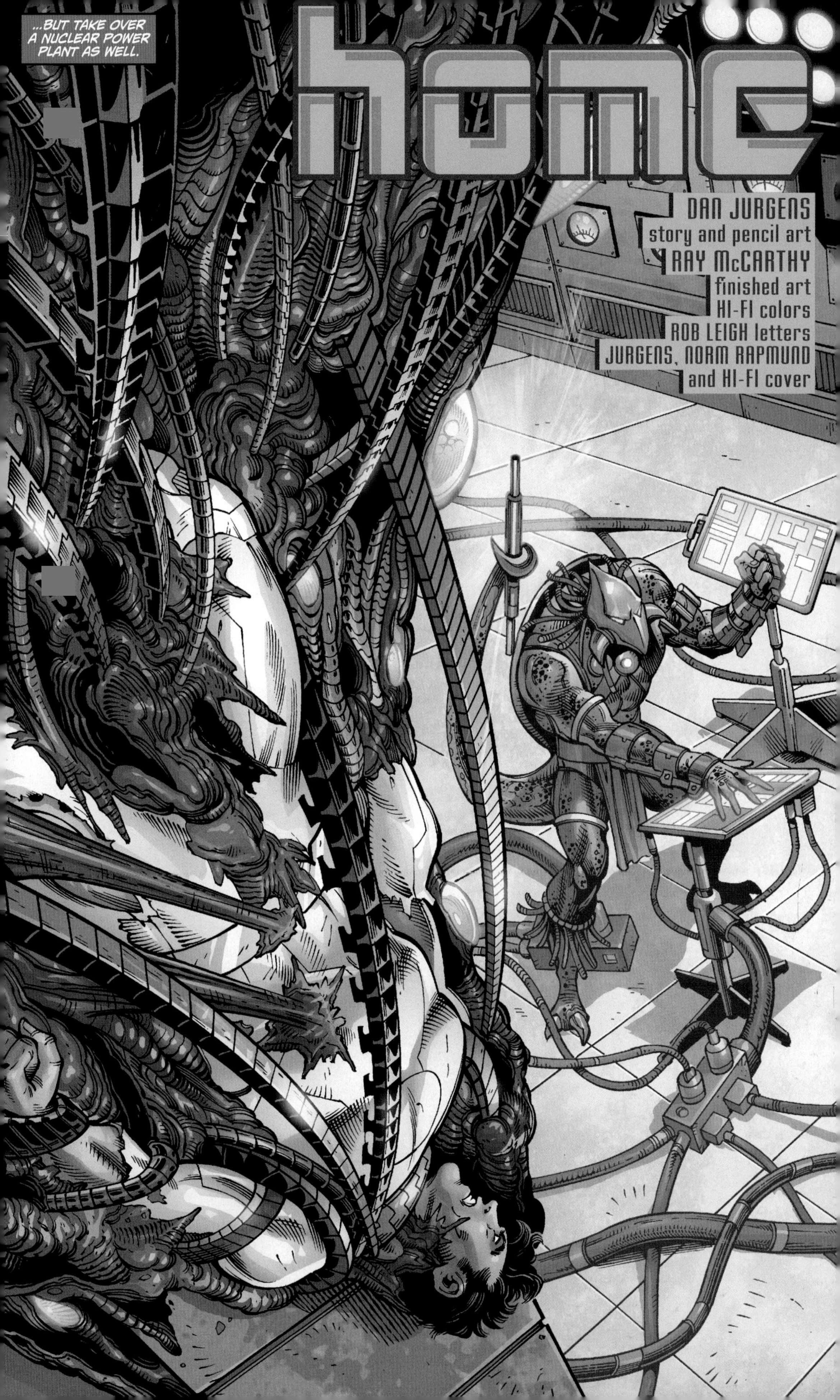
...BUT TAKE OVER A NUCLEAR POWER PLANT AS WELL.
HOME
DAN JURGENS story and pencil art
RAY McCARTHY finished art
HI-FI colors
ROB LEIGH letters
JURGENS, NORM RAPMUND and HI-FI cover

GATEWAY.

FOR OTHERS OF HIS KIND.

TO BRING THEM **HERE.**

AN ARMY OF CREATURES, WILLING TO WIPE OUT HUMAN LIFE.

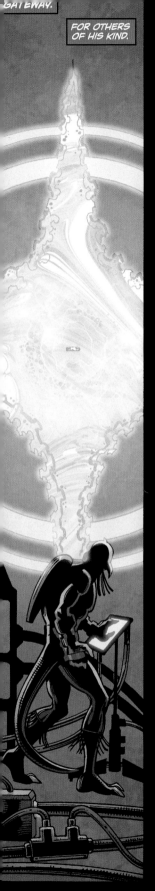

HAVE TO CHANGE THE EQUATION.

NO MORE WATCHING.

TIME TO ACT.

TOOSH

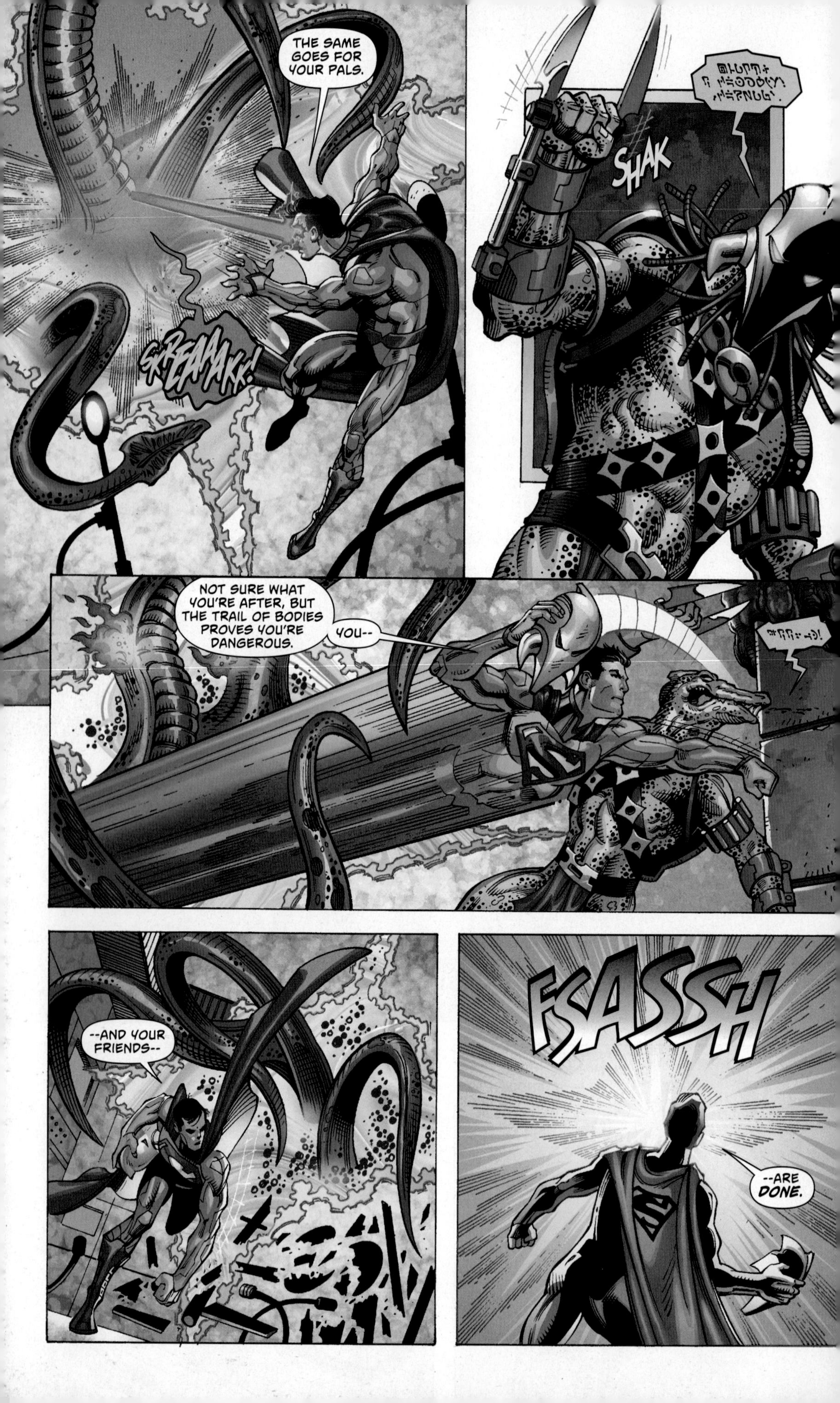

THE SAME GOES FOR YOUR PALS.
SKREEAAAKK!
SHAK
NOT SURE WHAT YOU'RE AFTER, BUT THE TRAIL OF BODIES PROVES YOU'RE DANGEROUS.
YOU--
--AND YOUR FRIENDS--
FSASSH
--ARE DONE.

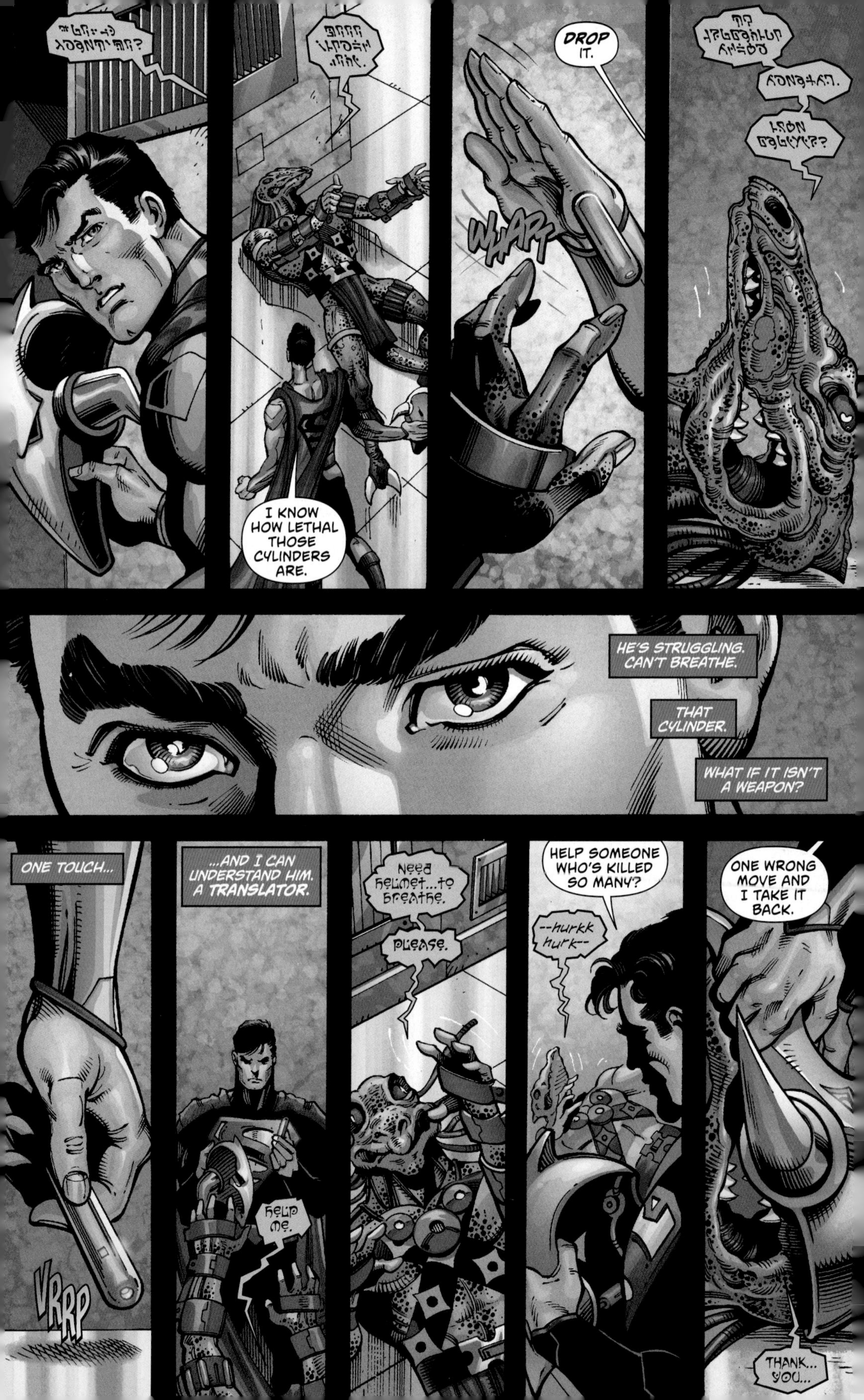
I KNOW HOW LETHAL THOSE CYLINDERS ARE.
DROP IT.
WHAP!
HE'S STRUGGLING. CAN'T BREATHE.
THAT CYLINDER.
WHAT IF IT ISN'T A WEAPON?
ONE TOUCH...
VRRP
...AND I CAN UNDERSTAND HIM. A TRANSLATOR.
HELP ME.
NEED HELMET...TO BREATHE.
PLEASE.
HELP SOMEONE WHO'S KILLED SO MANY?
--HURKK HURK--
ONE WRONG MOVE AND I TAKE IT BACK.
THANK... YOU...

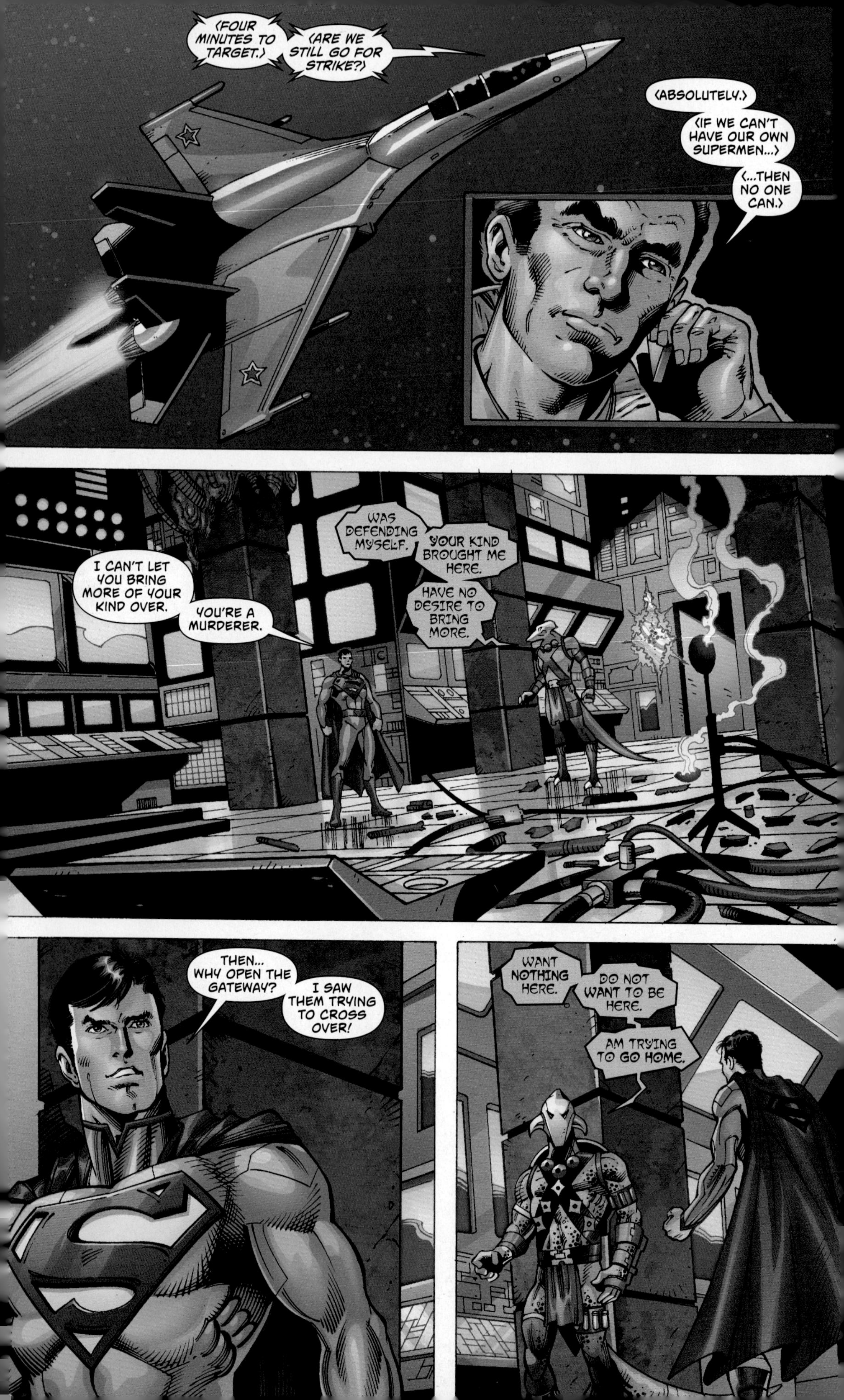

‹FOUR MINUTES TO TARGET.›
‹ARE WE STILL GO FOR STRIKE?›
‹ABSOLUTELY.›
‹IF WE CAN'T HAVE OUR OWN SUPERMEN...›
‹...THEN NO ONE CAN.›
I CAN'T LET YOU BRING MORE OF YOUR KIND OVER.
YOU'RE A MURDERER.
WAS DEFENDING MYSELF.
YOUR KIND BROUGHT ME HERE.
HAVE NO DESIRE TO BRING MORE.
THEN... WHY OPEN THE GATEWAY?
I SAW THEM TRYING TO CROSS OVER!
WANT NOTHING HERE.
DO NOT WANT TO BE HERE.
AM TRYING TO GO HOME.

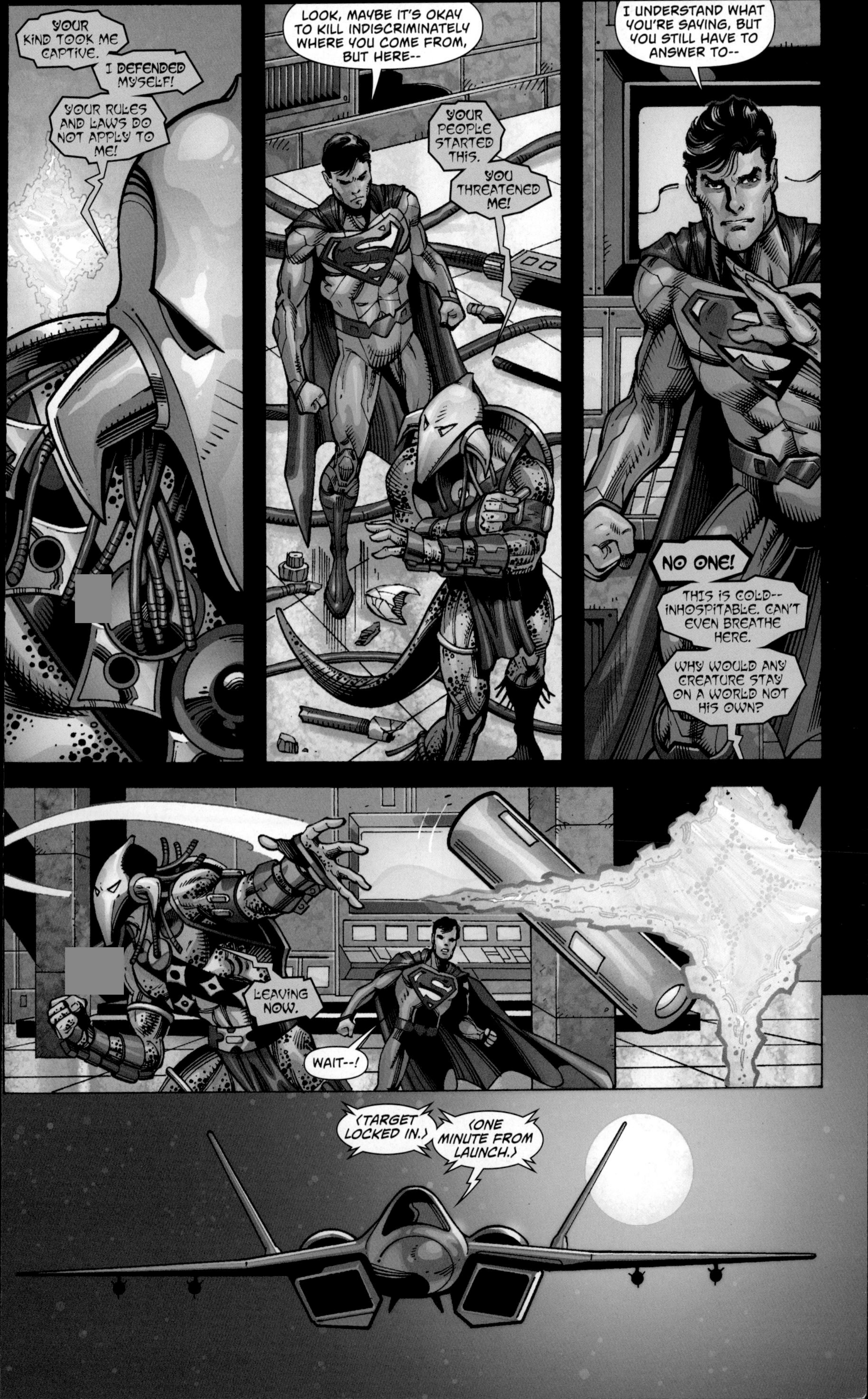
YOUR KIND TOOK ME CAPTIVE.
I DEFENDED MYSELF!
YOUR RULES AND LAWS DO NOT APPLY TO ME!
LOOK, MAYBE IT'S OKAY TO KILL INDISCRIMINATELY WHERE YOU COME FROM, BUT HERE--
YOUR PEOPLE STARTED THIS.
YOU THREATENED ME!
I UNDERSTAND WHAT YOU'RE SAYING, BUT YOU STILL HAVE TO ANSWER TO--
NO ONE!
THIS IS COLD-- INHOSPITABLE. CAN'T EVEN BREATHE HERE.
WHY WOULD ANY CREATURE STAY ON A WORLD NOT HIS OWN?
LEAVING NOW.
WAIT--!
<TARGET LOCKED IN.>
<ONE MINUTE FROM LAUNCH.>

THE RELATIVES OF THE PEOPLE YOU KILLED--

DON'T MATTER.

I DID WHAT I NEEDED TO TO SURVIVE.

NOW YOU HAVE FRIENDS TO HELP.

YES. YOU DON'T KNOW WHAT IT'S LIKE TO BE ALONE ON A STRANGE WORLD.

I'LL TAKE YOU WITH ME-- LET YOU SEE WHAT IT'S LIKE!

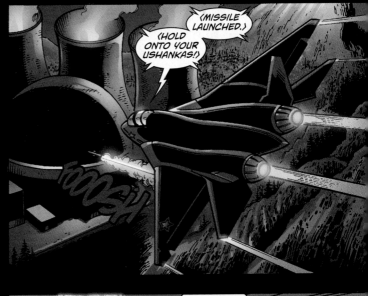

(MISSILE LAUNCHED.)

(HOLD ONTO YOUR USHANKAS!)

THAT SOUND! A MISSILE?

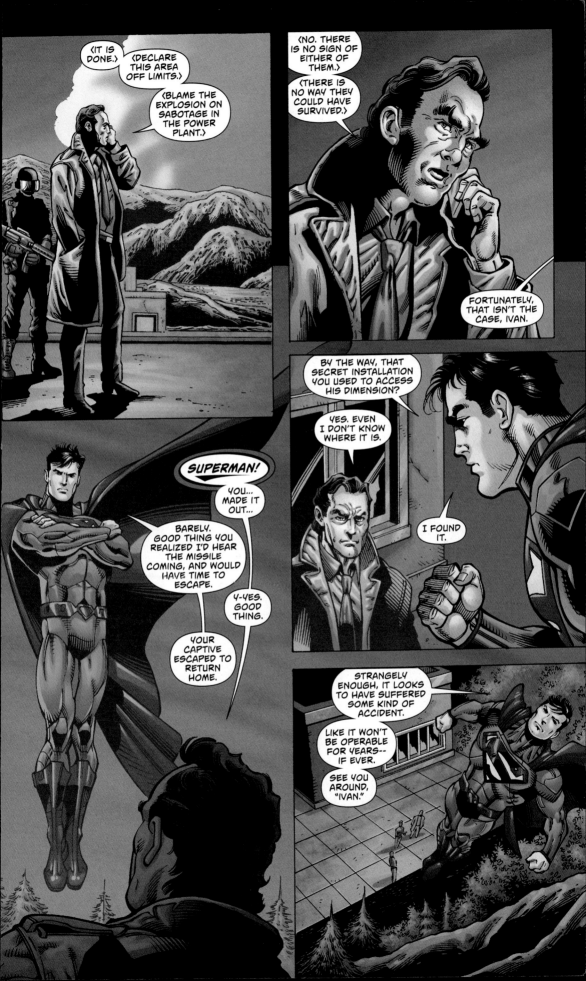

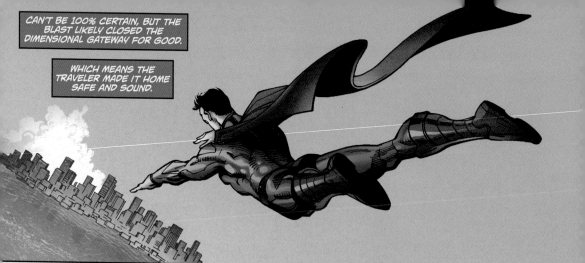

CAN'T BE 100% CERTAIN, BUT THE BLAST LIKELY CLOSED THE DIMENSIONAL GATEWAY FOR GOOD.

WHICH MEANS THE TRAVELER MADE IT HOME SAFE AND SOUND.

DESPITE HIS CRIMES, IT'S PROBABLY FOR THE BEST.

PUTTING THE FACILITY THAT CAPTURED HIM OUT OF COMMISSION WILL ENSURE WE DON'T SEE HIM AGAIN.

I CAN SYMPATHIZE WITH HIS PLIGHT.

I PROBABLY DON'T APPRECIATE WINDING UP ON EARTH AS MUCH AS I SHOULD.

TROUBLING THAT SOME STILL CONSIDER ME AN OUTSIDER THOUGH.

THAT THE RUSSIANS FELT THEY NEEDED THEIR OWN VERSION OF ME.

THEY SHOULD KNOW BY NOW THAT I CAN BE TRUSTED.

THAT I'M HERE TO HELP.

EVERYON

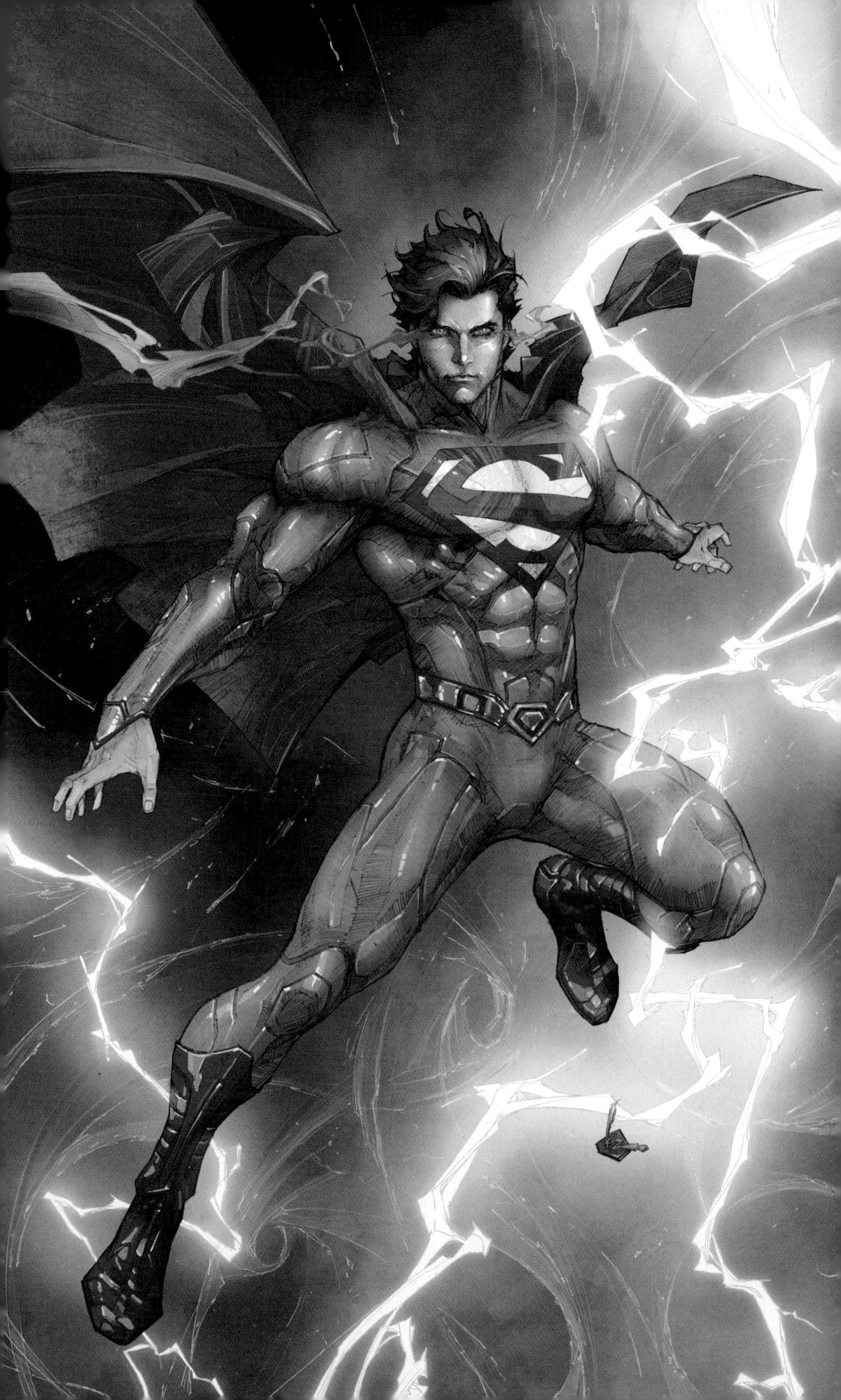

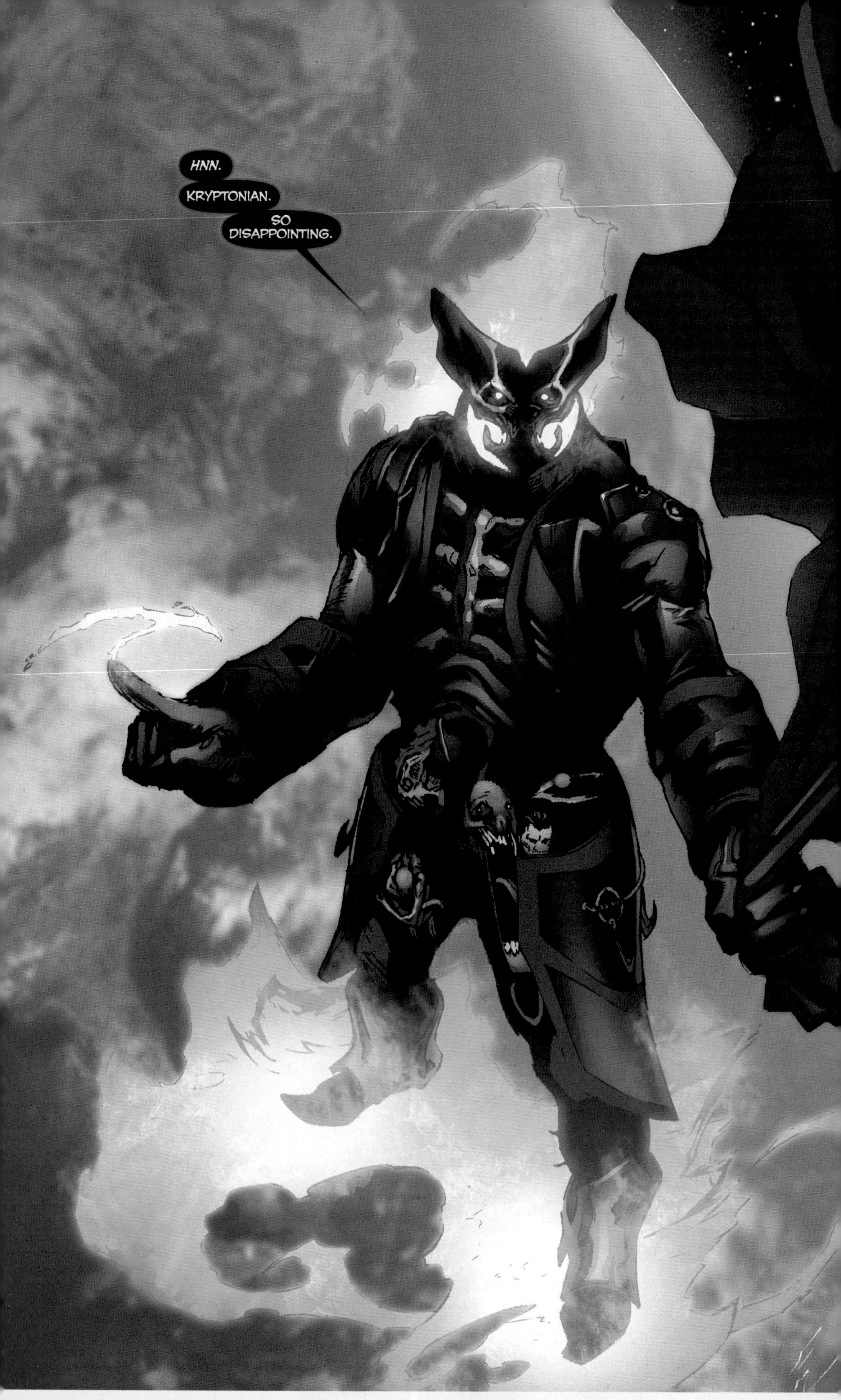
HNN.
KRYPTONIAN.
SO DISAPPOINTING.

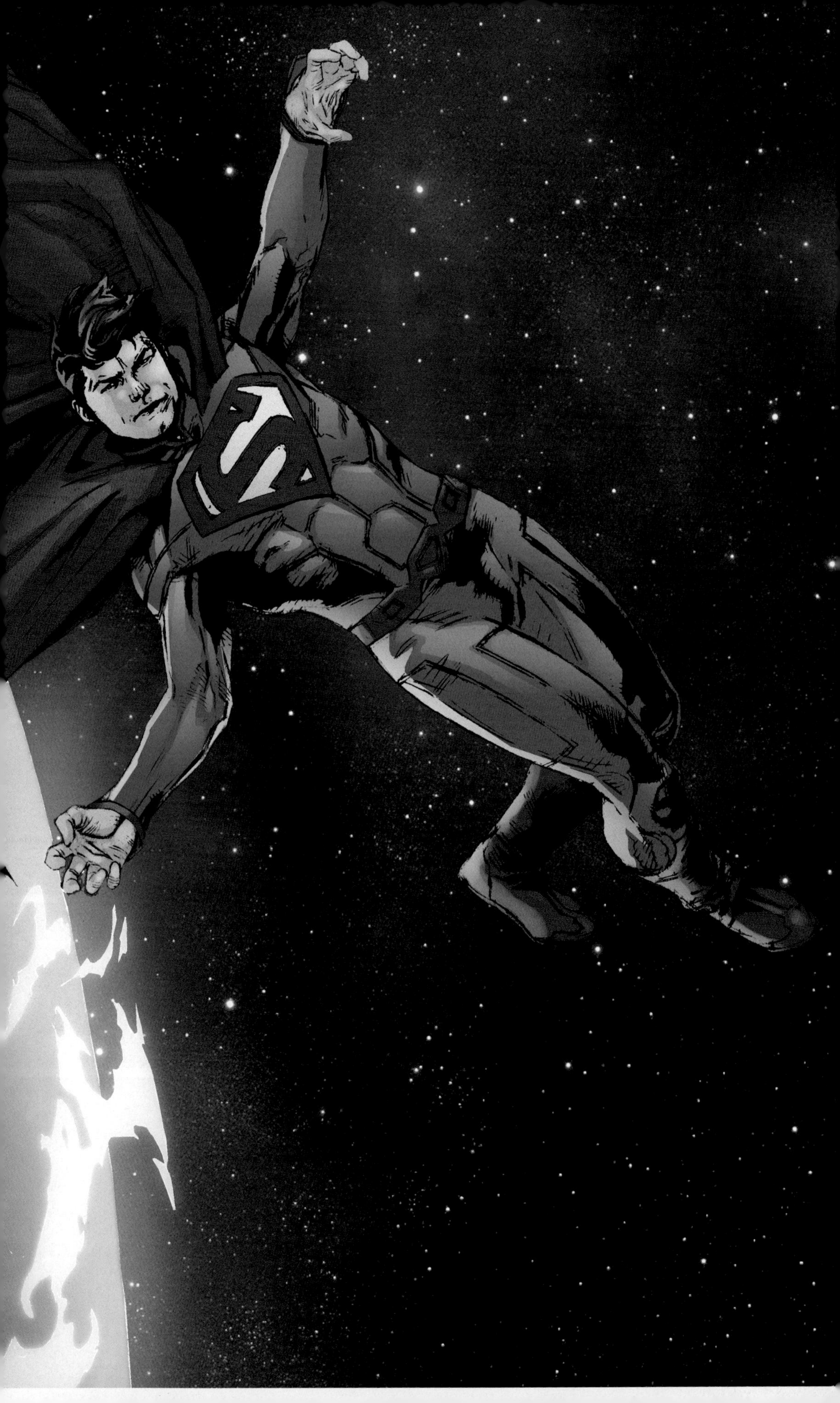

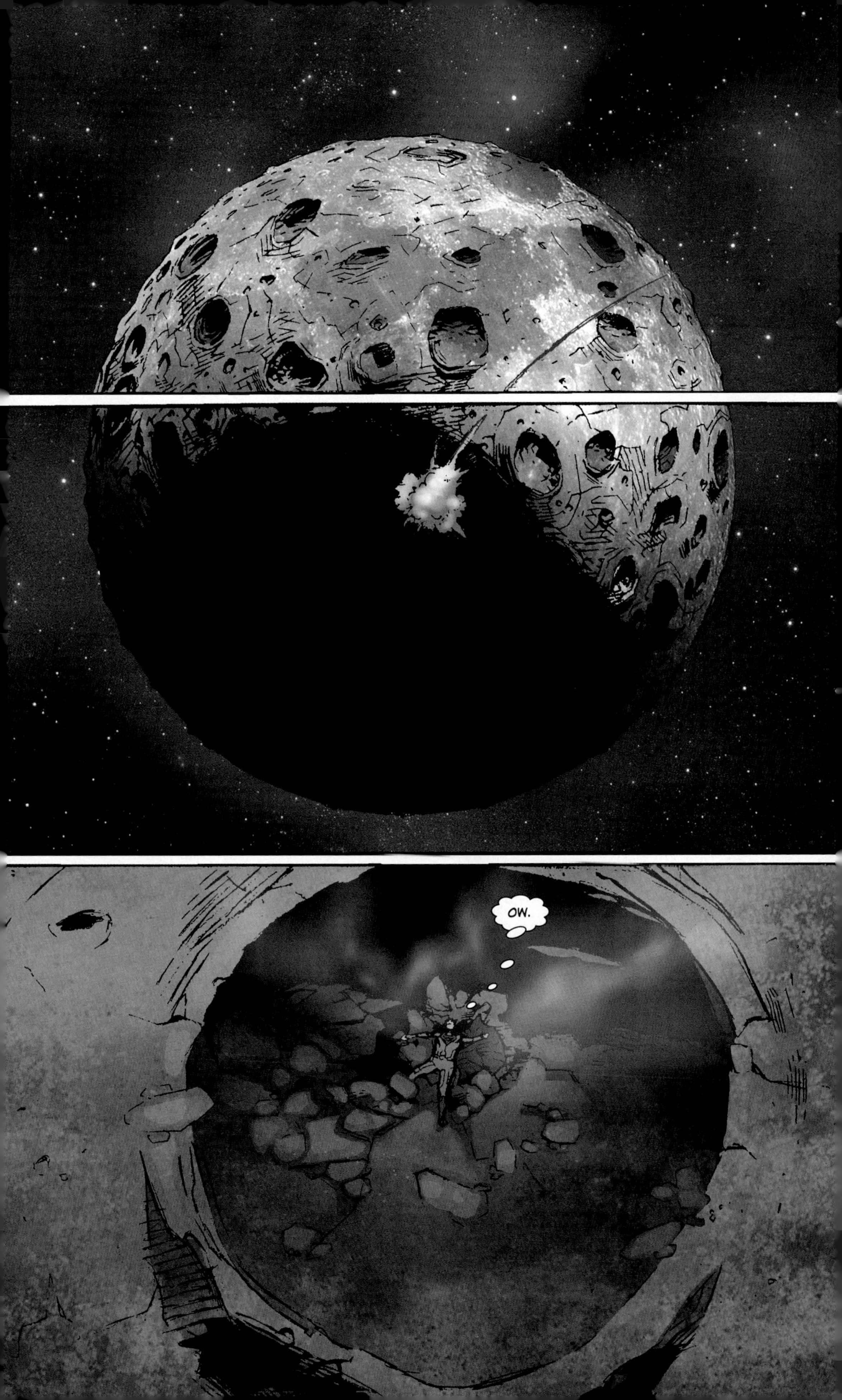
OW.

IT *IS* A DAEMONITE SHIP, BUT I SENSE A LIMITED CREW.

I AM CERTAIN THAT WAS THE KRYPTONIAN WHO IMPACTED WITH THE MOON.

...SPITE OUR RECENT... DIFFERENCES... I MUST INVOLVE *STORMWATCH*.

SURELY THEY WOULD SHUN THEIR USUAL ARROGANT ISOLATION IN ORDER TO--

THEY WILL NOT HELP YOU, SON OF *MA'ALECA'ANDRA*.

WHO ARE YOU?

I AM WHO I AM. UNLIKE YOU..."*JOHN JONES*."

YOUR NAME IS *SALU*. A DAEMONITE... AND RETAINER TO HELSPONT...?

YOUR *TELEPATHY* WORKS THROUGH THE *BLUE LIGHT OF TRUTH* THAT INFUSES ME?

IMPRESSIVE.

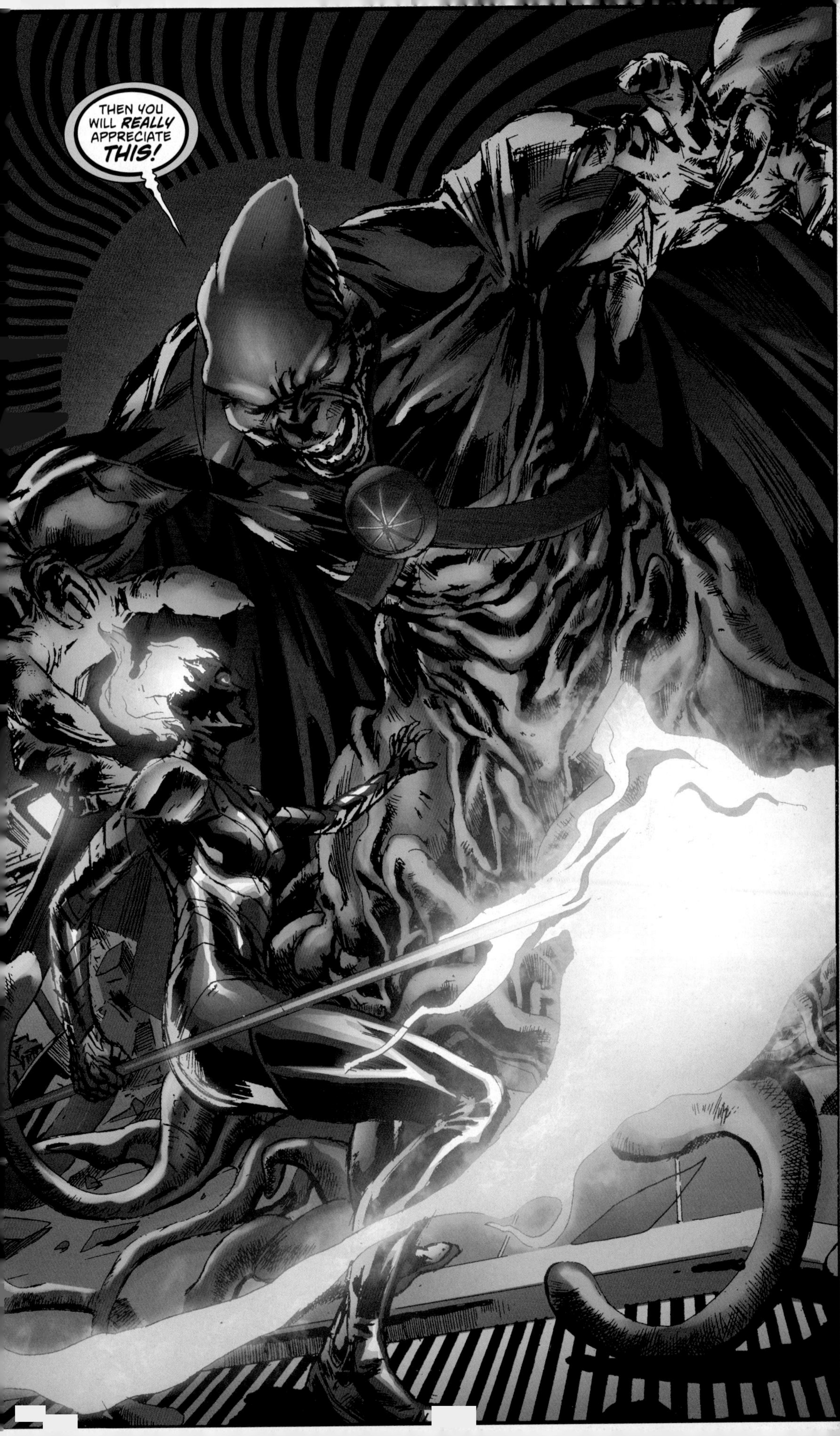
THEN YOU WILL REALLY APPRECIATE THIS!

NICE TO JUST RELAX WITHOUT WORRYING ABOUT *JASON* OR *ROY.*

THEY ARE MY FRIENDS AND THEY KEEP ME FROM FEELING *ALONE* ON THIS ALIEN WORLD--

--BUT SOMETIMES, THE QUIET IS A BLESSING. THE OCEANS OF THIS PLANET ARE--

--WAIT-- WHAT--?

FWSH HSH

MY MOTHER WA**MONARCH**, PRESIDING OVER THE RUINATION OF MY SPECIES. SHE CAST ME OUT FOR CALLING HER FOLLY.

THROUGH *PIRACY* THEN OUTRIGHT *CONQUEST,* I THEN SPENT HUNDREDS OF YEARS AMASSING AN *ARMADA*--

--THAT WOULD HELP ME RECLAIM MY HOME.

DISCOVERED THE BLUE FLAME--A CONDU OF TREMENDOUS *POWER* FOR MYSELF--

"--AND GIFTED M MOST FAITHFU FOLLOWERS WI BUT A *PORTION* O MY GREATNESS.

"AND SENT THEM OUT AS MY PILGRIMS IN SEARCH OF FERTILE LAND.

"BUT WE WERE NOT JUST CONQUERING WORLDS; IN THOSE MYRIAD SPECIES, WE WERE SEEKING THE HOPE OF *GENETIC SALVATION* FOR THE DAEM.

"AND THREE THOUSA YEARS AGO, WE FO THIS FERTILE BLUE C YOU CALL EARTH.

"MY LEADING GENETICIST, *SKUGARDT,* HAD ISOLATED AN *ACCELERANT* IN THE HUMAN POPULATION--

"-- A POTENT *METAGENE* TH IN DUE TIME, COULD EVOLVE BECOME THE *SALVATION* O MY PEOPLE.

"AND SO I LEFT MANY OF MY AGENTS BEHIND, TO LIVE AMONG THE HUMANS--TO MOLD AND PREPARE THEM FOR MY INEVITABLE RETURN.

"BUT IN MY ABSENCE, THEY GREW FECKLESS, SATED WITH THEIR CREATURE COMFORTS.

"THEY DIVIDED INTO FACTIONS, FIGHTING AMONG THEMSELVES, AND ALLOWING THE METAGENE TO MUTATE WITHOUT PROPER CONTROLS.

"SO NOW, THE TIME HAS COME--

START AT THE BEGINNING!

SUPERMAN: ACTION COMICS VOLUME 1: SUPERMAN AND THE MEN OF STEEL

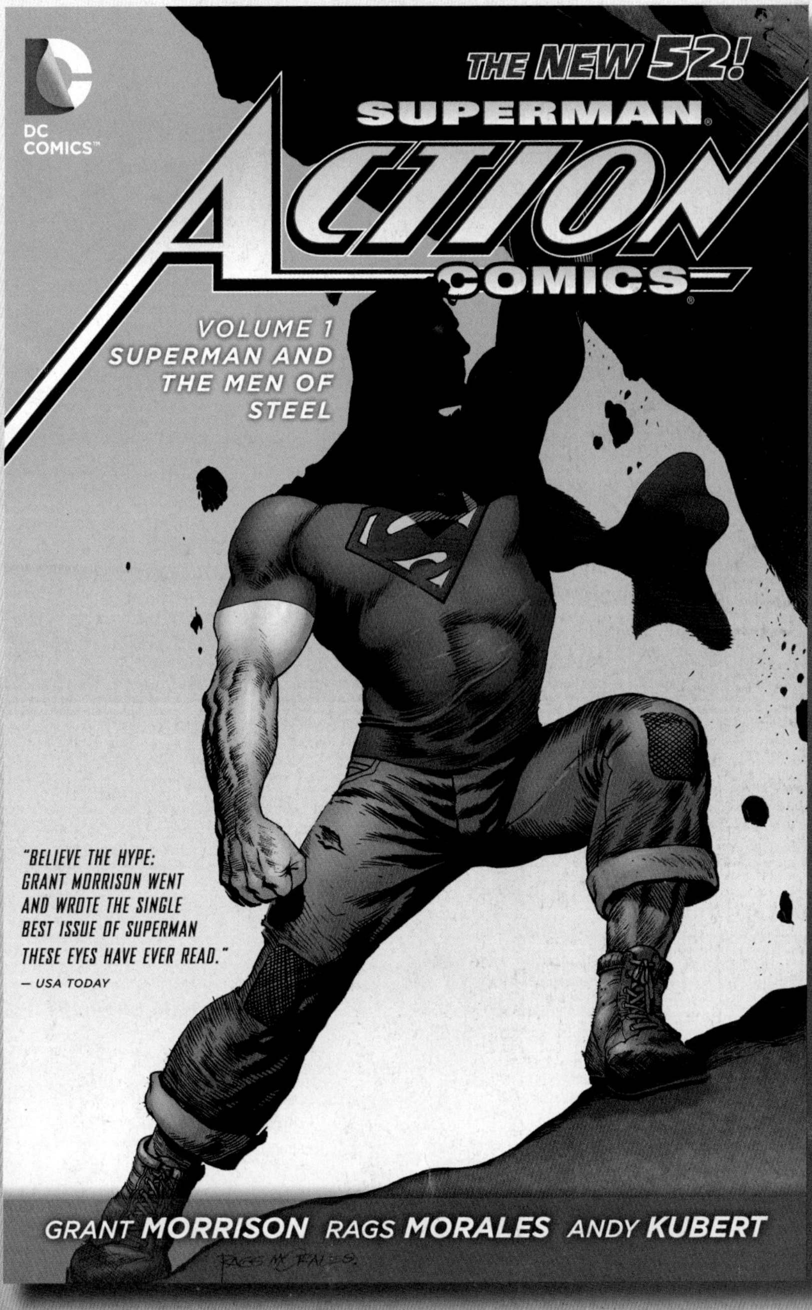

SUPERMAN VOLUME 1: WHAT PRICE TOMORROW?

GEORGE PEREZ JESÚS MERINO NICOLA SCOTT

SUPERGIRL VOLUME 1: THE LAST DAUGHTER OF KRYPTON

MICHAEL GREEN MIKE JOHNSON MAHMUD ASRAR

SUPERBOY VOLUME 1: INCUBATION

SCOTT LOBDELL R.B. SILVA ROB LEAN

THE NEW 52!

DC COMICS™

SUPERMAN ACTION COMICS

VOLUME 1 SUPERMAN AND THE MEN OF STEEL

GRANT **MORRISON** RAGS **MORALES** ANDY **KUBERT**

DC COMICS™

START AT THE BEGINNING!

JUSTICE LEAGUE VOLUME 1: ORIGIN

AQUAMAN
VOLUME 1:
THE TRENCH

THE SAVAGE
HAWKMAN VOLUME 1:
DARKNESS RISING

GREEN ARROW
VOLUME 1:
THE MIDAS TOUCH

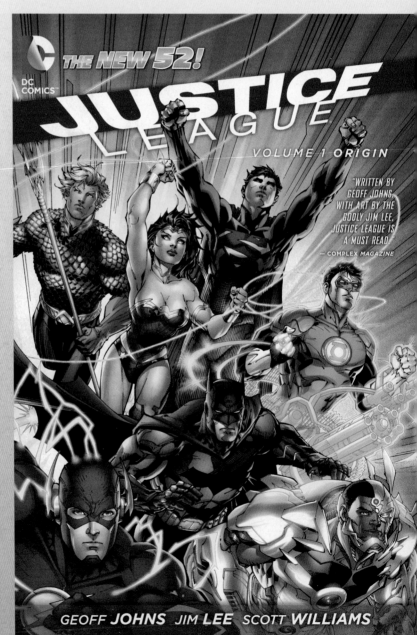